ACCA

Paper F2

Management accounting

The Complete Text

ACCA
pproved Publisher

KAPLAN
PUBLISHING

British library cataloguing-in-publication data

A catalogue record for this book is available from the British Library.

Published by:
Kaplan Publishing
Unit 2 The Business Centre
Molly Millars Lane
Wokingham
Berkshire
RG41 2QZ

ISBN 978 1 84710 232 4

Printed and bound in Great Britain by William Clowes Ltd, Beccles, Suffolk

Acknowledgements

We are grateful to the Association of Chartered Certified Accountants and the Chartered Institute of Management Accountants for permission to reproduce past examination questions. The answers have been prepared by Kaplan Publishing.

Contents

How to use these materials

These Kaplan Publishing learning materials have been carefully designed to make your learning experience as easy as possible and to give you the best chances of success in your examinations.

The product range contains a number of features to help you in the study process. They include:

1 Detailed study guide and syllabus objectives
2 Description of the examination
3 Study skills and revision guidance
4 Complete text or essential text
5 Question practice

The sections on the study guide, the syllabus objectives, the examination and study skills should all be read before you commence your studies. They are designed to familiarise you with the nature and content of the examination and give you tips on how best to approach your learning.

The complete text or essential text comprises the main learning materials and gives guidance as to the importance of topics and where other related resources can be found. Each chapter includes:

- The **learning objectives** contained in each chapter, which have been carefully mapped to the examining body's own syllabus learning objectives or outcomes. You should use these to check you have a clear understanding of all the topics on which you might be assessed in the examination.
- The **chapter diagram** provides a visual reference for the content in the chapter, giving an overview of the topics and how they link together.
- The **content** for each topic area commences with a brief explanation or definition to put the topic into context before covering the topic in detail. You should follow your studying of the content with a review of the **illustration/s**. These are worked examples which will help you to understand better how to apply the content for the topic.
- **Test your understanding** sections provide an opportunity to assess your understanding of the key topics by applying what you have learned to short questions. Answers can be found at the back of each chapter.
- **Summary diagrams** complete each chapter to show the important links between topics and the overall content of the paper. These diagrams should be used to check that you have covered and understood the core topics before moving on.
- **Question practice** is provided at the back of each text.

To help you find your way through the material you will find useful icons throughout each chapter:

Definition		Key definitions that you will need to learn from the core content.
Key exam points		Identifies topics that are key to success and are often examined.
Tricky topic		When reviewing these areas care should be taken and all illustrations and test your understanding exercises should be completed to ensure that the topic is understood.
Expandable text		Expandable text provides you with additional information about a topic area and may help you gain a better understanding of the core content. Essential text users can access this additional content on-line (read it where you need further guidance or skip over when you are happy with a topic).
Illustration	e.g	Worked examples help you understand the core content better.
Test your understanding		Exercises for you to complete to ensure that you have understood the topics just learned.

Paper introduction

Paper background

The aim of ACCA Paper F2, **Management accounting**, is to develop knowledge and understanding of how to prepare and process basic cost and quantitative information to support management in planning and decision-making in a variety of business contexts.

Objectives of the syllabus

- Explain the nature and purpose of cost accounting.
- Describe costs by classification, behaviour and purpose
- Apply essential business mathematics and using computer spreadsheet models.
- Explain and apply cost accounting techniques.
- Prepare and co-ordinate budgets and standard costing for planning, feedback and control.
- Use management accounting techniques to make and support decision-making.

Core areas of the syllabus

- The nature and purpose of cost and management accounting
- Cost classification, behaviour and purpose
- Business mathematics and computer spreadsheets
- Cost accounting techniques
- Budgeting and standard costing
- Short-term decision-making techniques

Syllabus objectives

We have reproduced the ACCA's syllabus below, showing where the objectives are explored within this book. Within the chapters, we have broken down the extensive information found in the syllabus into easily digestible and relevant sections, called **Content Objectives**. These correspond to the objectives at the beginning of each chapter.

Syllabus learning objective	Chapter reference
A THE NATURE AND PURPOSE OF COST AND MANAGEMENT ACCOUNTING	
1 Accounting for management	
(a) Distinguish between data and information.[1]	1
(b) Identify and explain the attributes of good information.[1]	1
(c) Outline the managerial processes of planning, decision making and control.[1]	1
(d) Explain the difference between strategic, tactical and operational planning.[1]	1
(e) Distinguish between cost, profit, investment and revenue centres.[1]	1
(f) Describe the differing needs for information of cost, profit, investment and revenue centre managers.[1]	1
2 Cost and management accounting and financial accounting	
(a) Describe the purpose and role of cost and management accounting within an organisation's management information system.[1]	1
(b) Compare and contrast financial accounting with cost and management accounting.[1]	1
B COST CLASSIFICATION, BEHAVIOUR AND PURPOSE	
1 Production and non-production costs	
(a) Explain and illustrate production and non-production costs.[1]	2
(b) Describe the different elements of production cost – materials, labour and overheads.[1]	2
(c) Describe the different elements of non-production cost – administrative, selling, distribution and finance.[1]	2
(d) Explain the importance of the distinction between production and non-production costs when valuing output and inventories.[1]	2
2 Direct and indirect costs	
(a) Distinguish between direct and indirect costs in manufacturing and non-manufacturing organisations.[1]	2

(b) Identify examples of direct and indirect costs in manufacturing and non-manufacturing organisations.[1] 2

(c) Explain and illustrate the concepts of cost objects, cost units and cost centres.[1] 2

3 Fixed and variable costs

(a) Describe and illustrate graphically different types of cost behaviour.[1] 2

(b) Explain and provide examples of costs that fall into the categories of fixed, stepped fixed and variable costs.[1] 2

(c) Use high/low analysis to separate the fixed and variable elements of total costs including situations involving stepped fixed costs and changes in the variable cost per unit.[2] 2

(d) Explain the structure of linear functions and equations.[1] 3

C BUSINESS MATHEMATICS AND COMPUTER SPREADSHEETS

1 Dealing with uncertainty

(a) Explain and calculate an expected value.[1] 3

(b) Demonstrate the use of expected values in simple decision making situations.[1] 3

(c) Explain the limitations of the expected value technique.[1] 3

Note: Decision trees and conditional profit tables are excluded.

2 Statistics for business

(a) Calculate a correlation coefficient and a coefficient of determination.[1] 3

(b) Explain the concepts in ((a) and interpret the coefficients calculated in (a).[1] 3

(c) Establish a linear function using regression analysis and interpret the results.[2] 3

3 Use of spreadsheet models

(a) Explain the role and features of a spreadsheet system.[1] Appendix

(b) Demonstrate a basic understanding of the use of spreadsheets.[1] Appendix

(c) Identify applications for spreadsheets in cost and management accounting.[1] Appendix

D COST ACCOUNTING TECHNIQUES

1 Accounting for materials

(a) Describe the different procedures and documents necessary for the ordering, receiving and issuing of materials from inventory.[1] 4

(b) Describe the control procedures used to monitor physical and 'book' inventory and to minimise discrepancies and losses.[1] 4

(c) Interpret the entries and balances in the material inventory account.[1] 4

(d) Identify and explain the costs of ordering and holding inventory.[1] 5

(e) Calculate and interpret optimal reorder quantities.[2] 5

(f) Calculate and interpret optimal reorder quantities when discounts apply.[1] 5

(g) Produce calculations to minimise inventory costs when stock is gradually replenished.[1] 5

(h) Describe and apply appropriate methods for establishing reorder levels where demand in the lead time is constant.[1] 5

2 Accounting for labour

(a) Calculate direct and indirect costs of labour.[1] 6

(b) Explain the methods used to relate input labour costs to work done.[1] 6

(c) Prepare the journal and ledger entries to record labour cost inputs and outputs.[1] 6

(d) Describe different remuneration methods time-based systems, piecework systems and individual and group incentive schemes.[1] 6

(e) Calculate the level, and analyse the costs and causes of labour turnover.[1] 6

(f) Explain and calculate labour efficiency, capacity and production volume ratios.[1] 6

(g) Interpret the entries in the labour account.[1] 6

3 Accounting for overheads

(a) Explain the different treatment of direct and indirect expenses.[1] 7

(b) Describe the procedures involved in determining production overhead absorption rates.[1] 7

(c) Allocate and apportion production overheads to cost centres using an appropriate basis.[1] 7

(d) Reapportion service cost centre costs to production cost centres (using the reciprocal method where service cost centres work for each other).[2] 7

(e) Select, apply and discuss appropriate bases for absorption rates.[2] 7

(f) Prepare journal and ledger entries for manufacturing overheads incurred and absorbed.[1] 7

(g) Calculate and explain the under- and over-absorption of overheads.[1] 7

(h) Apply methods of relating non-production overheads to cost units.[1] 7

4 Marginal and absorption costing

(a) Explain the importance of and apply the concept of contribution.[1] 8
(b) Demonstrate and discuss the effect of absorption and marginal costing on inventory valuation and profit determination.[2] 8
(c) Calculate profit or loss under-absorption and marginal costing.[2] 8
(d) Reconcile the profits or losses calculated under-absorption and marginal costing.[2] 8
(e) Describe the advantages and disadvantages of absorption and marginal costing.[1] 8

5 Job and batch costing

(a) Describe the characteristics of job and batch costing.[1] 11
(b) Describe the situations where the use of job or batch costing would be appropriate.[1] 11
(c) Prepare cost records and accounts in job and batch costing situations.[1] 11
(d) Establish job costs from given information.[1] 11

6 Process costing

(a) Describe the characteristics of process costing.[1] 11
(b) Describe the situations where the use of process costing would be appropriate.[1] 11
(c) Explain the concepts of normal and abnormal losses and abnormal gains.[1] 11
(d) Calculate the cost per unit of process outputs.[1] 11
(e) Prepare process accounts involving normal and abnormal losses and abnormal gains.[1] 11
(f) Calculate and explain the concept of equivalent units.[1] 11
(g) Apportion process costs between work remaining in process and transfers out of a process using the weighted average and FIFO methods.[1] 11
(h) Prepare process accounts in situations where work remains incomplete.[2] 11
(i) Prepare process accounts where losses and gains are identified at different stages of the process.[1] 11
(j) Distinguish between by-products and joint products.[1] 11
(k) Value by-products and joint products at the point of separation.[1] 11
(l) Prepare process accounts in situations where by-products and/or joint products occur.[2] 11

Note: Situations involving work in process and losses in the same process are excluded.

7 Service/operation costing

(a) Identify situations where the use of service/operation costing is appropriate.[1] 12

(b) Illustrate suitable unit cost measures that may be used in different service/operation situations.[1] 12

(c) Carry out service cost analysis in simple service industry situations.[1] 12

E BUDGETING AND STANDARD COSTING

1 Nature and purpose of budgeting

(a) Explain why organisations use budgeting.[1] 13

(b) Explain the administrative procedures used in the budgeting process.[1] 13

(c) Describe the stages in the budgeting process.[1] 13

2 Functional budgets

(a) Explain the term 'principal budget factor'.[1] 13

(b) Prepare budgets for sales, production, materials (usage and purchases), labour and overheads.[1] 13

3 Flexible budgets and standard costing

(a) Explain and prepare fixed, flexible and flexed budgets.[1] 13

(b) Explain the purpose and principles of standard costing.[1] 14

(c) Establish the standard cost per unit under absorption and marginal costing.[1] 14

4 Basic variance analysis under absorption and marginal costing

(a) Calculate the following variances:[1] 14

- (i) sales price and volume
- (ii) materials total, price and usage
- (iii) labour total, rate and efficiency
- (iv) variable overhead total, expenditure and efficiency
- (v) fixed overhead total, expenditure and, where appropriate, volume, capacity and efficiency.

(b) Interpret all the variances in 4(a).[1] 14

(c) Explain possible causes of all the variances in 4(a).[1] 14

(d) Describe the interrelationships between the variances in 4(a).[1] 14

(e) Calculate actual or standard figures where the variances in 4(a) are given.[1] 14

5 Reconciliation of budgeted profit and actual profit

(a) Reconcile budgeted profit with actual profit under standard absorption costing.[1]

(b) Reconcile budgeted profit or contribution with actual profit or contribution under standard marginal costing.[1]

F SHORT-TERM DECISION-MAKING TECHNIQUES

1 Cost-volume-profit (CVP) analysis

(a) Calculate and interpret a break-even point and a margin of safety.[2] 8

(b) Understand and use the concepts of a target profit or revenue and a contribution to sales ratio.[2] 8

(c) Identify the elements in traditional and contribution break-even charts and profit/volume charts.[1] 8

(d) Apply CVP analysis to single product situations.[2] 8

Note: Multi-product break-even charts and profit/volume charts are excluded.

2 Relevant costing

(a) Explain the concept of relevant costing.[1] 9

(b) Calculate the relevant costs for materials, labour and overheads.[2] 9

(c) Calculate the relevant costs associated with non-current assets.[1] 9

(d) Explain and apply the concept of opportunity cost.[1] 9

3 Limiting factors

(a) Identify a single limiting factor.[1] 10

(b) Determine the optimal production plan where an organisation is restricted by a single limiting factor.[2] 10

(c) Formulate a linear programming problem involving two variables.[1] 10

(d) Determine the optimal solution to a linear programming problem using a graphical approach.[1] 10

(e) Use simultaneous equations, where appropriate, in the solution of a linear programming problem.[1] 10

The superscript numbers in square brackets indicate the intellectual depth at which the subject area could be assessed within the examination. Level 1 (knowledge and comprehension) broadly equates with the Knowledge module, Level 2 (application and analysis) with the Skills module and Level 3 (synthesis and evaluation) to the Professional level. However, lower level skills can continue to be assessed as you progress through each module and level.

The examination

Examination format

The syllabus is assessed by a two-hour paper or computer-based examination. Questions will assess all parts of the syllabus and will contain both computational and non-computational elements:

	Number of marks
Forty 2-mark questions	80
Ten 1-mark questions	10
	90

Total time allowed: 2 hours

Paper-based examination tips

Divide the time you spend on questions in proportion to the marks on offer. One suggestion **for this exam** is to allocate 1 and 1/3 minutes to each mark available, so a 2-mark question should be completed in approximately 2 minutes 40 seconds.

If you **get completely stuck** with a question, leave space in your answer book and **return to it later**.

Multiple-choice questions: Read the questions carefully and work through any calculations required. If you don't know the answer, eliminate those options you know are incorrect and see if the answer becomes more obvious. Guess your final answer rather than leave it blank if necessary.

Computer-based examination (CBE) - tips

Be sure you understand how to use the software before you start the exam. If in doubt, ask the assessment centre staff to explain it to you.

Questions are **displayed on the screen** and answers are entered using keyboard and mouse. At the end of the exam, you are given a certificate showing the result you have achieved.

Do not attempt a CBE until you have **completed all study material** relating to it. **Do not skip any of the material** in the syllabus.

Read each question very carefully.

Double-check your answer before committing yourself to it.

Answer every question – if you do not know an answer, you don't lose anything by guessing. Think carefully before you **guess**.

With a multiple-choice question, eliminate first those answers that you know are wrong. Then choose the most appropriate answer from those that are left.

Remember that **only one answer to a multiple-choice question can be right.** After you have eliminated the ones that you know to be wrong, if you are still unsure, guess. But only do so after you have double-checked that you have only eliminated answers that are definitely wrong.

Don't panic if you realise you've answered a question incorrectly. Getting one question wrong will not mean the difference between passing and failing.

Study skills and revision guidance

This section aims to give guidance on how to study for your ACCA exams and to give ideas on how to improve your existing study techniques.

Preparing to study

Set your objectives

Before starting to study decide what you want to achieve - the type of pass you wish to obtain. This will decide the level of commitment and time you need to dedicate to your studies.

Devise a study plan

Determine which times of the week you will study.

Split these times into sessions of at least one hour for study of new material. Any shorter periods could be used for revision or practice.

Put the times you plan to study onto a study plan for the weeks from now until the exam and set yourself targets for each period of study – in your sessions make sure you cover the course, course assignments and revision.

If you are studying for more than one paper at a time, try to vary your subjects as this can help you to keep interested and see subjects as part of wider knowledge.

When working through your course, compare your progress with your plan and, if necessary, re-plan your work (perhaps including extra sessions) or, if you are ahead, do some extra revision/practice questions.

Effective studying

Active reading

You are not expected to learn the text by rote, rather, you must understand what you are reading and be able to use it to pass the exam and develop good practice. A good technique to use is SQ3Rs – Survey, Question, Read, Recall, Review:

1 **Survey** the chapter – look at the headings and read the introduction, summary and objectives, so as to get an overview of what the chapter deals with.

2 **Question** – whilst undertaking the survey, ask yourself the questions that you hope the chapter will answer for you.

3 **Read** through the chapter thoroughly, answering the questions and making sure you can meet the objectives. Attempt the exercises and activities in the text, and work through all the examples.

4 **Recall** – at the end of each section and at the end of the chapter, try to recall the main ideas of the section/chapter without referring to the text. This is best done after a short break of a couple of minutes after the reading stage.

5 **Review** – check that your recall notes are correct.

You may also find it helpful to re-read the chapter to try to see the topic(s) it deals with as a whole.

Note-taking

Taking notes is a useful way of learning, but do not simply copy out the text. The notes must:

- be in your own words
- be concise
- cover the key points
- be well-organised
- be modified as you study further chapters in this text or in related ones.

Trying to summarise a chapter without referring to the text can be a useful way of determining which areas you know and which you don't.

Three ways of taking notes:

Summarise the key points of a chapter.

Make linear notes – a list of headings, divided up with subheadings listing the key points. If you use linear notes, you can use different colours to highlight key points and keep topic areas together. Use plenty of space to make your notes easy to use.

Try a diagrammatic form – the most common of which is a mind-map. To make a mind-map, put the main heading in the centre of the paper and put a circle around it. Then draw short lines radiating from this to the main sub-headings, which again have circles around them. Then continue the process from the sub-headings to sub-sub-headings, advantages, disadvantages, etc.

Highlighting and underlining
You may find it useful to underline or highlight key points in your study text – but do be selective. You may also wish to make notes in the margins.

Revision
The best approach to revision is to revise the course as you work through it. Also try to leave four to six weeks before the exam for final revision. Make sure you cover the whole syllabus and pay special attention to those areas where your knowledge is weak. Here are some recommendations:

Read through the text and your notes again and condense your notes into key phrases. It may help to put key revision points onto index cards to look at when you have a few minutes to spare.

Review any assignments you have completed and look at where you lost marks – put more work into those areas where you were weak.

Practise exam standard questions under timed conditions.

If you are stuck on a topic find somebody (a tutor) to explain it to you.

Read good newspapers and professional journals, especially ACCA's **Student Accountant** – this can give you an advantage in the exam.

Ensure you **know the structure of the exam** – how many questions and of what type you will be expected to answer. During your revision attempt all the different styles of questions you may be asked.

Further reading

You can find further reading and technical articles under the student section of ACCA's website.

chapter

1

The nature and purpose of management accounting

Chapter learning objectives

Upon completion of this chapter you will be able to:

- describe the difference between data and information
- explain, using the 'ACCURATE' acronym the attributes of good information
- describe, in overview, the managerial processes of: planning, decision making and control
- explain the characteristics of and difference between strategic, tactical and operational planning
- explain the characteristics and differences between cost, profit, investment and revenue centres
- describe the different information needs of managers of cost, profit, investment and revenue centres
- describe the purpose and role of cost and management accounting within an organisation's management information system
- compare and contrast, for a business, financial accounting with cost and management accounting.

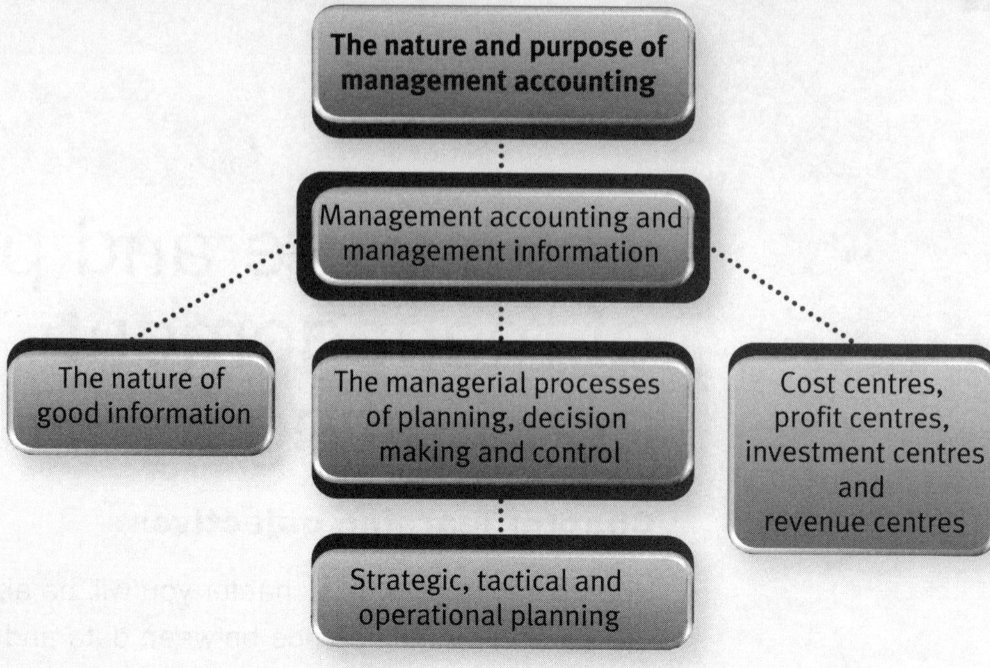

1 The nature of good information

1.1 Data and information

'Data' means facts. Data consists of numbers, letters, symbols, raw facts, events and transactions which have been recorded but not yet processed into a form suitable for use.

Information is data which has been processed in such a way that it is meaningful to the person who receives it (for making decisions).

- The terms data and information are often used interchangeably in everyday language. Make sure that you can distinguish between the two.
- As data is converted into information, some of the detail of the data is eliminated and replaced by summaries which are easier to understand.

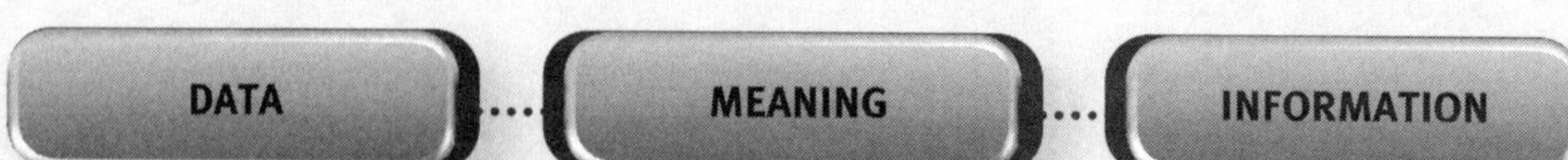

e.g

Illustration 1 – The nature of good information

In management accounting the accounting system records a large number of facts (data) about materials, labour, expenses and other transactions. If management were to look at the individual items relating to materials, labour, expenses and so on, they would not be very meaningful.

These facts and figures are analysed and summarised to produce management information i.e. information that is used by management to plan and control the activities of the organisation. This information usually takes the form of accounts which are more meaningful and of more use to management than raw data.

1.2 Attributes of good information

Information is provided to management to assist them with planning, controlling operations and making decisions. Management decisions are likely to be better when they are provided with better quality information.

The attributes of good information can be identified by the 'ACCURATE' acronym as shown below:

- **A – Accurate**
- **C – Complete**
- **C – Cost-effective**
- **U – Understandable**
- **R – Relevant**
- **A – Accessible**
- **T – Timely**
- **E – Easy to use!**

Expandable text

We can look at the attributes of good information in more detail:

- **A – Accurate** – Information should be as accurate as it needs to be. The degree of accuracy required will depend on the reason why the information is needed. A problem in accounting can be that reports are produced showing figures to the nearest dollar, when managers are only interested in figures to the nearest hundred thousand or ten thousand. On the other hand, when calculating the cost of a unit of product manufactured in a factory, managers might want the cost to be accurate to the nearest cent.

- **C – Complete** – Information should be as complete as it needs to be, but it should not be excessive. Managers should be given all the information they need to make their decisions, but it is often helpful to draw their attention to what seems significant. In control reports, for example, actual results might be compared with planned results, with differences between actual and plan reported as 'variances'.

  A report that highlights the most significant information, such as the biggest variances, can help to draw management attention to what is important. Sometimes, management only want to be informed when something exceptional or out-of-the-ordinary has happened. Reporting on this basis is called reporting by exception.

- **C – Cost-effective –** The value of information should not exceed the cost of producing it. Management information has a value because it helps a manager to make decisions. If a decision by a manager is different from what it would have been without the information, the value of the information could be measured by the amount of money that has been saved as a result. The value of information results from actions by decision makers who use the information to improve profitability. This value should not be greater than the costs involved in obtaining it.

- **U – Understandable –** It should be understandable. A manager should be able to understand what the information is telling him. If he doesn't understand it, he will not use it to make a decision. If he misunderstands it, he might make a bad decision. There can be a particular problem with the use of technical language ('jargon'), and accountants should always be careful about the way in which they present financial information to non-financial managers.

- **R – Relevant –** It should have a purpose and be relevant for that purpose. There is no point in providing a manager with a report if the manager does not know why he has been given it, or what he is expected to do with it. Similarly, the information within a report should be relevant to its purpose and should not contain details that can be ignored.

- **A – Accessible –** Information should be accessible via the appropriate channels of communication and to the right people. A 'channel' of information refers to the method by which the information is given, such as verbally, in a formal report, in an informal report, by e-mail, by electronic file transfer, and so on. It also refers to the individual or department or external organisation that provides the information.

  The appropriate channel of communication varies according to circumstances and the nature of the information. For example, it will depend on how quickly it is needed, how much information has to be communicated, how far the information has to be sent and the costs of sending it in different ways. Within a business, management information should be directed to the manager or managers who can use it and do something with it.

In the context of responsibility accounting, information about costs and revenues should be reported to the manager responsible, who is in a position to control them. There is little value to be gained in reporting costs to a manager who has no control over them.

- **T – Timely –** It should be timely. This means that it should be provided to a manager in time for the manager to do something with it. For example, suppose that a business produces monthly performance reports for its cost centres, and that in May the manager of cost centre X receives a report about actual costs incurred by the centre in January. This information would be over three months old, and the cost centre manager is likely to ignore it because it is not relevant to his current situation.

  Similarly, suppose that a senior management team want to decide on their strategy for overseas expansion, and ask for a report on market conditions in Southern Africa. If they want to make their decision in February, a report submitted in March will be of no value, because the decision will already have been taken.

- **E – Easy** to use!

Test your understanding 1

List the attributes of good information.

2 The managerial processes of planning, decision making and control

The main functions that management are involved with are:

- planning
- decision making
- control.

2.1 Planning

- Planning involves establishing the objectives of an organisation and formulating relevant strategies that can be used to achieve those objectives.
- Planning can be either short-term (tactical planning) or long-term (strategic planning).
- Planning is looked at in more detail in the next section of this chapter.

2.2 Decision making

Decision making involves considering information that has been provided and making an informed decision.

- In most situations, decision making involves making a choice between two or more alternatives.
- The first part of the decision-making process is planning.
- The second part of the decision-making process is control.

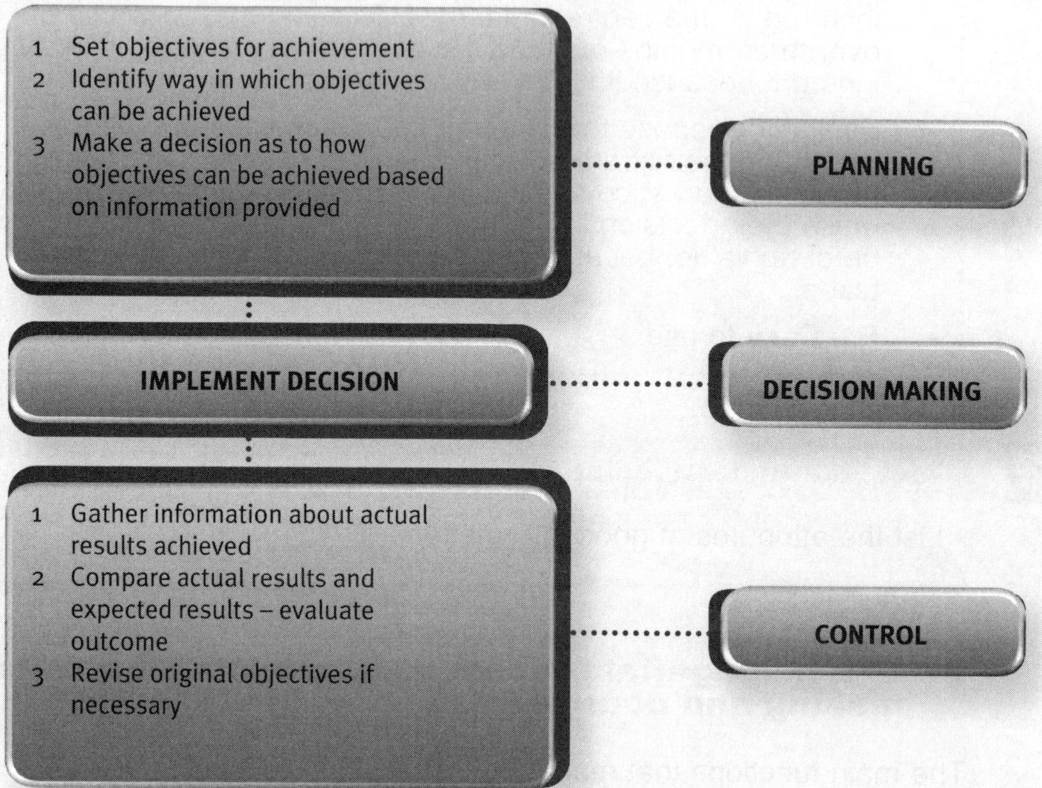

2.3 Control

Control is the second part of the decision-making process. Information relating to the actual results of an organisation is reported to managers.

- Managers use the information relating to actual results to take control measures and to re-assess and amend their original budgets or plans.
- Internally-sourced information, produced largely for control purposes, is called feedback.
- The 'feedback loop' is demonstrated in the following illustration.

e.g

Illustration 2 – The managerial processes of planning, decision making and control

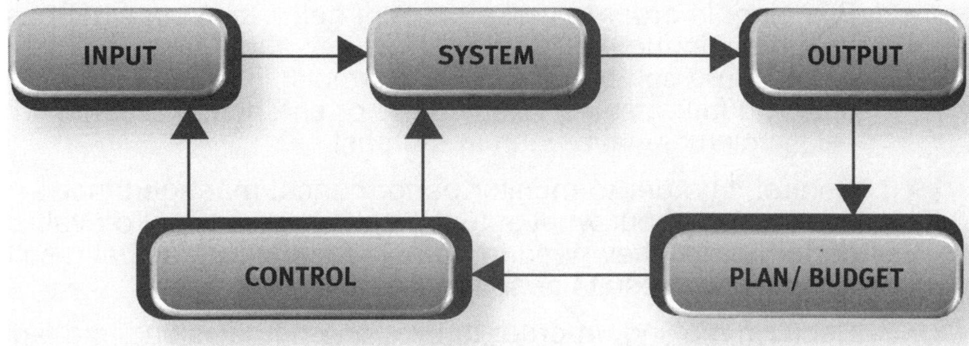

Here, management prepare a plan, which is put into action by the managers with control over the input resources (labour, money, materials, equipment and so on). Output from operations is measured and reported ('fed back') to management, and actual results are compared against the plan in control reports. Managers take corrective action where appropriate, especially in the case of exceptionally bad or good performance. Feedback can also be used to revise plans or prepare the plan for the next period.

Test your understanding 2

	Planning	Control	Decision making
Preparation of the annual budget for a cost centre			
Revise budgets for next period for a cost centre			
Implement decisions based on information provided			
Set organisation's objectives for next period			
Compare actual and expected results for a period			

Required:

Complete the table shown above, identifying each function as either planning, decision making or control.

Expandable text

Managers must have information in order to do their job i.e. in order to plan, control and make decisions.

- Planning. In order to make plans, it helps to know what has happened in the past so that decisions about what is achievable in the future can be made. For example, if a manager is planning future sales volumes, he or she needs to know what sales volumes have been in the past.
- Control. In order to monitor performance, managers need information about what actual results have been. To evaluate performance, they need to be able to compare actual results with planned results or some other target.
- Decision making. In order to take one-off decisions, managers need reliable information to compare the different courses of action available and understand what the consequences might be of choosing each of them.

3 Strategic, tactical and operational planning

3.1 Levels of planning

There are three different levels of planning (known as 'planning horizons').These three levels differ according to their time span and the seniority of the manager responsible for the tasks involved.

- Strategic planning – senior managers formulate long-term objectives (goals) and plans (strategies) for an organisation.
- Tactical planning – senior managers make short-term plans for the next year.
- Operational planning – all managers (including junior managers) are involved in making day-to-day decisions about what to do next and how to deal with problems as they arise.

A simple hierarchy of management tasks can be presented as follows.

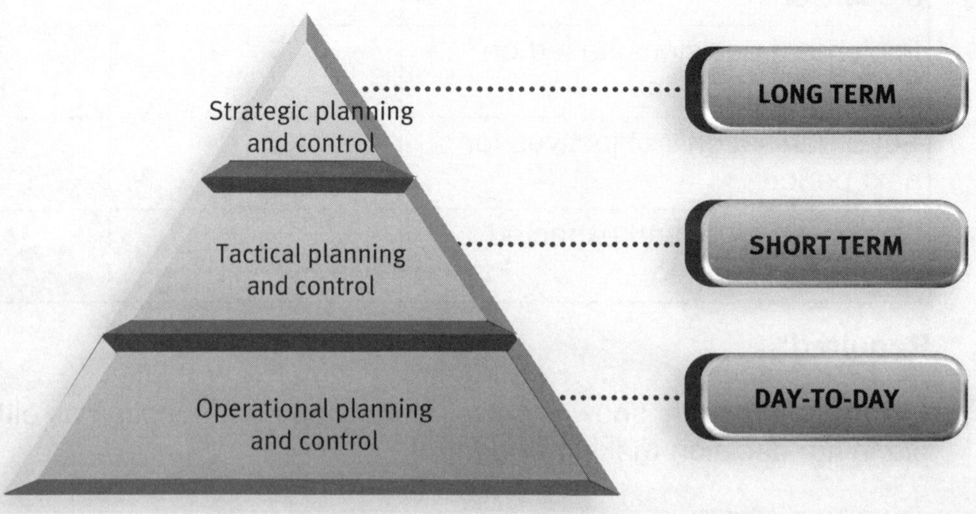

e.g

Illustration 3 – Strategic, tactical and operational planning

The table shown below illustrates the three different categories of planning.

	Private school	Profit-making business
Objective	To provide a high quality of education so that, within five years, 95% of pupils achieve grades A or B in their final examinations.	To achieve a 20% return on capital every year. To increase earnings per share by 10% every year for the next five years.
Strategic plans	Reduce class sizes. Raise new funds to invest $1 million in new equipment and facilities. Attract the highest quality of teacher by paying good salaries.	Cut costs by 15% in domestic markets. Expand into markets in Asia. Increase domestic market share by 10% in the next five years.
Tactical plans	Set a target for this year for examination results. Increase the number of teachers by 10% by the end of the year. Plan the launch of a fund-raising campaign.	Carry out a cost reduction program next year. Establish business relationships with customers in Asia and carry out market research. Increase the size of the work force in order to improve total sales.
Operational plans	Prepare teaching schedules for the next term. Monitor the marks gained by students in mock examinations. Provide whiteboard training to teaching staff.	Obtain prices from more than one supplier before purchasing materials. Offer a bulk purchase discount of 10% to a major customer.

4 Cost centres, profit centres, investment centres and revenue centres

4.1 Responsibility accounting

Responsibility accounting is based on identifying individual parts of a business which are the responsibility of a single manager.

A **responsibility centre** is an individual part of a business whose manager has personal responsibility for its performance. The main responsibility centres are:

- cost centre
- profit centre
- investment centre
- revenue centre.

4.2 Cost centres

A **cost centre** is a production or service location, function, activity or item of equipment whose costs are identified and recorded.

- For a paint manufacturer cost centres might be: mixing department; packaging department; administration; or selling and marketing departments.
- For an accountancy firm, the cost centres might be: audit; taxation; accountancy; word processing; administration; canteen. Alternatively, they might be the various geographical locations, e.g. the London office, the Cardiff office, the Plymouth office.
- Cost centre managers need to have information about costs that are incurred and charged to their cost centres.
- The performance of a cost centre manager is judged on the extent to which cost targets have been achieved.

4.3 Profit centres

A **profit centre** is a part of the business for which both the costs incurred and the revenues earned are identified.

- Profit centres are often found in large organisations with a divisionalised structure, and each division is treated as a profit centre.
- Within each profit centre, there could be several costs centres and revenue centres.
- The performance of a profit centre manager is measured in terms of the profit made by the centre.
- The manager must therefore be responsible for both costs and revenues and in a position to plan and control both.
- Data and information relating to both costs and revenues must be collected and allocated to the relevant profit centres.

Illustration 4 – Responsibility accounting

For a paint manufacturer, profit centres might be the wholesale division and the retail division. For an accountancy firm the profit centres might be the individual locations or the type of business undertaken (audit, consultancy, accountancy etc). Clearly all profit centres can also be cost centres, but not all cost centres can be profit centres. For instance the costs of an employees' canteen can be ascertained, thus it could be a cost centre. But if it earns no revenue, then it cannot be a profit centre.

4.4 Investment centres

Managers of investment centres are responsible for investment decisions as well as decisions affecting costs and revenues.

- Investment centre managers are therefore accountable for the performance of capital employed as well as profits (costs and revenues).
- The performance of investment centres is measured in terms of the profit earned relative to the capital invested (employed). This is known as the return on capital employed (ROCE).
- ROCE = Profit/Capital employed.

4.5 Revenue centres

A **revenue centre** is a part of the organisation that earns sales revenue. It is similar to a cost centre, but only accountable for revenues, and not costs.

- Revenue centres are generally associated with selling activities, for example, a regional sales managers may have responsibility for the regional sales revenues generated.
- Each regional manager would probably have sales targets to reach and would be held responsible for reaching these targets.
- Sales revenues earned must be able to be traced back to individual (regional) revenue centres so that the performance of individual revenue centre managers can be assessed.

5 Management accounting and management information

5.1 Financial accounting

Financial accounting involves recording the financial transactions of an organisation and summarising them in periodic financial statements for external users who wish to analyse and interpret the financial position of the organisation.

- The main duties of the financial accountant include: maintaining the bookkeeping system of the nominal ledger, payables control account, receivables control account and so on and to prepare financial statements as required by law and accounting standards.
- Information produced by the financial accounting system is usually insufficient for the needs of management. Managers usually want to know about: the costs of individual products and services and the profits made by individual products and services
- In order to obtain this information, details are needed for each cost, profit, investment and revenue centre. Such information is provided by cost accounting and management accounting systems.

Expandable text

The role of accountants within an organisation is to set up and operate information systems. Much of this information is financial in nature.

- A business must keep accounting records, for legal purposes. Accounting records are needed to prepare financial statements at the end of each accounting period, and financial statements provide a basis for an assessment of tax on the profits.
- Companies are required to prepare annual financial statements in a form set out by the Companies Act and in compliance with generally-accepted accounting practice. Company accounts must also be audited.
- Financial accountants and bookkeepers have the task of maintaining the ledger system of accounting records, from which the financial statements will be prepared.

The financial accounts can be a source of management information. In general, however, they are insufficient for management's requirements.

A simplified income statement of XYZ Company, prepared by a financial accountant, is shown below:

XYZ Company
Income statement for period X

	$	$
Sales		2,000,000
Cost of sales		
Materials consumed	800,000	
Wages	400,000	
Production expenses	150,000	
		1,350,000
Gross profit		650,000
Marketing expenses	150,000	
General administrative expenses	100,000	
Financing costs	40,000	
		290,000
Net profit		360,000

This profit statement may be adequate to give shareholders a superficial picture of the trading results of the whole business. However, it doesn't give managers enough information about the business performance. Managers need much more detail to answer questions such as:

- Which of our products sell best? How much sales revenue do we earn from each product or product line?
- How much profit do we earn from each product?
- Do we make a loss with any of our products?
- How does the cost per unit sold compare with the cost per unit last year?
- Are costs higher than expected, and if so, in which areas?
- How much more would we have needed to sell to make a profit of $500,000 for the year?

Managers want to know about the costs of individual products and services and the profits they make. Detailed financial information, about costs, revenues, profits and returns, is needed for each cost centre, revenue centre, profit centre and investment centre.

The basic financial accounting system is not capable of providing this information.

Cost accounting and management accounting systems, which can vary in practice between a simple budgeting system and a large and complex information system, provide the detailed information that managers require.

5.2 Cost accounting

Cost accounting is a system for recording data and producing information about costs for the products produced by an organisation and/or the services it provides. It is also used to establish costs for particular activities or responsibility centres.

- Cost accounting involves a careful evaluation of the resources used within the enterprise.
- The techniques employed in cost accounting are designed to provide financial information about the performance of the enterprise and possibly the direction that future operations should take.
- The terms 'cost accounting' and 'management accounting' are often used to mean the same thing.

5.3 Management accounting

Management accounting has cost accounting at its essential foundation.

The main differences between management accounting and cost accounting are as follows:

- Cost accounting is mainly concerned with establishing the historical cost of a product/service.
- Management accounting is concerned with historical information but it is also forward-looking. It is concerned with both historical and future costs of products/services. (For example, budgets and forecasts).
- Management accounting is also concerned with providing non-financial information to managers.
- Management accounting is essentially concerned with offering advice to management based upon information collected (management information).
- Management accounting may include involvement in planning, decision making and control.

Expandable text

Non-financial information

- Information provided by cost accounting systems is financial in nature. Financial information is important for management because many objectives of an organisation are financial in nature, such as making profits and avoiding insolvency. Managers also need information of a non-financial nature.
- At a strategic level, management need to know about developments in their markets and in the economic situation.

They also need to know about any new technology that emerges, and about the activities of competitors.

- At a tactical level, they might want to know about issues such as product or service quality, speed of handling customer complaints, customer satisfaction levels, employee skills levels and employee morale.
- At an operational level, they may want to know about the number of rejects per machine, the lead time for delivering materials and the number of labour and machine hours available.
- The management accounting systems in many organisations are able to obtain non-financial as well as financial information for reporting to management. The importance of non-financial information within the reporting system should not be forgotten.

5.4 Differences between management accounting and financial accounting

The following illustration compares management accounting with financial accounting.

e.g

Illustration 5 – Management accounting and management information

	Management accounting	**Financial accounting**
Information mainly produced for	Internal use: e.g. managers and employees	External use: e.g. shareholders, creditors, lenders, banks, government.
Purpose of information	To aid planning, controlling and decision making	To record the financial performance in a period and the financial position at the end of that period.
Legal requirements	None	Limited companies must produce financial accounts.
Formats	Management decide on the information they require and the most useful way of presenting it	Format and content of financial accounts intending to give a true and fair view should follow accounting standards and company law.
Nature of information	Financial and non-financial.	Mostly financial.
Time period	Historical and forward-looking.	Mainly an historical record.

5.5 The role of management accounting within an organisation's management information system

The management information system of an organisation is likely to be able to prepare the following:

- annual statutory accounts
- budgets and forecasts
- product profitability reports
- cash flow reports
- capital investment appraisal reports
- standard cost and variance analysis reports
- returns to government departments, e.g. VAT returns.

Management information is generally supplied to management in the form of reports. Reports may be routine reports prepared on a regular basis (e.g. monthly) or they may be prepared for a special purpose (e.g. ad hoc report).

Chapter summary

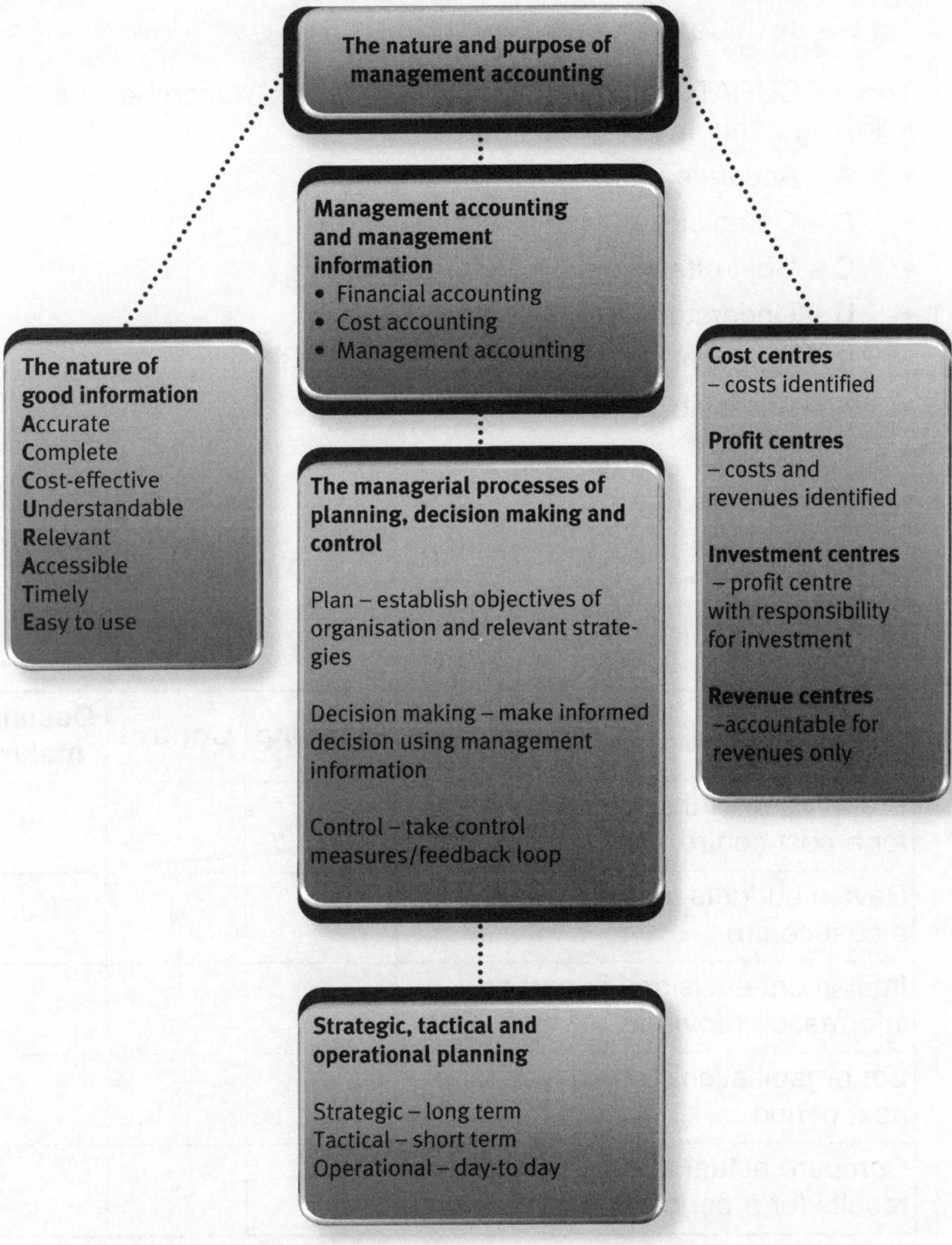

Test your understanding answers

Test your understanding 1

The 'ACCURATE' acronym should help you to remember the following attributes of good information.

- **A** – Accurate
- **C** – Complete
- **C** – Cost-effective
- **U** – Understandable
- **R** – Relevant
- **A** – Accessible
- **T** – Timely
- **E** – Easy to use.

Test your understanding 2

	Planning	**Control**	**Decision making**
Preparation of the annual budget for a cost centre	√		√
Revise budgets for next period for a cost centre		√	√
Implement decisions based on information provided			√
Set organisation's objectives for next period	√		√
Compare actual and expected results for a period		√	√

Note that all planning and control functions are part of the decision-making process and are therefore identified as being both. The only exception is 'implement decisions based on information provided' which is not part of planning and control, but the one decision-making task that there is.

chapter

2

Types of cost and cost behaviour

Chapter learning objectives

- Explain for a manufacturing business, the distinction between production and non-production costs
- Describe, for a manufacturing business, the different elements of production cost - materials, labour and overheads
- Describe, for a manufacturing business, the different elements of non-production cost - administrative, selling, distribution and finance
- Explain the importance of the distinction between production and non-production costs when valuing output and inventories for a business
- Distinguish between, and give examples of, direct and indirect costs in manufacturing and non-manufacturing organisations
- Explain and illustrate the concepts of cost objects, cost units and cost centres for organisations in general
- Describe, using graphs, the following types of cost behaviour and give examples of each: fixed costs; variable costs; stepped fixed costs; and semi-variable costs
- Use high/low analysis to separate the fixed and variable elements of total costs including situations involving stepped fixed costs and changes in the variable cost per unit
- Explain the structure of linear functions and equations (of the form y = a + bx)

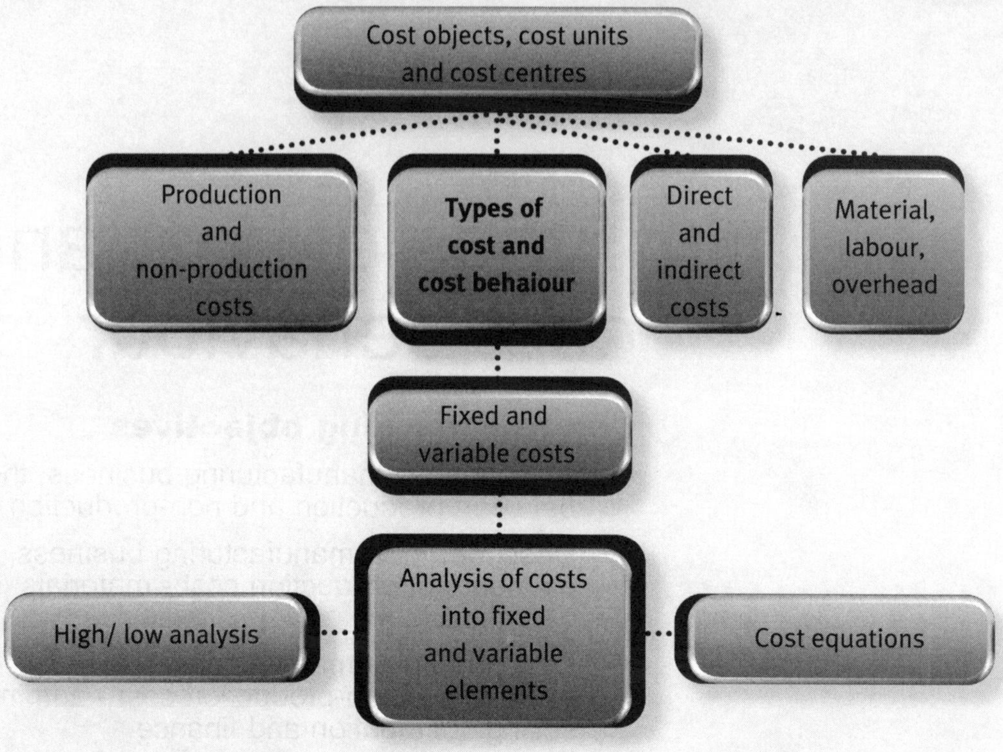

1 Production and non-production costs

1.1 Classifying costs

Costs can be classified in a number of different ways.

- Element - costs are classified as materials, labour or expenses (overheads).
- Nature - costs are classified as being direct or indirect.
- Behaviour - costs are classified as being fixed, variable, semi-variable or stepped fixed.
- Function - costs are classified as being production or non-production costs.

1.2 Classification by element

The main cost elements that you need to know about are materials, labour and expenses.

- Materials - all costs of materials purchased for production or non-production activities. For example, raw materials, components, cleaning materials, maintenance materials and stationery.
- Labour costs - all staff costs relating to employees on the payroll of the organisation.
- Expenses - all other costs which are not materials or labour. This includes all bought-in services, for example, rent, telephone, sub-contractors and costs such as the depreciation of equipment.

1.3 Classification by function - production costs

Production costs are the costs which are incurred when raw materials are converted into finished goods and part-finished goods (work in progress).

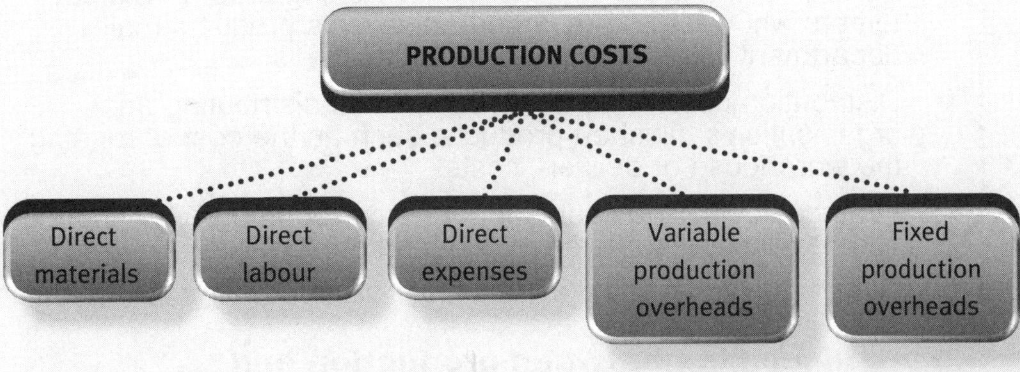

Expandable text

- Direct materials - the direct materials that go into making a product. For example, cloth in the manufacture of shirts.
- Direct labour - the cost of labour directly engaged in making a product. For example, the wages of the machinists making the shirts.
- Direct expenses - the cost of expenses directly involved in making a product. For example, the depreciation of the sewing machines used to make the shirts.
- Variable production overheads - overheads that vary in direct proportion to the quantity of product manufactured. For example, code of fuel used to run machinery.
- Fixed production overheads - overheads that are fixed whatever the quantity of product manufactured. For example, rent of the factory.

1.4 Classification by function - non-production costs

Non-production costs are costs that are not directly associated with the production processes in a manufacturing organisation.

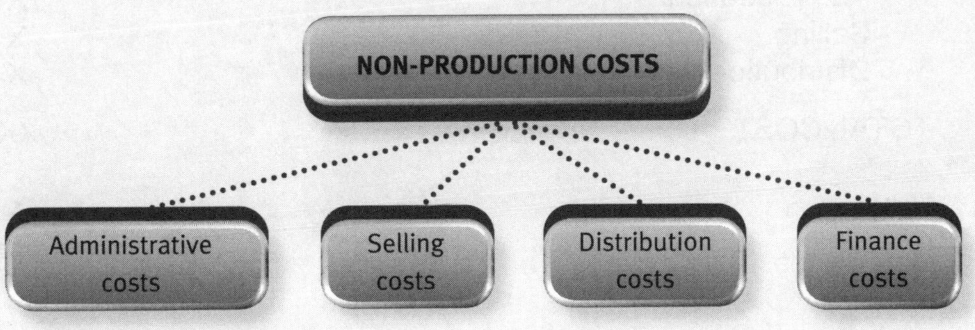

Expandable text

- Administrative costs - the costs involved in running the general administration departments of an organisation, for example, the accounts department.
- Selling costs - costs associated with taking orders from customers who wish to buy an organisation's products (sales department costs) and also marketing costs.
- Distribution costs - the costs involved in distributing an organisation's finished products, such as the cost of running the warehouse or delivery costs.
- Finance costs - the costs that are incurred in order to finance an organisation, for example, loan interest.

1.5 Distinguishing between production and non-production costs

Once costs have been analysed as being production or non-production costs, management may wish to collect the costs together on a cost card. A cost card (or unit cost card) lists out all of the costs involved in making one unit of a product.

COST CARD - statement of the total cost of one unit of a product

	$
Direct materials	X
Direct labour	X
Direct expenses	X
PRIME COST	XX
Variable production overheads	X
MARGINAL PRODUCTION COST	XX
Fixed production overheads	X
TOTAL PRODUCTION COST	XX
Non-production overheads:	
Administration	X
Selling	X
Distribution	X
TOTAL COST	XX
Profit	X
Sales price	XXX

Expandable text

- The total production cost is the marginal production cost (total direct costs) plus any fixed production overheads.
- It is important that the total production cost of a product is clearly identified as being such. Non-production costs must be analysed separately.
- This is because when finished products are transferred to the warehouse as finished goods, they are transferred at a value that reflects the direct manufacturing costs that were involved in producing them, i.e. total production cost.
- When finished goods are transferred to the warehouse, this is where they remain until they are sold to customers or held as inventory.
- When inventory is sold, it is important that it is given a value that reflects the 'cost of sale' of the product, so that a profit can be calculated and reported in the income statement.
- Similarly, at the end of an accounting period, inventory is valued and reported in the balance sheet of an organisation at its total production cost.
- It is important, therefore, that the production costs and the non-production costs are clearly distinguished for the purposes of valuing output and inventories.

Test your understanding 1

Complete the following table by classifying each expense correctly.

Cost	**Classification**
Overalls for machine workers	
Cost of printer cartridges in general office	
Salary of factory supervisor	
Salary of payroll supervisor	
Rent of warehouse for storing goods ready for sale	
Loan interest	
Salary of factory security guard	
Early settlement discounts for customers who pay early	
Salary of the Chairman's PA	
Road tax licence for delivery vehicles	
Bank overdraft fee	
Salesmens' commissions	

Classifications
1 = Production
2 = Selling
3 = Distribution
4 = Administrative
5 = Finance

2 Direct and indirect costs

2.1 Direct costs

Direct costs are costs which can be directly identified with a specific cost unit or cost centre. There are three main types of direct cost:

- direct materials - for example, cloth for making shirts
- direct labour - for example, the wages of the workers stitching the cloth to make the shirts
- direct expenses - for example, the cost of maintaining the sewing machine used to make the shirts.

The total of direct costs is known as the prime cost.

2.2 Indirect costs

Indirect costs are costs which cannot be directly identified with a specific cost unit or cost centre. Examples of indirect costs include the following:

- indirect materials - these include materials that cannot be traced to an individual shirt, for example, cotton
- indirect labour - for example, the cost of a supervisor who supervises the shirtmakers
- indirect expenses - for example, the cost of renting the factory where the shirts are manufactured.

The total of indirect costs is known as overheads.

Test your understanding 2

Identify whether the following costs are materials, labour or expenses and whether they are direct or indirect.

Cost	Materials, labour or expense	Direct or indirect?
The hire of tools or equipment		
Rent of a factory		
Packing materials, e.g. cartons and boxes		
Supervisors' salaries		
Oil for lubricating machines		
Wages of factory workers involved in production		
Depreciation of equipment		

Test your understanding 3

(a) Which of the following would be classed as indirect labour?

A Assembly workers

B A stores assistant in a factory store

C Plasterers in a building company

D An audit clerk in an accountancy firm

(b) Direct costs are:

A costs which can be identified with a cost centre but not a single cost unit

B costs which can be identified with a single cost unit

C costs which can be attributed to an accounting period

D none of the above.

3 Fixed and variable costs

3.1 Cost behaviour

Costs may be classified according to the way that they behave. Cost behaviour is the way in which input costs vary with different levels of activity. Cost behaviour tends to classify costs as one of the following:

- variable cost
- fixed cost
- stepped fixed cost
- semi-variable cost.

3.2 Variable costs

Variable costs are costs that tend to vary in total with the level of activity. As activity levels increase then total variable costs will also increase.

- Variable costs can be shown graphically as follows:

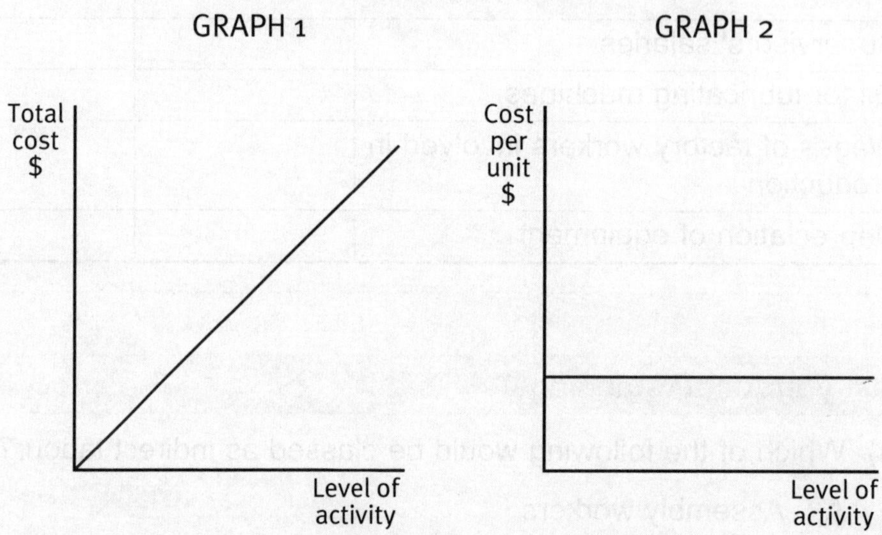

- Note that as total costs increase with activity levels, the cost per unit of variable costs remains constant.
- Examples of variable costs include direct costs such as raw materials and direct labour.

Expandable text

- Variable costs in total change in direct proportion to the level of activity (graph 1) i.e. as level of activity rises, total cost rises at the same rate.
- If the direct cost of materials is two kilograms at $2 per kg for each widget, this amounts to $4 per widget.
- Total materials cost is $4 if one unit is made, $8 if two units are made and $800 if 200 units are made.
- The variable cost per unit is constant at $4 per widget (graph 2) i.e. it is a constant $4 per unit.

3.3 Fixed costs

A fixed cost is a cost which is incurred for an accounting period, and which, within certain activity levels remains constant.

- Fixed costs can be shown graphically as follows:

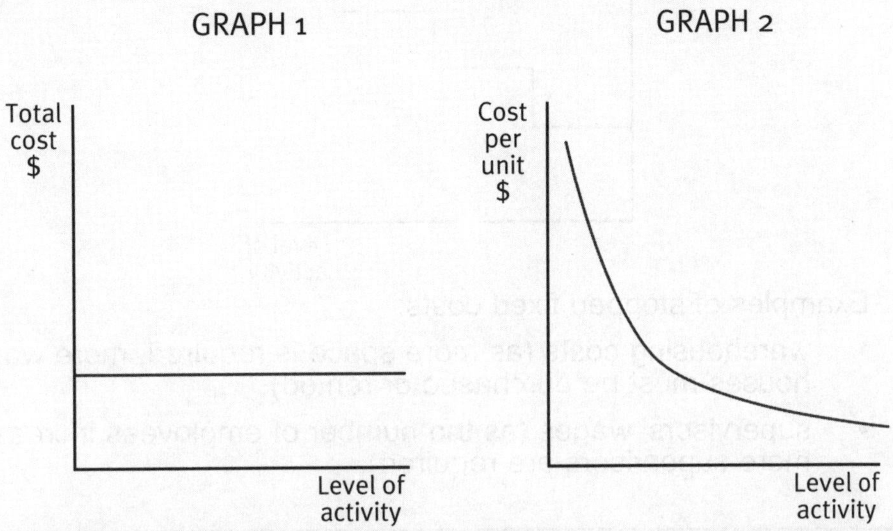

- Note that the total cost remains constant over a given level of activity but that the cost per unit falls as the level of activity increases.
- Examples of fixed costs:
  - rent
  - business rates
  - executive salaries.

Expandable text

- If factory rent is $5,000 per month, this cost will be incurred whether 2 widgets are made, or 200 widgets are made - graph 1 demonstrates this.
- If 2 widgets are made the fixed cost per unit is $\frac{\$5,000}{2}$, i.e. $2,500 per widget.
- If 200 widgets are made the fixed cost per unit is $\frac{\$5,000}{200}$, i.e. $25 per widget.
- Therefore, the fixed cost per unit falls at a reducing rate but never reaches zero - graph 2 demonstrates this.

3.4 Stepped fixed costs

This is a type of fixed cost that is only fixed within certain levels of activity. Once the upper limit of an activity level is reached then a new higher level of fixed cost becomes relevant.

- Stepped fixed costs can be shown graphically as follows:

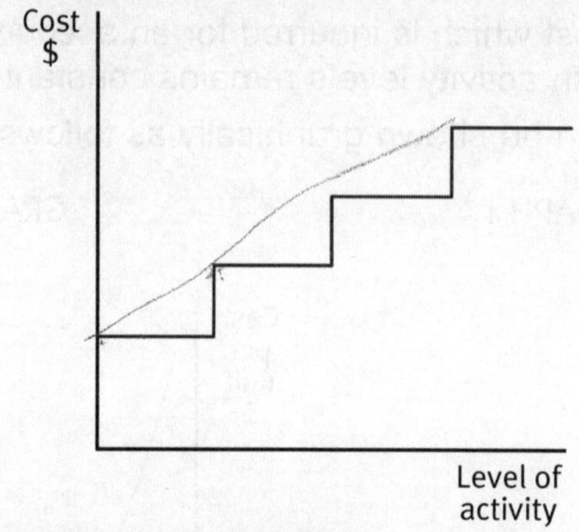

- Examples of stepped fixed costs:
  - warehousing costs (as more space is required, more warehouses must be purchased or rented)
  - supervisors' wages (as the number of employees increases, more supervisors are required).

Expandable text

- For production of up to 50 widgets, only one supervisor is required but if production is between 50 and 100 widgets, two supervisors are required.
- The cost of one supervisor is $18,000 per annum and the cost of two supervisors is therefore $36,000.
- The fixed costs therefore increase in steps as shown in the stepped fixed cost graph above.

3.5 Semi-variable costs

Semi-variable costs contain both fixed and variable cost elements and are therefore partly affected by fluctuations in the level of activity.

- Semi-variable costs can be shown graphically as follows:

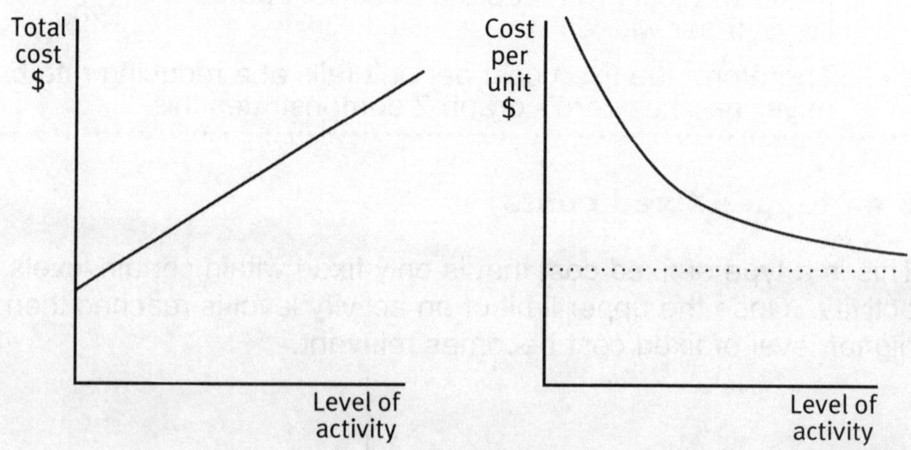

- Examples of semi-variable costs:
  - electricity bills (fixed standing charge plus variable cost per unit of electricity consumed)
  - telephone bills (fixed line rental plus variable cost per call).

Test your understanding 4

Classify the following items of expenditure according to their behaviour i.e. as fixed, variable, semi-variable or stepped fixed costs.

(1) Monthly rent
(2) Council tax charge
(3) Bank loan interest
(4) Petrol
(5) Electricity bill
(6) Telephone bill
(7) Annual salary
(8) Depreciation of one, two and three factory machines
(9) Raw materials

Test your understanding 5

Study the following graphs and then answer the questions shown below.

Graph 1

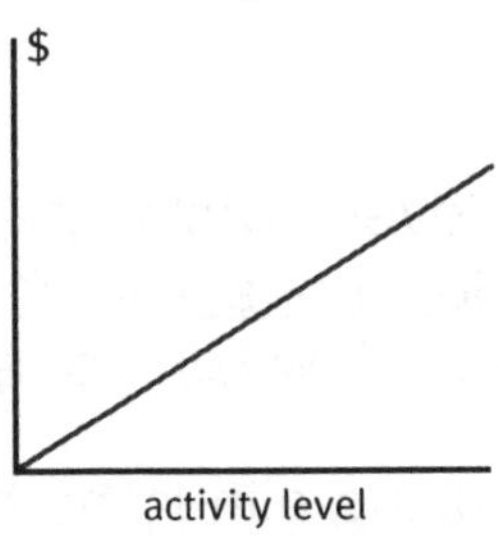

Graph 2

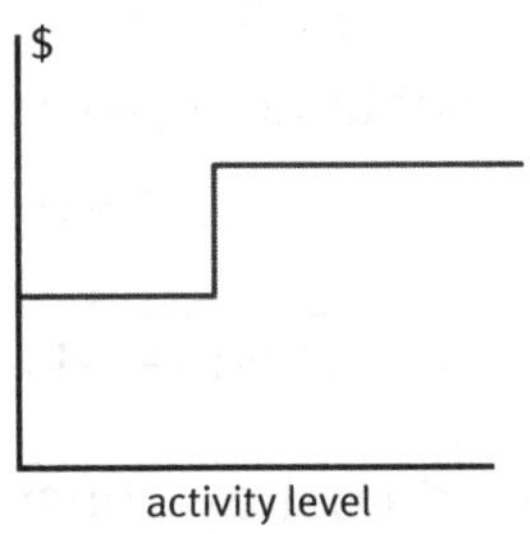

Graph 3

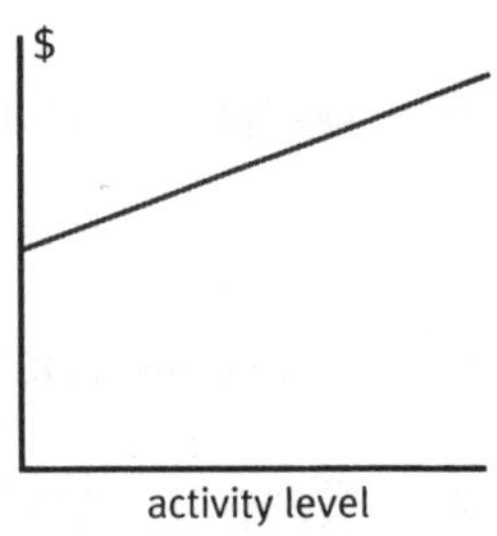

Graph 4

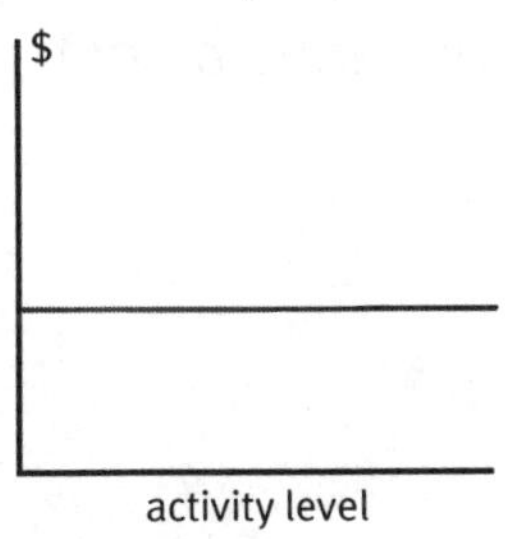

Graph 5

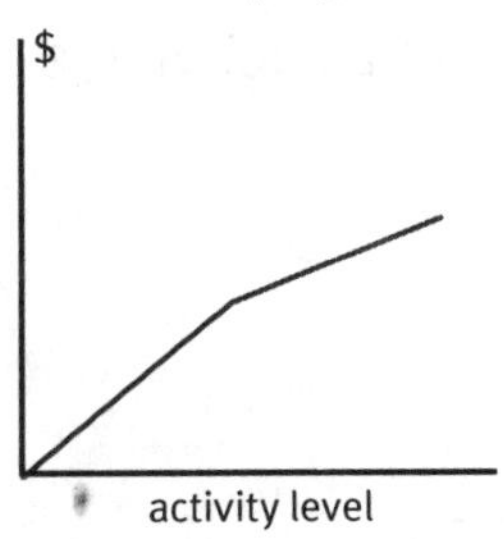

Graph 6

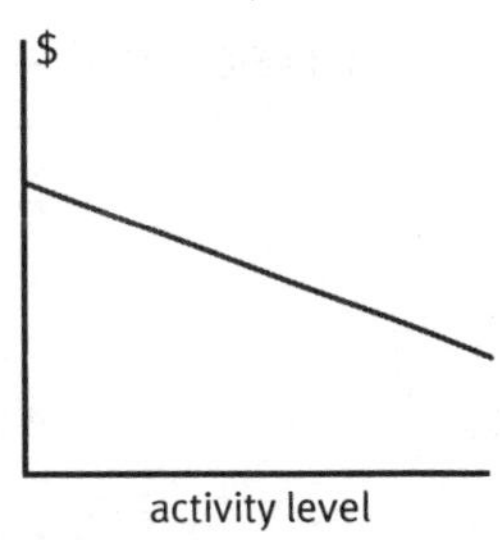

A fixed cost is shown in graph	
A variable cost is shown in graph	
A semi-variable cost is shown in graph	
Fixed cost per unit is shown in graph	
Variable cost per unit is shown in graph	
A stepped fixed cost is shown in graph	

4 Analysis of costs into fixed and variable elements

4.1 Cost estimation

A number of methods exist for analysing semi-variable costs into their fixed and variable elements. The two main methods are:

- high/low method
- least squares regression - (we will look at this in the next chapter).

4.2 High/low method

- **Step 1** - select the highest and lowest activity levels, and their associated costs

  (Note: do not take the highest and lowest costs)

- **Step 2** - find the variable cost per unit

$$\text{Variable cost per unit} = \frac{\text{Cost at high level of activity} - \text{cost at low level of activity}}{\text{High level of activity} - \text{low level of activity}}$$

- **Step 3** - find the fixed cost by substitution, using either the high or low activity level.

  Fixed cost = Total cost at activity level - Total variable cost

Expandable text

Assumptions of the high/low method are as follows:

- the cost under consideration is potentially semi-variable (ie it has both fixed and variable elements)
- the linear model of cost behaviour is valid ie y = a + bx (we will study this in more detail later on in this chapter).

Making a distinction between fixed and variable costs might be used:

- in product costing
- to analyse profitability of a product or department
- to help managers to make decisions about increasing/decreasing activity levels
- to estimate future costs (forecasting and budgeting)
- to estimate what costs should have been (for budgetary control and performance assessment).

e.g

Illustration 1 – Analysis of costs into fixed and variable elements

Output (Units)	Total cost ($)
200	7,000
300	8,000
400	9,000

Required:

(a) Find the variable cost per unit.
(b) Find the total fixed cost.
(c) Estimate the total cost if output is 350 units.
(d) Estimate the total cost if output is 600 units.

Solution

(a) Variable cost per unit = $\frac{\$9{,}000 - \$7000}{400 - 200} = \frac{\$2000}{200}$ = \$10 per unit

(b) Total fixed cost by substituting at high activity level:

Total cost	=		$9,000
Total variable cost	=	400 x $10	$4,000
∴ Fixed cost	=		$5,000

(c) If output is 350 units:

Variable cost	=	350 x $10 =	$3,500
Fixed cost	=		$5,000
Total cost	=		$8,500

(d) If output is 600 units:

Variable cost	=	600 x $10	$6,000
Fixed cost	=		$5,000
Total cost	=		$11,000

Test your understanding 6

The total costs incurred at various output levels in a factory have been measured as follows:

Output (units)	Total cost ($)
26	6,566
30	6,510
33	6,800
44	6,985
48	7,380
50	7,310

Required:

Using the high/low method, analyse the total cost into fixed and variable components.

4.3 High/low method with stepped fixed costs

Sometimes fixed costs are only fixed within certain levels of activity and increase in steps as activity increases (i.e. they are stepped fixed costs).

- The high/low method can still be used to estimate fixed and variable costs.
- Adjustments need to be made for the fixed costs based on the activity level under consideration.

e.g

Illustration 2 – Analysis of costs into fixed and variable elements

An organisation has the following total costs at three activity levels:

Activity level (units)	4,000	6,000	7,500
Total cost	$40,800	$50,000	$54,800

Variable cost per unit is constant within this activity range and there is a step up of 10% in the total fixed costs when the activity level exceeds 5,500 units.

What is the total cost at an activity level of 5,000 units?

A $44,000

B $44,800

C $45,400

D $46,800

Solution:

A

Calculate the variable cost per unit by comparing two output levels where fixed costs will be the same:

Variable cost per unit = [(54,800 - 50,000) ÷ (7,500 - 6,000)] = $3.20

Total fixed cost above 5,500 units = [54,800 - (7,500 x 3.20)] = $30,800

Total fixed cost below 5,500 units = (10 ÷ 11) x 30,800 = $28,000

Total cost for 5,000 units = [(5,000 x 3.20) + 28,000] = $44,000

4.4 High/low method with changes in the variable cost per unit

Sometimes there may be changes in the variable cost per unit, and the high/low method can still be used to determine the fixed and variable elements of semi-variable costs. The variable cost per unit may change because:

- prices may be forecast to increase in future periods
- bulk discounts may be available for purchasing resources in large quantities.

e.g

Illustration 3 – Analysis of costs into fixed and variable elements

The following information relates to the manufacture of Product LL in 20X8:

Output (Units)	Total cost ($)
200	7,000
300	8,000
400	8,600

For output volumes above 350 units the variable cost per unit falls by 10%. (Note: this fall applies to all units - not just the excess above 350).

Required:

Estimate the cost of producing 450 units of Product LL in 20X9.

Solution

Variable cost per unit (<350) = $\frac{\$8{,}000 - \$7{,}000}{300 - 200} = \frac{\$1{,}000}{100}$ = \$10 per unit

Total cost at 300 units =			$8,000
Total variable cost	=	300 x $10	$3,000
∴ Fixed cost	=		$5,000

If output is 450 units in 20X9:

Variable cost	=	450 x $9(W1) =	$4,050
Fixed cost	=		$5,000
Total cost	=		$9,050

W1 Variable cost per unit in 20X9 (when output > 350 units) = $10 x 0.9 = $9 per unit

Test your understanding 7

The total costs incurred in 20X3 at various output levels in a factory have been measured as follows:

Output (units)	Total cost ($)
26	6,566
30	6,510
33	6,800
44	6,985
48	7,380
50	7,310

When output is 80 units or more, another factory unit must be rented and fixed costs therefore increase by 100%.

Variable cost per unit is forecast to rise by 10% in 20X4.

Required:

Calculate the estimated total costs of producing 100 units in 20X4.

Expandable text

The main advantage of the high/low method is that it is easy to understand and easy to use.

The limitations of the high/low method are as follows:

- it relies on historical cost data and assumes this data can reliably predict future costs
- it assumes that activity levels are the only factor affecting costs
- it uses only two values (highest and lowest) to predict future costs and these results may be distorted because of random variations which may have occurred.

5 Cost equations

5.1 Equation of a straight line

The equation of a straight line is a linear function and is represented by the following equation:

y = a + bx

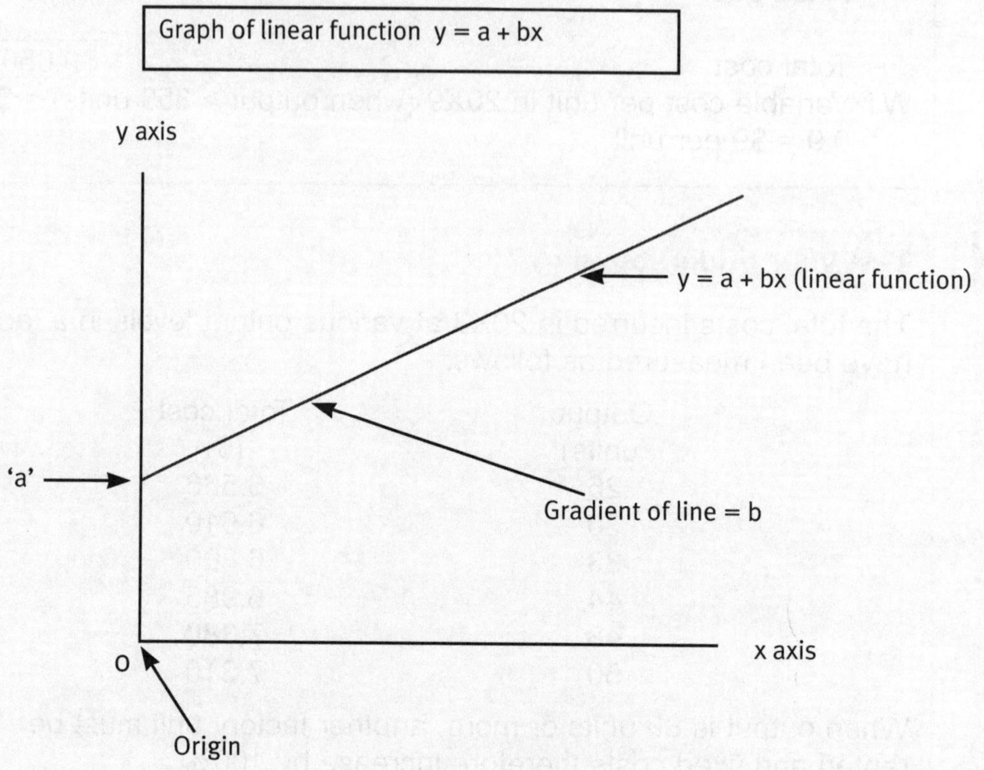

- 'a' is the intercept, i.e. the point at which the line y = a + bx cuts the y axis (the value of y when x = 0).
- 'b' is the gradient/slope of the line y = a + bx (the change in y when x increases by one unit).
- 'x' = independent variable .
- 'y' = dependent variable (its value depends on the value of 'x').

5.2 Cost equations

Cost equations are derived from historical cost data. Once a cost equation has been established, like the high/low method, it can be used to estimate future costs. Cost equations have the same formula as linear functions:

- 'a' is the fixed cost per period (the intercept)
- 'b' is the variable cost per unit (the gradient)
- 'x' is the activity level (the independent variable)
- 'y' is the total cost = fixed cost + variable cost (dependent on the activity level)

Suppose a cost has a cost equation of y = $5,000 + 10x, this can be shown graphically as follows:

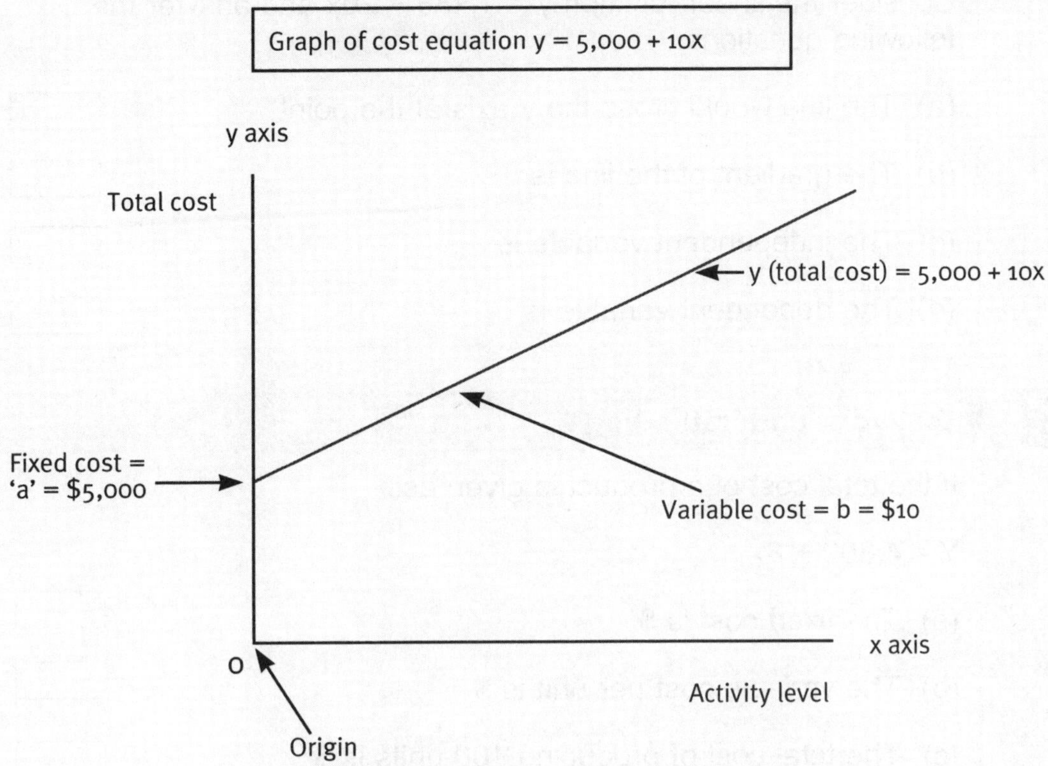

e.g

Illustration 4 – Cost equations

If y = 8,000 + 40x

(a) Fixed cost = $ [ ]

(b) Variable cost per unit = $ [ ]

(c) Total cost for 200 units = $ [ ]

Solution

(a) Fixed cost = $ 8000

(b) Variable cost per unit = $ 40

(c) Total cost for 200 units = $ 16,000 (see working)

Working

Fixed cost = $8,000

Variable cost = 200 x $40 = $8,000

Total cost = fixed cost + variable cost = $8,000 + $8,000 = $16,000

Test your understanding 8

Consider the linear function y = 1,488 + 20x and answer the following questions.

(a) The line would cross the y axis at the point

(b) The gradient of the line is

(c) The independent variable is

(d) The dependent variable is

Test your understanding 9

If the total cost of a product is given as:

Y = 4,800 + 8x

(a) The fixed cost is $

(b) The variable cost per unit is $

(c) The total cost of producing 100 units is $

6 Cost objects, cost units and cost centres

6.1 Analysing costs

Management will require a variety of different cost summaries, including:

- costs for a particular product - cost unit or cost object
- costs for use in the preparation of external financial reports
- costs for a particular department - cost centre
- costs that may be useful for decision making
- costs that are useful for planning and control.

6.2 Cost objects

A cost object is any activity for which a separate measurement of cost is undertaken.

Examples of cost objects:

- cost of a product
- cost of a service (e.g. insurance policy)
- cost of running a department
- cost of running a regional office.

6.3 Cost units

A cost unit is a unit of product or service in relation to which costs are ascertained.

Examples of cost units:

- a room (in a hotel)
- a litre of paint (paint manufacturers)
- in-patient (in a hospital).

6.4 Cost centres

A cost centre is a production or service location, function, activity or item of equipment for which costs can be ascertained.

Examples of cost centres:

- a department
- a machine
- a project
- a ward (in a hospital).

6.5 Cost cards

The following costs are brought together and recorded on a cost card:

- direct materials
- direct labour
- direct expenses
- prime cost (total direct costs)
- variable production overheads
- fixed production overheads
- non-production overheads.

e.g

Illustration 5 – Cost objects, cost units and cost centres

A cost card for a hand-made wooden train set is shown below.

- The cutting and assembly department and the painting department are cost centres.
- One hand-made wooden train set is a cost unit (but may also be classed as a cost object).

Cost card for hand-made wooden train set

		$
Direct materials		
Wood	5m2 @ $2.50 per m2	12.50
Paint	0.1 litre at $10 per litre	1.00
Direct labour		
Cutting and assembly department	0.5 hours at $6.00 per hour	3.00
Painting department	1.0 hours @ $7.00 per hour	7.00
Direct expenses	Licence fee @ $2 per train set	2.00
PRIME COST		25.50
Variable production overheads		
Power for electric saws	0.25 hours @ $2.00 per hour	0.50
MARGINAL PRODUCTION COST		26.00
Fixed production overheads	1.5 labour hours @ $10.00 per labour hour	15.00
TOTAL PRODUCTION COST		41.00
Non-production overheads:		
Administration, selling and distribution	20% of total production cost	8.20
TOTAL COST		49.20
Profit	30% of total cost	14.76
Sales price		63.96

Test your understanding 10

(a) A cost unit is:

A the cost per hour of operating a machine.

B the cost per unit of electricity consumed.

C a unit of product or service in relation to which costs are ascertained.

D a measure of work output in a standard hour.

(b) A cost centre is:

A a function or location for which budgets are prepared.

B a unit of product for which costs can be ascertained.

C a function or location for which costs can be ascertained.

D an activity for which costs can be estimated.

Chapter summary

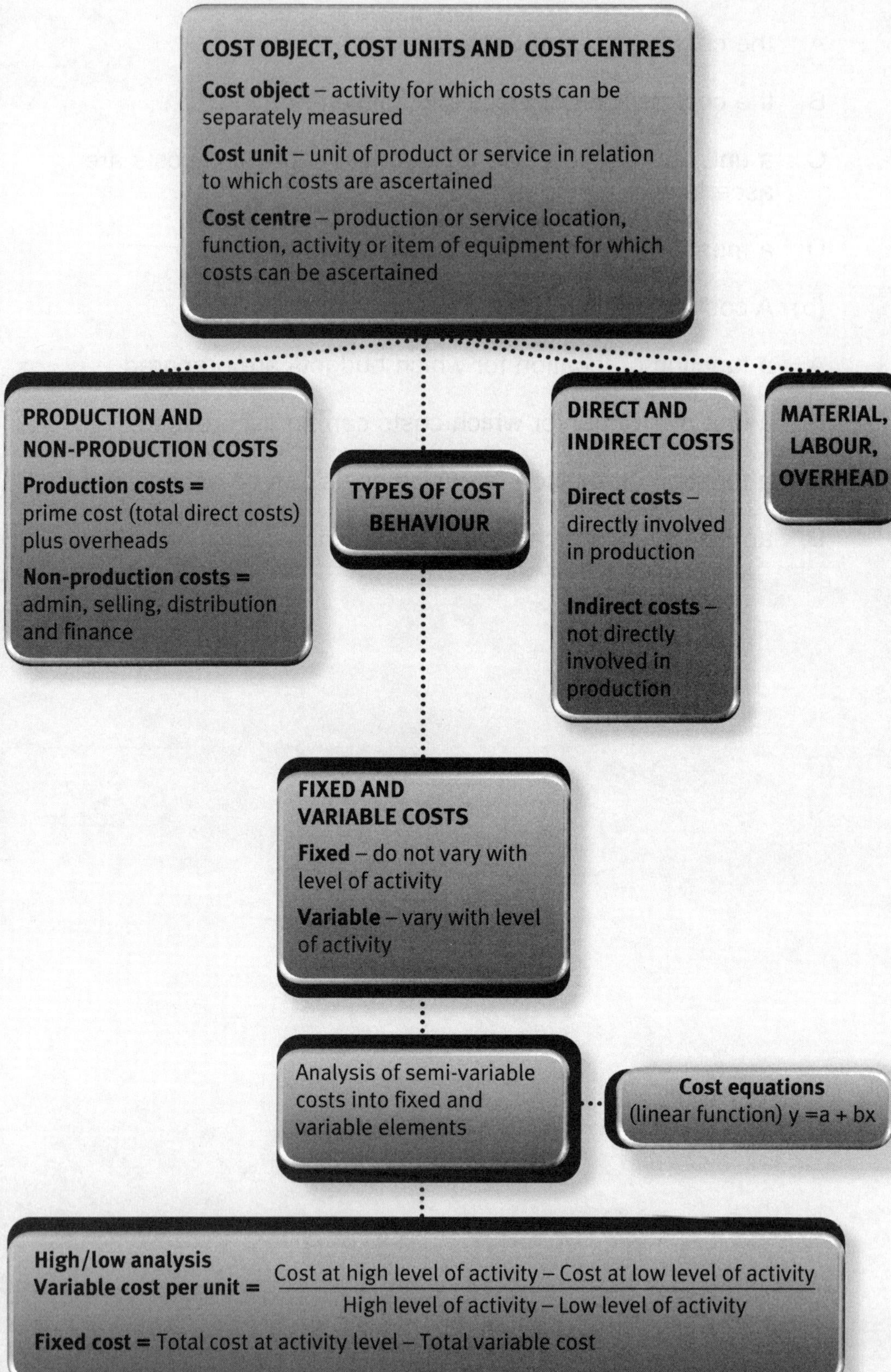

Test your understanding answers

Test your understanding 1

Cost	Classification
Overalls for machine workers	1
Cost of printer cartridges in general office	4
Salary of factory supervisor	1
Salary of payroll supervisor	4
Rent of warehouse for storing goods ready for sale	3
Loan interest	5
Salary of factory security guard	1
Early settlement discounts for customers who pay early	2
Salary of the Chairman's PA	4
Road tax licence for delivery vehicles	3
Bank overdraft fee	5
Salesmens' commissions	2

Test your understanding 2

Cost	Materials, labour or expense	Direct or indirect?
The hire of tools or equipment	Expense	Direct
Rent of a factory	Expense	Indirect
Packing materials, e.g. cartons and boxes	Material	Direct
Supervisors' salaries	Labour	Indirect
Oil for lubricating machines	Material	Indirect
Wages of factory workers involved in production	Labour	Direct
Depreciation of equipment	Expense	Indirect

Test your understanding 3

(a) B Store assistants are not directly involved in producing the output (goods or services) of an organisation.

(b) B This is a basic definition question. Direct costs are costs which can be identified with a single cost unit, or cost centre.

Test your understanding 4

The items of expenditure would be analysed as follows.

(1) Fixed
(2) Fixed
(3) Fixed
(4) Variable
(5) Semi-variable
(6) Semi-variable
(7) Fixed
(8) Stepped fixed
(9) Variable

Note that the depreciation charge for the factory machines (8) is a stepped fixed cost because as activity increases to such a level that a second and third machine are required, the fixed cost will double and then treble.

Test your understanding 5

A fixed cost is shown in graph	4
A variable cost is shown in graph	1
A semi-variable cost is shown in graph	3
Fixed cost per unit is shown in graph	6
Variable cost per unit is shown in graph	4
A stepped fixed cost is shown in graph	2

Test your understanding 6

Variable cost per unit = $\frac{\$7,310 - \$6,566}{50 - 26} = \frac{\$744}{24}$ = $31 per unit

Substituting at high activity level:

Total cost	=		$7,310
Total variable cost	=	50 x $31	$1,550
∴ Fixed cost	=		$5,760

Test your understanding 7

Variable cost per unit (20X3) = $\frac{\$7,310 - \$6,566}{50 - 26} = \frac{\$744}{24}$ = $31 per unit

Substituting at high activity level:

Total cost	=		$7,310
Total variable cost	=	50 x $31	$1,550
∴ Fixed cost (in 20X3)	=		$5,760

Estimated total costs of producing 100 units in 20X4:

Variable cost	=	100 x $31 x 1.1	$3,410
Fixed cost	=	$5,760 x 2 =	$11,520
Total cost	=		$14,930

Test your understanding 8

(a) The line would cross the y axis at the point	1,488
(b) The gradient of the line is	20
(c) The independent variable is	x
(d) The dependent variable is	y

Test your understanding 9

(a) The fixed cost is $	4,800
(b) The variable cost per unit is $	8
(c) The total cost of producing 100 units is $	5,600

Working

Fixed cost = $4,800

Variable cost = 100 x $8 = $800

Total cost = fixed cost + variable cost = $4,800 + $800 = $5,600

Test your understanding 10

(a) C - a cost unit is a unit of product or service in relation to which costs are ascertained.

(b) C - a cost centre is a function or location for which costs can be ascertained.

chapter

3

Business mathematics

Chapter learning objectives

Upon completion of this chapter you will be able to:

- explain, calculate and demonstrate the use of an expected value in simple decision-making situations
- explain the limitations of the expected value technique, excluding the use of decision trees and conditional profit tables
- establish a linear function using regression analysis and interpret the results including areas where care is needed (extrapolation and the relevant range)
- calculate a correlation coefficient and a coefficient of determination, interpreting and explaining r and r^2.

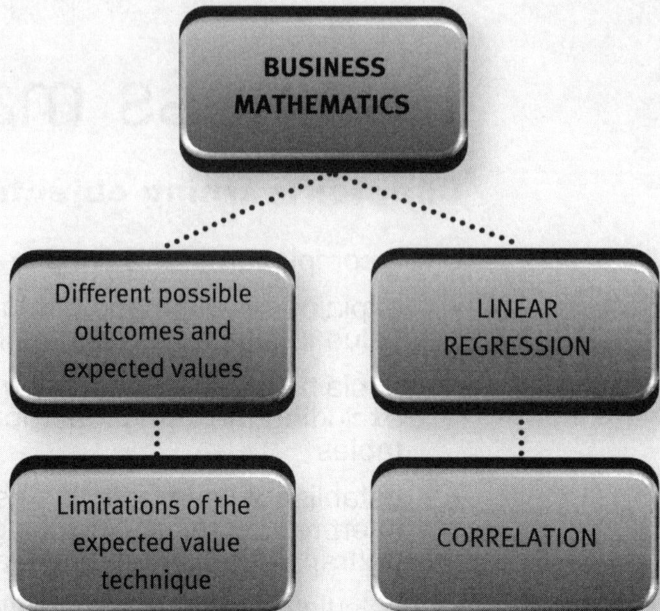

1. Different possible outcomes and expected values

1.1 Expected values

An expected value is a long run average. It is the weighted average of a probability distribution.

- The formula for an expected value is as follows.

  Expected value (EV) = $\sum px$

  Where:

  $\sum$ = 'sum of'

  p = probability of the outcome occurring

  x = the outcome

- Expected values are used in simple decision-making situations in order to decide the best course of action for a company.
- Probabilities are based on an analysis of past data. It is assumed that the past is a good indicator of the future.

- When using expected values to assess projects, accept projects only if the EV is positive. If the EV is negative (i.e. an expected loss) the project should be rejected.
- If deciding between projects which all have positive EVs then the project with the highest expected value should be chosen.

Expandable text

Expected values

The expected value of a particular action is the sum of the values of the possible outcomes each multiplied by their respective probabilities.

If the probability of winning \$x is p then the expectation (or expected value) is p x \$x.

This is rather a mathematical (or theoretical) concept as will be seen from the following example.

On the throw of a dice \$5 is to be paid for a six, \$4 for a five, \$3 for a four and nothing for a 1, 2 or 3. The expectation is calculated as follows:

P(6)	= 1/6	∴	expectation	=	1/6	x	\$5	=	\$0.83
P(5)	= 1/6	∴	expectation	=	1/6	x	\$4	=	\$0.67
P(4)	= 1/6	∴	expectation	=	1/6	x	\$3	=	\$0.50
P(1, 2 or 3)	= 3/6	∴	expectation	=	3/6	x	\$0	=	\$0.00
			Total						\$2.00

The expected winnings is \$2.

In fact a person playing a game of this type will either win \$5 or \$4 or \$3 or nothing. They cannot actually win \$2. The expectation is the amount they can expect to win per game, on average, over a long series of games. It is also a fair price to pay for playing the game.

This same approach can be applied to decision making. Two or more possible courses of action may be open to a company and the only basis on which they can make a decision is that of expected values (usually profits).

Decision analysis

A decision is a choice between two or more alternatives.

- Certainty or uncertainty? Decisions may be taken under conditions of certainty, for example, I have received an offer to sell my car for \$5,000. Should I accept the offer?

- The decision has a simple yes/no choice which can be evaluated:

  Accept - receive $5,000 and have no car.

  Reject - keep the car but do not receive $5,000.
- Alternatively the decision may involve:
  - keeping the car
  - trying to sell it privately for $5,000
  - trying to sell it at auction for $4,800.
- Clearly the outcome of (b) and (c) is uncertain; the car may not be sold at all, and if it is sold the proceeds may not be for the sums suggested.
- Most decisions which a company's management has to make can be described as decisions made under uncertainty. The essential features of making a decision under uncertain conditions are:
  - the decision maker is faced with a choice between several alternative courses of action
  - each course of action may have several possible outcomes, dependent on a number of uncertain factors, i.e. even when a decision has been made the outcome is by no means certain
  - which choice is made will depend upon the criteria used by the decision maker in judging between the outcomes of the possible courses of action.

e.g

Illustration 1 – Different possible outcomes and expected values

A company has recorded the following daily sales over the last 200 days.

Daily sales (units)	Number of days
100	40
200	60
300	80
400	20

Required:

Calculate the expected sales level in the future.

Solution

We can convert the above results into a probability distribution (i.e. show the range of possible outcomes and their associated probabilities) as follows:

Daily sales (units)	Probability
100	40/200 = 0.2
200	60/200 = 0.3
300	80/200 = 0.4
400	20/200 = 0.1

(Note that the probabilities add up to one.)

The expected value ('EV') of the future sales is calculated as follows:

EV = $\sum px$ = sum of (daily sales x probability)

= (0.2 x 100) + (0.3 x 200) + (0.4 x 300) + (0.1 x 400) = 240 units

Note that the daily sales are the 'outcome' in the situation given here.

So what does this mean?

- On average we will sell 240 units a day.
- On a particular day we will sell 100 or 200 or 300 or 400, so the average (240) cannot actually happen.

Test your understanding 1

A company is bidding for three contracts, which are awarded independently of each other. The Board estimates its chances of winning contract X as 50%, of winning contract Y as 1 in 3, and of winning contract Z as 1 in 5. The profits from X, Y and Z are estimated to be $40,000, $60,000 and $100,000 respectively.

The expected value to the company of the profits from all three contracts will be closest to ($000):

A 40

B 60

C 90

D 100

2 Limitations of the expected value technique

There are a number of limitations of using the expected value technique to evaluate decisions.

- Probablities used in expected value calculations are usually based on past data and are therefore likely to be estimates. There is a danger, therefore, that these estimates are likely to be unreliable because they are not accurate.

- Expected values are not always suitable for making one-off decisions. This is because expected values are long-term averages and the conditions surrounding a one-off decision may be difficult to estimate.
- Expected value calculations do not take into account the 'time value of money' and the fact that $1,000 now is worth less than $1,000 in five years' time. EV calcuations are based on the value of money 'today' only.
- Expected values only take into account some of the factors surrounding a decision, and not all of them. For example, they do not look at the decision taker's attitude to risk which will vary from person to person.

3 Linear regression analysis

3.1 Line of best fit

Consider the following data which relates to the total costs incurred at various output levels in a factory:

Output (units)	Total cost ($)
26	6,566
30	6,510
33	6,800
44	6,985
48	7,380
50	7,310

If the data shown above is plotted on a graph, it will look like this.

Scattergraph showing total costs incurred at various output levels in a factory

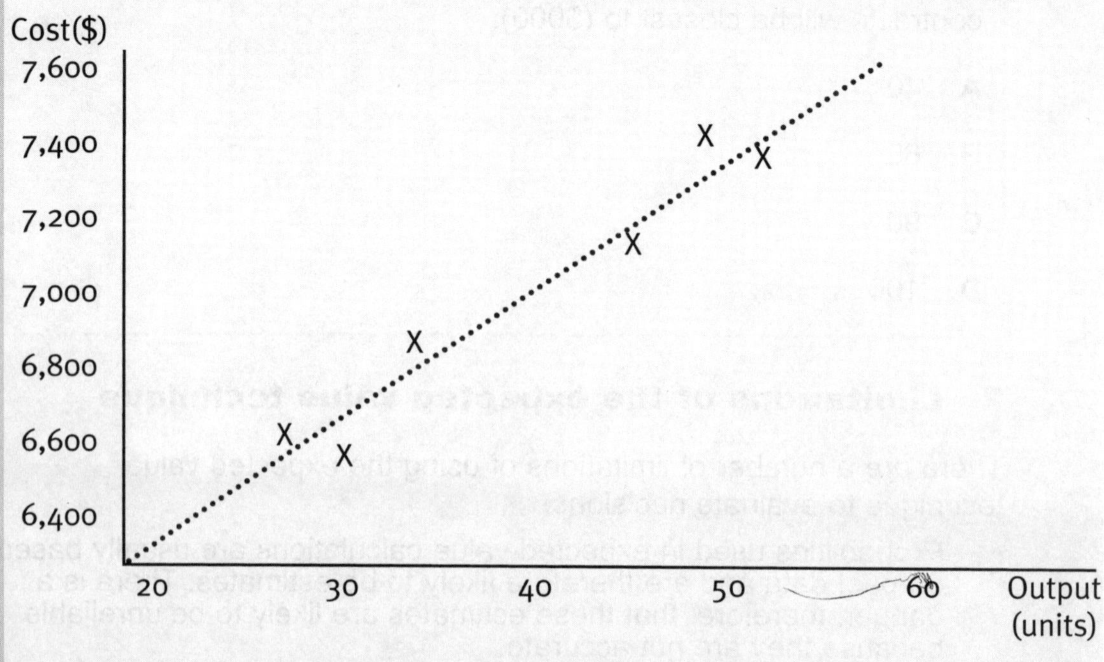

- A graph like this is known as a scattergraph (or scatter chart).
- A scattergraph can be used to make an estimate of fixed and variable costs by drawing a 'line of best fit' through the points which represents all of the points plotted.
- The line of best fit is a cost equation (or linear function) of the form y = a + bx where a = fixed costs and b = variable cost per unit.
- Regression analysis can be used to establish the equation of the line of best fit, and therefore, the fixed and variable costs.

3.2 Establishing a linear function

Regression analysis, like the high/low method, can be used to predict the linear relationship between two variables (the linear function y = a + bx).

- Linear regression (or regression analysis) calculates the values of 'a' and 'b' from past cost data using the following formulae:

$$a = \frac{\Sigma y}{n} - \frac{b\Sigma x}{n}$$

$$b = \frac{n\Sigma xy - \Sigma x\Sigma y}{n\Sigma x^2 - (\Sigma x)^2}$$

- 'a' is the fixed cost per period (the intercept)
- 'b' is the variable cost per unit (the gradient)
- 'x' is the activity level (the independent variable)
- 'y' is the total cost = fixed cost + variable cost (dependent on the activity level)
- Σ means 'sum of'
- n is the sample size

The regression formulae shown above (for calculating values for 'a' and 'b') are provided in your exam. Don't waste valuable time learning them by heart, but do make sure that you know how to use them properly!

e.g

Illustration 2 – Linear regression analysis

We can establish the linear cost function of the graph shown above by using the data in paragraph 3.1 as follows.

Output (units) (x)	Total cost ($) (y)	xy	x^2
26	6,566	170,716	676
30	6,510	195,300	900
33	6,800	224,400	1,089
44	6,985	307,340	1,936
48	7,380	354,240	2,304
50	7,310	365,500	2,500
231	41,551	1,617,496	9,405

$\Sigma x = 231$
$\Sigma y = 41{,}551$
$\Sigma xy = 1{,}617{,}496$
$\Sigma x^2 = 9{,}405$
$n = 6$

Now we apply the formula for calculating b.

$$b = \frac{n\Sigma xy - \Sigma x\Sigma y}{n\Sigma x^2 - (\Sigma x)^2}$$

$$b = \frac{6\times1{,}617{,}496 - 231\times41{,}551}{6\times9{,}405 - 231^2} = \frac{106{,}695}{3{,}069} = 34.765$$

Now we apply the formula for calculating a.

$$a = \frac{\Sigma y}{n} - \frac{b\Sigma x}{n}$$

$$a = \frac{41{,}551}{6} - 34.765\,\frac{231}{6} = 5{,}587$$

a = fixed cost per period = $5,587 (to the nearest $)

b = variable cost per unit = $34.77 to 2 decimal places

The cost equation is: y = 5,587 + 34.77x

OR Total cost = $5,587 + $34.77 × units

3.3 Where care is needed

- Regression lines can be used with confidence to calculate intermediate values of variables, i.e. values within the known range ("interpolation").
- Generally speaking, extrapolation must be treated with caution, since once outside the relevant range (range of known values) other factors may influence the situation, and the relationship which has been approximated as linear over a limited range may not be linear outside that range.
- In addition the mathematics will produce an equation even if there is no clear 'cause and effect' relationship between the two sets of figures. The strength of this relationship is explored under 'correlation' below. Particular care must be taken when the number of readings is low.

Expandable text

- For example, in **Illustration 2**, the linear cost equation was estimated to be y = 5,587 + 34.77x. This equation can be used to estimate the total cost for a given output level within the relevant range ie between 26 and 50 units. This is known as interpolation and it is one of the main uses of regression lines.
- It is also possible to extend regression lines beyond the range of values used in their calculation (the relevant range). It is then possible to calculate values of the variables that are outside the limits of the original data. This is known as extrapolation.
- The problem with extrapolation is that it assumes that the relationship already calculated is still valid. This may or may not be so.
- For example, if output were increased outside the given range there might come a point where economies of scale reduce costs and total costs might actually fall. So, the graph as seen from the known range (left figure below) might extend as in the right figure below.

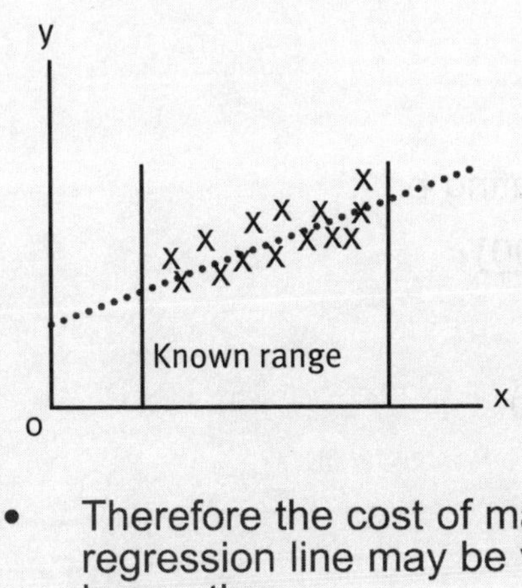

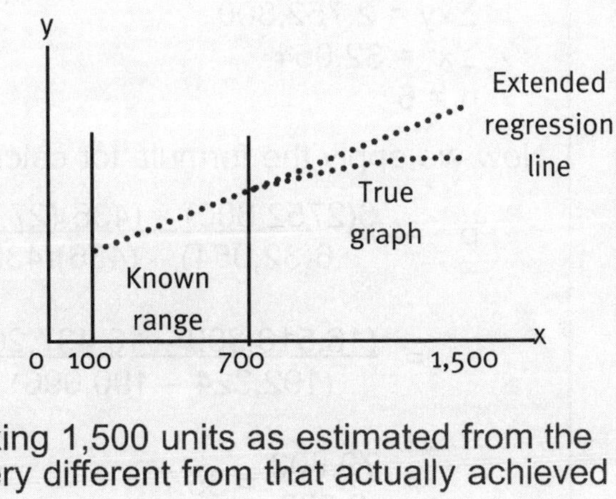

- Therefore the cost of making 1,500 units as estimated from the regression line may be very different from that actually achieved in practice.

e.g

Illustration 3 – Linear regression analysis

Bronze recorded the following costs for the past six months.

Month	Activity level Units	Total cost $
1	80	6,500
2	60	6,200
3	72	6,400
4	75	6,500
5	83	6,700
6	66	5,400

Required:

(a) Estimate the fixed costs per month and variable cost per unit using linear regression analysis.

(b) Estimate the total costs for the following activity levels in a month.

(i) 75 units

(ii) 90 units

Solution

(a)

x	y $	xy	x^2
80	6,500	520,000	6,400
60	6,200	372,000	3,600
72	6,400	460,800	5,184
75	6,500	487,500	5,625
83	6,700	556,100	6,889
66	5,400	356,400	4,356
436	37,700	2,752,800	32,054

$\Sigma x = 436$

$\Sigma y = 37{,}700$

$\Sigma xy = 2{,}752{,}800$

$\Sigma x^2 = 32{,}054$

$n = 6$

Now we apply the formula for calculating b.

$$b = \frac{6(2752{,}800) - (436)(27{,}700)}{6(32{,}054) - (436)(436)}$$

$$= \frac{(16{,}516{,}800 - 16{,}437{,}200)}{(192{,}324 - 190{,}096)}$$

$$= \frac{79{,}600}{2{,}228} = 35.7$$

Now we apply the formula for calculating a.

$$a = \frac{37,700}{6} - 35.7\left(\frac{436}{6}\right)$$

$$= 6,283 - 2,594$$

$$= 3,689$$

The cost equation is y = 3,689 + 35.7x
Fixed costs per month = $3,689
Variable cost per unit = $35.7

(b) (i) When x = 75

Total costs = 3,689 + 35.7 (75) = $6,367

The relevant range is between 60 and 83 units. This estimate of total costs should be fairly reliable as it lies in the range of known data.

(ii) When x = 90

Total costs = 3,689 + 35.7 (90) = $6,902
However, it should be noted that the linear function y = 3,689 + 35.7x only holds for the relevant range i.e. between 60 and 83 units. An activity level of 90 is outside the known range and it cannot be assumed that the linear relationship y = 3,689 + 35.7x is still valid.

Test your understanding 2

A company is investigating its current cost structure. An analysis of production levels and costs over the first six months of the year has revealed the following:

Month	Production level (units) (000s)	Production cost ($000)
January	9.125	240
February	10.255	278
March	9.700	256
April	10.500	258
May	11.000	290
June	11.500	300

Required:

(a) Use regression analysis to identify:

(i) Variable cost per unit.

(ii) Monthly fixed costs.

(b) It is expected that in July, production will be 12,000 units. Estimate the cost of July's production and comment on the accuracy of your estimate.

4 Correlation

4.1 Correlation

- Correlation measures the strength of the relationship between two variables. In particular, whether movements are related, e.g. does spending more on advertising necessarily result in more sales?
- One way of measuring 'how correlated' two variables are is by drawing a graph (scattergraph or scatter chart) to see if any visible relationship exists. The 'line of best fit' drawn on a scattergraph indicates a possible linear relationship.
- When correlation is strong, the estimated line of best fit should be more reliable.
- Another way of measuring 'how correlated' two variables are is to calculate a correlation coefficient, r, and to interpret the result.

4.2 Different degees of correlation

Variables may be either perfectly correlated, partially correlated or uncorrelated.The different degrees of correlation can be shown graphically on scattergraphs as follows.

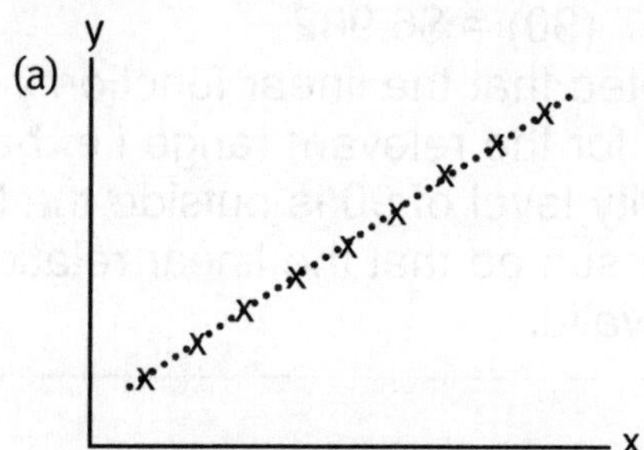

Perfect positive linear

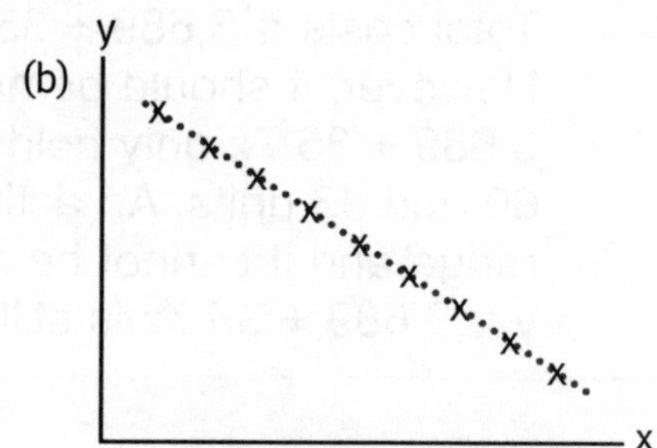

Perfect negative linear

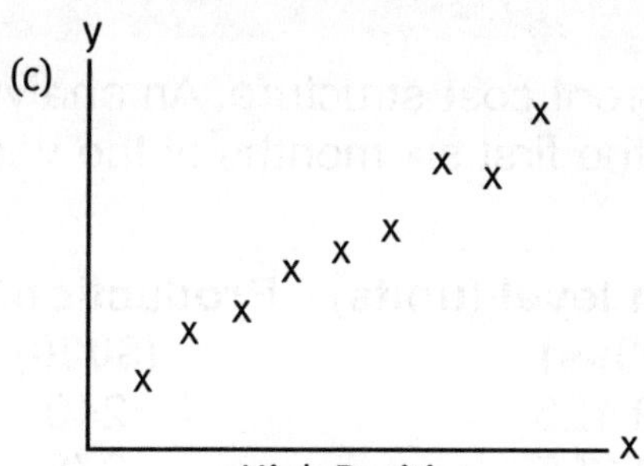

High Positive

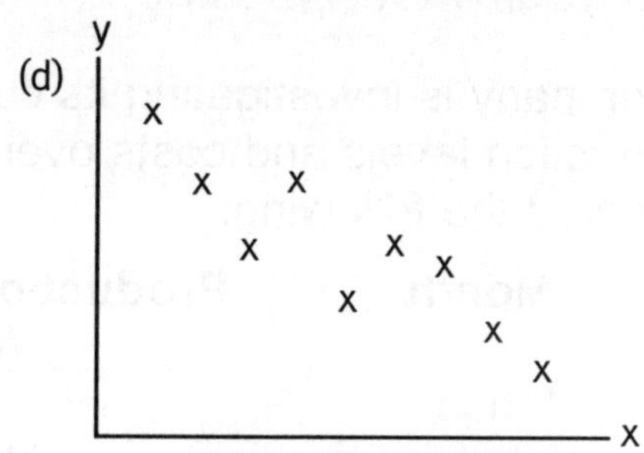

Moderate negative

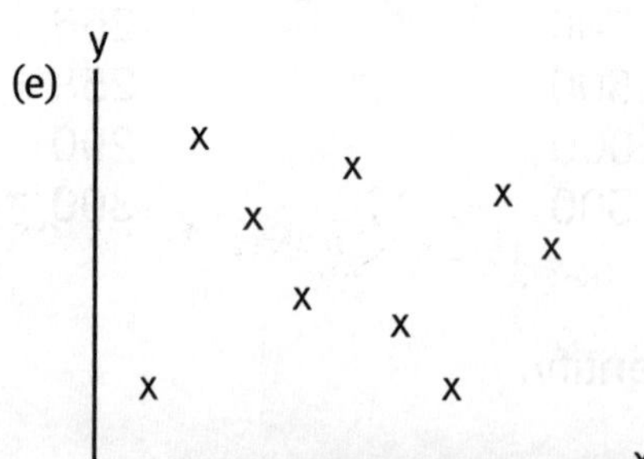

No correlation

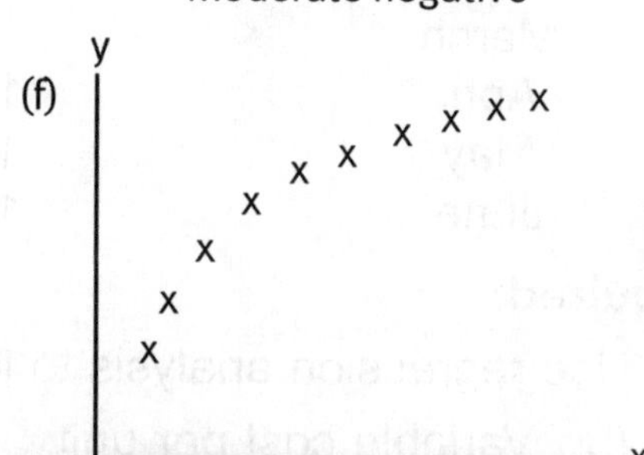

Non-linear or curvilinear

Expandable text

- Perfect correlation means that if all the pairs of values were plotted, they would lie on a straight line. This is because a linear relationship exists between the two variables.
- Partial (or moderate) correlation means that there is no exact linear relationship between two variables but that high/low values of one variable tend to be associated with high/low values of the other variable.
- Uncorrelated means that there is no correlation between the two variables.
- Perfect negative correlation means that low values of one variable are associated with high values of another (and vice versa).
- Perfect positive correlation means that high values of one variable are associated with high values of another OR low values of one variable are associated with low values of another.

4.3 The correlation coefficient

An alternative to drawing a graph each time you want to know whether two variables are correlated, and the extent of the correlation if there is any, is to calculate the correlation coefficient (r) and to interpret the result.

- The correlation coefficient, r, measures the strength of a linear relationship between two variables. It can therefore give an indication of how reliable the estimated linear function is for a set of data.
- For example, the linear function of the scattergraph in paragraph 3.1 was estimated to be y = 5,587 + 34.77x. If we were to calculate the associated correlation coefficient we could get some idea of how reliable our estimated linear function was.
- The correlation coefficient can only take on values between –1 and +1.

  r = + 1 indicates perfect positive correlation

  r = 0 indicates no correlation

  r = – 1 indicates perfect negative correlation.
- The correlation coefficient is calculated using the following formula:

$$r = \frac{n\Sigma x^2 - \Sigma x \Sigma y}{\sqrt{(n\Sigma x^2 - (\Sigma x)^2)(n\Sigma y^2 - (\Sigma y)^2)}}$$

Note: This formula is given to you in the exam.

e.g

Illustration 4 – Correlation

The following table shows the number of units of a good produced and the total costs incurred.

Units produced	Total costs $
100	40,000
200	45,000
300	50,000
400	65,000
500	70,000
600	70,000
700	80,000

Required:

Calculate the correlation coefficient for the data given and comment on the result obtained.

Solution

The calculation is set out as follows, where x is the activity level in units of hundreds and y is the cost in units of $1,000.

x	y	xy	x^2	y^2
1	40	40	1	1,600
2	45	90	4	2,025
3	50	150	9	2,500
4	65	260	16	4,225
5	70	350	25	4,900
6	70	420	36	4,900
7	80	560	49	6,400
28	420	1,870	140	26,550

$\Sigma x = 28,$
$\Sigma y = 420$
$\Sigma xy = 1,870$
$\Sigma x^2 = 140$
$\Sigma y^2 = 26,550$
$n = 7$

Now we apply the formula for calculating r.

$$r = \frac{(7 \times 1,870) - (28 \times 420)}{\sqrt{((7 \times 140) - (28 \times 28))((7 \times 26,550) - (420 \times 420))}}$$

$$= \frac{13,090 - 11,760}{\sqrt{(980 - 784)(185,850 - 176,400)}}$$

$$= \frac{1,330}{\sqrt{(196 \times 9,450)}}$$

$$= +\ 0.98$$

A correlation coefficient of + 0.98 indicates a high degree of positive correlation between the variables. In general, the closer that r is to +1 (or – 1) the higher the degree of correlation.

Test your understanding 3

If $\Sigma x = 440$, $\Sigma y = 330$, $\Sigma x^2 = 17,986$, $\Sigma y^2 = 10,366$, $\Sigma xy = 13,467$ and $n = 11$, then the value of r, the coefficient of correlation, to two decimal places, is:

A 0.98

B 0.63

C 0.96

D 0.59

If you calculate a correlation coefficient with a value >+1 or <-1 go back and check your calculation again as you will have got the wrong answer. Remember - the value of the correlation coefficient can only lie in the range -1 to +1.

4.4 Coefficient of determination

The coefficient of determination is the square of the correlation coefficient, and so is denoted by r^2.

- The coefficient of determination is a measure of how much of the variation in the dependent variable is 'explained' by the variation of the independent variable.
- The variation not accounted for by variations in the independent variable will be due to random fluctuations, or to other specific factors that have not been identified in considering the two-variable problem.

- For example, if r = 0.98, r^2 = 0.96 or 96%.
- This means that 96% of the variation in the dependent variable (y) is explained by variations in the independent variable (x). This would be interpreted as high correlation.
- For example, the linear function y = 5,587 + 34.77x is plotted (as a 'line of best fit') in paragraph 3.1. The associated correlation coefficient was calculated to be 0.957, and the coefficient of determination, r^2, is therefore:

  r^2 = 0.9572 = 0.92 or 92%
- This means that 92% of the variations in total costs is explained by variations in the level of activity. The other 8% of variations in total costs are assumed to be due to random fluctuations.

Note: With both correlation coefficients and coefficients of determination there is the possibility that the calculated figure does not indicate true correlation. 'Spurious' correlation can occur when the behaviour of both sets of figures is due to a third factor, e.g. a strengthening currency will make demand for both imported cigars and CD players rise. The correlation between sales of cigars and CD players would be high despite no causal relationship.

Chapter summary

Limitations of the expected value technique

- Probabilities based on past data - estimates
- Not always suitable for one-off decisions
- Do not take into account 'time value money'
- Do not take into account all factors surrounding a decision

Different possible outcomes and expected values

An expected value is a long run average. it is the weighted average of a probability distribution.

expected value (ev) = Σpx

BUSINESS MATHEMATICS

Linear regression

- Used to predict linear relationship (linear cost function) between two variables
- Formulae to calculate 'a' (fixed costs) and 'b' (variable costs) are provided in your exam
- Linear cost function only holds for the 'relevant' range

Correlation

- Correlation measures strength of relationship between two variables
- Measured by correlation coefficient, r (formula given in exam)
- Coefficient of determination, r , measures how much the variation in the dependent variable is 'explained' by the variation in the independent variable

Test your understanding answers

Test your understanding 1

B $EV = 40,000 \times 0.5 + 60,000 \times \frac{1}{3} + 100,000 \times \frac{1}{5} = 60,000$

Test your understanding 2

(a)

Month	**Production level (units)** x (000s)	**Production cost** y $000	**xy**	**x^2**
January	9.125	240	2,190	83.265
February	10.255	278	2,851	105.165
March	9.700	256	2,483	94.090
April	10.500	258	2,709	110.250
May	11.000	290	3,190	121.000
June	11.500	300	3,450	132.250
Totals	62.080	1,622	16,873	646.021

(i) Variable cost = b

$$= \frac{6 \text{ x } 16,873 - 62.080 \text{ x } 1,622}{6 \text{ x } 646.020 - 62.080^2}$$

$$= \frac{544,780}{22,197} = \$24.54$$

(ii) Fixed cost = a

$$= \frac{1,622}{6} - 24.54 \frac{62.080}{6} = \$16.426 \text{ (in thousands)}$$

(b) The estimated cost of 12,000 units will be given by the linear cost equation:

y = $16.426 + $24.54x

y = 16.426 + (24.54 x12) = $310.906

It should be noted that since this is outside the range of values for which costs are known it might be inaccurate. For example there may be stepped fixed cost such as an additional supervisor that is required at 11,800 units.

Test your understanding 3

$$r = \frac{11 \times 13{,}467 - 440 \times 330}{\sqrt{(11 \times 17{,}986 - 400^2)(11 \times 10{,}366 - 330^2)}} = 0.63$$

chapter

4

Ordering and accounting for inventory

Chapter learning objectives

Upon completion of this chapter you will be able to:

- describe, for a manufacturing business, the different procedures and documents necessary for the ordering, receiving and issuing of materials from inventory
- interpret the entries and balances in the material inventory account for a manufacturing business
- describe the control procedures that can be used in a manufacturing business to monitor physical and 'book' inventory and to minimise discrepancies and losses.

1 Accounting procedures for ordering and issuing inventory

Accounting and control procedures for ordering and issuing inventory include the following functions:

- ordering
- purchasing
- receiving
- issuing
- storing and stocktaking.

1.1 Ordering, purchasing and receiving inventory

The procedures for ordering, purchasing and receiving materials are as follows.

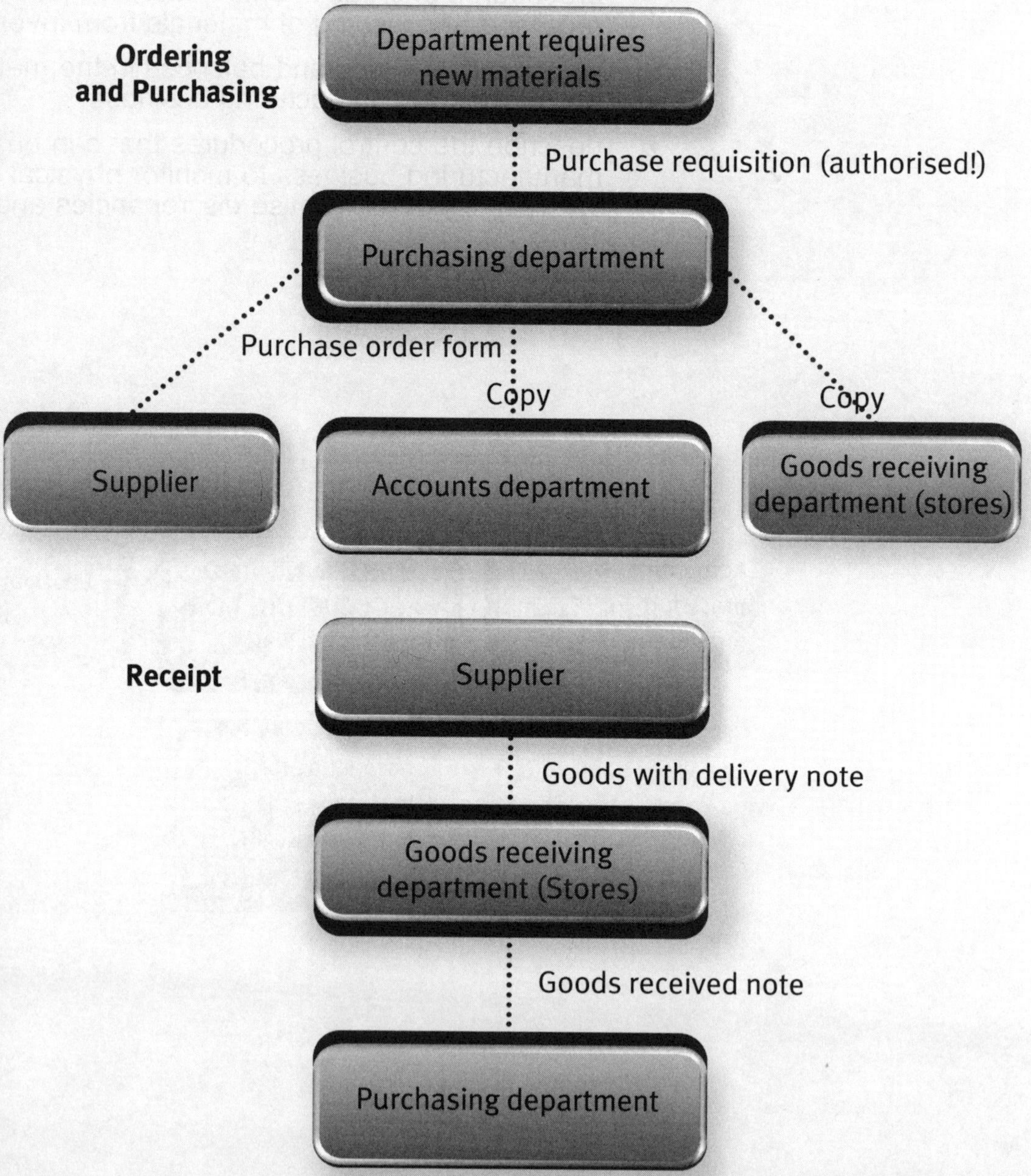

Expandable text

- When a department requires new materials, a **purchase requisition** is completed (including authorisation by the relevant manager) and sent to the **purchasing department**.
- On receipt of a properly authorised requisition, the purchasing department will select a supplier and create an order on a **purchase order form**.
- The purchase order form is sent to the supplier and copies are also sent to the accounts department and the goods receiving department.
- On receipt of the goods, the goods receiving department will check the goods against the relevant purchase order, and check the **delivery note** which accompanies the goods. Full details of the goods are then entered onto a **goods received note (GRN)**.
- A copy of the GRN is attached to the relevant purchase order and they are both sent to the purchasing department where they are matched to the relevant supplier's purchase invoice. Once approved, the **purchase invoice** can be paid.

Specimen forms for the ordering, purchasing and receipt of inventory are shown in the illustration below.

1.2 Issuing inventory

The accounting procedures for issuing inventory are as follows.

- **Materials requisition notes** are issued to production departments. Their purpose is to authorise the storekeeper to release the goods which have been requisitioned and to update the stores records.
- **Materials returned notes** are used to record any unused materials which are returned to stores. They are also used to update the stores records.
- **Materials transfer notes** document the transfer of materials from one production department to another. They are also used to update the stores records.

e.g

Illustration 1 – Accounting procedures for ordering and issuing inventory

Some specimen documents that are used in the ordering, receiving and issuing of inventory are illustrated as follows.

PURCHASE REQUISITION

Date ....20...........

Serial No: ....

Purpose*: inventory/special capital equipment/(budget reference)

*Delete as appropriate

Quantity and units	Description	Materal code	Job or dept. code	Delivery required		Purchase order		
				Date	Place	No.	Date	Supplier

Origination department .... Authorisation ....

PURCHASE ORDER

To: ....

....

....

Serial No: ....

Date: ....

Purchase Req. No: ....

Please supply, in accordance with the attached conditions

Quantity	Description	Code	Delivery date	Price	Per

Your quotation ....

To be delivered, carriage paid, to .... Terms

Please quote our Purchase Order number on all correspondence.

For ABC Ltd

....

GOODS RECEIVED NOTE

To: .... Serial No: ....

.... Date issued: ....

Carrier: .... Purchase Order No: ....

Date of delivery: ....

Description	Code	Quantity	Packages	Gross Weight

INSPECTION REPORT			Received by: ....
Quantity passed	Quantity rejected	Remarks	Required by: ....
			Accepted: ....
Inspector	Date		Date: ....

MATERIAL REQUISITION

Charge job/
Cost Centre No: .... Serial No: ....

Date: ....

Code No.	Description	Quantity or weight	Cost office only				
			Rate	Unit	$	$	Stores ledger

Authorised by:	Storekeeper:	Prices entered by:
Received by:	Bin card entered:	Calculations checked:

Test your understanding 1

A goods received note (GRN) provides (tick all that apply):

- [ ] Information used to update inventory records.
- [ ] Information to check that the correct price has been recorded on the supplier's invoice.
- [ ] Information to check that the correct quantity of goods has been recorded on the supplier's invoice.
- [ ] Information to record any unused materials which are returned to stores.

2 Accounting for inventory – the material inventory account

2.1 Material inventory account

Materials held in store are an asset and are recorded in the balance sheet of a company.

Accounting transactions relating to materials are recorded in the **material inventory account**.

Material inventory account

Debit entries reflect an **increase** in inventory	Credit entries reflect a **decrease** in inventory
• purchases	• issues to production
• returns to stores	• returns to suppliers

The illustration below shows how the material inventory account is drawn up.

e.g

Illustration 2 – Accounting for inventory

Material inventory account

	$000		$000
Opening balance (1)	33	Work-in-progress (4)	137
Creditors (2)	146	Materials returned to suppliers (5)	2
		Production overhead account (6)	4
Materials returned to stores (3)	4		
		Income statement (7)	3
		Closing balance (8)	37
	183		183

1 The opening balance of materials held in inventory at the beginning of a period is shown as a debit in the material inventory account.

2 Materials purchased on credit are debited to the material inventory account.

3 Materials returned to stores cause inventory to increase and so are debited to the material inventory account.

4 Direct materials used in production are transferred to the work-in-progress account by crediting the material inventory account.

5 Materials returned to suppliers cause inventory levels to fall and are therefore 'credited out' of the material inventory account.

6 Indirect materials are not a direct cost of manufacture and are treated as overheads. They are therefore transferred to the production overhead account by way of a credit to the material inventory account.

7 Any material write-offs are 'credited out' of the material inventory account and transferred to the income statement where they are written off.

8 The balancing figure on the material inventory account is the closing balance of material inventory at the end of a period. It is also the opening balance at the beginning of the next period.

Test your understanding 2

Transaction	Debit which account?	Credit which account?
Issue materials to production.		
Purchase new materials on credit.		
Materials returned to store from production.		
Materials written off.		
Indirect materials transferred to production overheads.		

2.2 Inventory valuation

- When inventory is received into stores from different suppliers and at different prices every week, it is important that it is valued in a consistent way so that closing inventory values and issues from stores can be valued accurately.
- You are probably aware that inventory is usually valued at the lower of cost and net realisable value. However, various methods are used to value closing inventory and issues from stores in management accounting.
- There are three main inventory valuation methods:
  - **FIFO**
  - **LIFO**
  - **Weighted average cost.**
- **First In First Out – FIFO** assumes that materials are issued out of stock in the order in which they were delivered into inventory.
- **Last In First Out – LIFO** assumes that materials are issued out of inventory in the reverse order to which they were delivered into inventory.
- **Weighted average cost – AVCO** values all items of inventory and issues at an average price. The average price is calculated after each receipt of goods. The average price is calculated by dividing the total purchase costs to date by the total units received to date.

These valuation methods are outside the F2 syllabus.

3 Physical inventory and book inventory

3.1 Perpetual inventory

Perpetual inventory is the recording as they occur of receipts, issues and the resulting balances of individual items of inventory in either quantity or quantity and value.

- Inventory records are updated using **stores ledger cards** and **bin cards**.
- **Bin cards** also show a record of receipts, issues and balances of the quantity of an item of inventory handled by stores.
- As with the stores ledger card, bin cards will show materials received (from purchases and returns) and issued (from requisitions).
- A typical stores ledger card is shown below.

STORES LEDGER CARD

Description: .... Unit: .... Location: .... Code: ....
Maximum: .... Minimum: .... Reorder level: .... Reorder quantity: ....

Receipts			Issues			On order		
Date/ref	Quantity	$	Date/ref	Quantity	$	Date/ref	Quantity	$

3.2 Stocktaking

The process of stocktaking involves checking the physical quantity of inventory held on a certain date and then checking this balance against the balances on the stores ledger (record) cards or bin cards. Stocktaking can be carried out on a **periodic basis** or a **continuous basis.**

- **Periodic stocktaking** involves checking the balance of every item of inventory on the same date, usually at the end of an accounting period.
- **Continuous stocktaking** involves counting and valuing selected items of inventory on a rotating basis. Specialist teams count and check certain items of inventory on each day. Each item is checked at least once a year with valuable items being checked more frequently.

- Any differences (or discrepancies) which arise between 'book' inventory and physical inventory must be investigated.
- In theory any differences, as recorded in the stores ledger or the bin card, must have arisen through faulty recording.
- Once the discrepancy has been identified, the stores ledger card is adjusted in order that it reflects the true physical inventory count.
- Any items which are identified as being **slow-moving** or **obsolete** should be brought to the attention of management as soon as possible.
- Management will then decide whether these items should be disposed of and written off to the income statement.
- Slow-moving items are those inventory items which take a long time to be used up.
- Obsolete items are those items of inventory which have become out of date and are no longer required.

Expandable text

Inventory losses and waste

- Inventory losses may be quantified by comparing the physical quantity of an item held with the balance quantity recorded on the bin card and/or stores ledger card.
- There are two categories of loss: those which occur because of theft, pilferage, damage or similar means and those which occur because of the breaking of bulk receipts into smaller quantities.
- It is the second of these which are more commonly referred to as waste.
- Inventory losses must be written off against profits as soon as they occur. If the value to be written off is significant then an investigation should be made of the cause.
- When waste occurs as a result of breaking up bulk receipts, it is reasonable to expect that the extent of such wastage could be estimated in advance based upon past records. Either of two accounting treatments could then be used:
  - Issues continue to be made and priced without any adjustment and the difference at the end of the period is written off.
  - Alternatively, the issue price is increased to compensate for the expected waste.
- Suppose that a 100 metre length of copper is bought for $99. The estimated loss caused by cutting into shorter lengths as required is 1%.
  The issue price could be based on the expected issues of 99 metres, i.e. $1 per metre rather than pricing the copper at:

  $$\text{Issue price} = \frac{\$99}{100} = \$0.99/\text{metre}$$

3.3 Control procedures to minimise discrepancies and losses

The level of investment in inventory and the labour costs of handling and recording/controlling them is considerable in many organisations. It is for this reason that organisations must have control procedures in place in order to minimise discrepancies and losses.

Problem	Control procedure
Ordering goods at inflated prices.	Use of standard costs for purchases. Quotation for special items.
Fictitious purchases.	Separation of ordering and purchasing. Physical controls over materials receipts, usage and inventory.
Shortages on receipts.	Checking in all goods inwards at gate. Delivery signatures.
Losses from inventory.	Regular stocktaking. Physical security procedures.
Writing off obsolete or damaged inventory which is good.	Control of responsible official over all write-offs.
Losses after issue to production department.	Records of all issues. Standard usage allowance.

e.g

Illustration 3 – Physical inventory and book inventory

Complete the following table by filling in a description of each item in the right-hand column.

Periodic stocktaking	
Continuous stocktaking	
Perpetual inventory	
Slow-moving stock	
Obsolete stock	

Solution

Periodic stocktaking	Check balance of every item of inventory on the same date, usually at the end of an accounting period.
Continuous stocktaking	Count and value selected items of inventory on a rotating basis. Specialist teams count and check certain stock items on each day.
Perpetual inventory	Record, as they occur, receipts, issues and the resulting balances of individual items of inventory in either quantity or quantity and value.
Slow-moving stock	Those inventory items which take a long time to be used up.
Obsolete stock	Those items of inventory which have become out of date and are no longer required.

Test your understanding 3

The perpetual inventory system is:

A Where the inventory levels are checked on a continuous basis.

B Where enough inventory is always available to meet production.

C Where the different inventory records are continually compared to ensure agreement.

D Where the inventory balance is shown after each movement.

Chapter summary

ORDERING AND ACCOUNTING FOR INVENTORY

ACCOUNTING PROCEDURES FOR ORDERING AND ISSUING INVENTORY

Order:
Purchase requisition
Purchase order form

Receive:
Delivery note
Goods received note

Issue:
Materials requisition note
Materials returned note
Materials transfer note

PHYSICAL INVENTORY AND BOOK INVENTORY

Physical inventory checked via stocktaking:

Periodic – Check every item at end of accounting period.

Continuous – Count and value selected items on rotating basis.

Book inventory updated via stores ledger (record) cards and bin cards as inventory received and issued – perpetual inventory system.

Accounting for inventory – the material inventory account

ENTRIES IN THE MATERIAL INVENTORY ACCOUNT

Material inventory account debited when inventory increases:

- Purchases
- Materials returned to store

Material inventory account credited when inventory decreases:

- Transfers to WIP (production)
- Materials returned to suppliers
- Indirect materials transferred to production overheads
- Inventory write-offs

BALANCE IN THE MATERIAL INVENTORY ACCOUNT

Closing balance at end of period represents inventory held and may be valued as follows:

- **FIFO**
- **LIFO**
- **AVCO**

Test your understanding answers

Test your understanding 1

- [x] Information used to update inventory records.
- [ ] Information to check that the correct price has been recorded on the supplier's invoice.
- [x] Information to check that the correct quantity of goods has been recorded on the supplier's invoice.
- [ ] Information to record any unused materials which are returned to stores.

Test your understanding 2

Transaction	**Debit which account?**	**Credit which account?**
Issue materials to production.	Work-in-progress.	Material inventory account.
Purchase new materials on credit.	Material inventory account.	Creditors.
Materials returned to store from production.	Material inventory account.	Work-in-progress account.
Materials written off.	Income statement.	Material inventory account.
Indirect materials transferred to production overheads.	Production overhead account.	Material inventory account.

Test your understanding 3

D by definition

chapter

5

Order quantities and reorder levels

Chapter learning objectives

Upon completion of this chapter you will be able to:

- identify and explain the costs of ordering and holding inventory, distinguishing between fixed and variable costs
- from given data, calculate and interpret the economic order quantities
- from given data, calculate and interpret the economic order quantities when quantity discounts are available
- produce calculations to minimise inventory costs when stock is gradually replenished
- describe and apply appropriate methods for establishing reorder levels where demand in the lead time is constant.

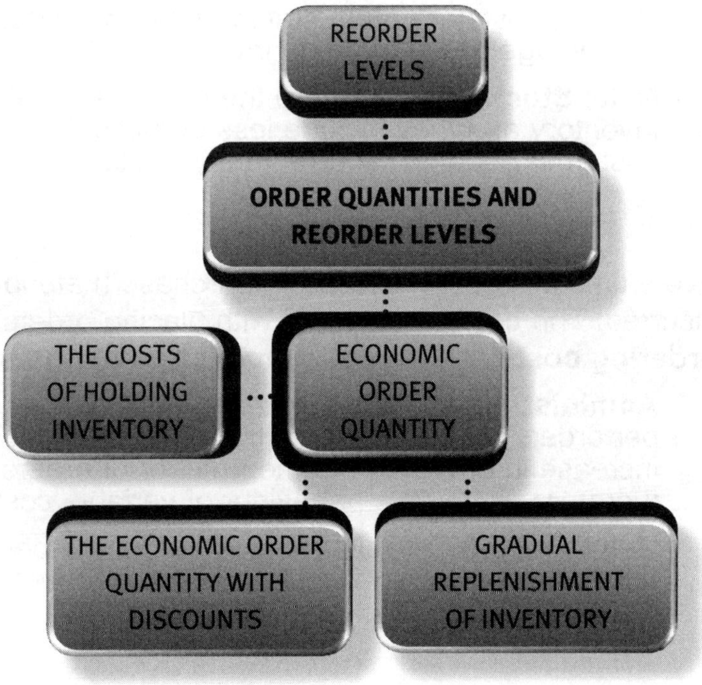

1 The costs of holding inventory

1.1 Reasons for holding inventory

The main reason that an organisation will hold inventory is in order to make sure that customer demands are met as soon as possible.

- If customer demands are met, customers will be happy.
- If customers are happy, sales and, therefore, profits will increase.
- Holding raw material inventory will prevent hold-ups in the production process of manufacturing companies.

1.2 Holding costs

Costs associated with holding inventory are known as **holding costs**.

- Holding costs include the following:
  – interest on capital tied up in inventory
  – cost of storage space
  – cost of insurance.
- **Buffer inventory** is a basic level of inventory held for emergencies and to prevent stock-outs from occurring. It is also known as safety inventory or the minimum inventory level.
- **Holding costs** can be distinguished between fixed holding costs and variable holding costs.
- **Fixed holding costs** include the cost of storage space and the cost of insurance. Note that the cost of storage space may be a stepped fixed cost if increased warehousing is needed when higher volumes of inventory are held.
- **Variable holding costs** include interest on capital tied up in inventory. The more inventory that is held, the more capital that is tied up.
- Holding costs are often stated as being valued at a certain percentage of the average inventory held.
- Note: **Stock-out costs** are the costs associated with running out of inventory and they include loss of sales, loss of customers (and customer goodwill) and reduced profits.

1.3 Ordering costs

Every time an order is placed to purchase materials, an **order cost** is incurred. The costs associated with placing orders are known as **ordering costs** and include **administrative costs** and **delivery costs**.

- **Administrative costs** of placing an order are usually a fixed cost per order. The total administrative costs of placing orders will increase in proportion to the number of orders placed. They therefore exhibit the behaviour of variable costs.
- **Delivery costs** are usually a fixed charge per delivery (order). The total delivery costs will also increase in direct proportion to the

number of deliveries in a period, and therefore behave as variable costs.

- If inventory levels are too low, there is a danger that the number of stock-outs will increase and there will therefore be an increase in the number of orders placed.
- An increase in the number of orders will cause a corresponding increase in **ordering costs**.
- It is essential, therefore, to maintain inventory at a level (known as the optimum level) where the total of holding costs, ordering costs and stock-out costs are at a minimum. This is the main objective of stock control.

e.g

Illustration 1 – The cost of holding inventory

A company uses components at the rate of 6,000 units per year, which are bought in at a cost of £1.20 each from the supplier. The company orders 1,000 units each time it places an order and the average inventory held is 500 units. It costs $20 each time to place an order, regardless of the quantity ordered.

The total holding cost is 20% per annum of the average inventory held.

The annual holding cost will be $ [ ]

The annual ordering cost will be $ [ ]

Solution

The annual holding cost will be $ 120

The annual ordering cost will be $ 120

Workings

Annual holding cost = average inventory held x cost per unit x 20%

= 500 units x $1.20 x 20%

= $120

Annual ordering cost = $\frac{\text{Annual usage}}{\text{Order size}}$ x $20

= $\frac{6,000}{1,000}$ x $20

= $120

Test your understanding 1

A company has recorded the following details for Component 427 which is sold in boxes of 10 components.

Ordering cost	$32 per order placed
Purchase price	$20 per box of 10 components
Holding cost	10% of purchase price
Monthly demand	1,500 components

Component 427 is currently ordered in batches of 240 boxes at a time. The average inventory held is 120 boxes.

Required:

Calculate the annual holding cost and the annual ordering cost for Component 427.

2 The economic order quantity (EOQ)

2.1 EOQ

The EOQ is the reorder quantity which minimises the total costs associated with holding and ordering stock (i.e. (holding costs + ordering costs) are at a minimum at the EOQ).

We can estimate the EOQ graphically by plotting holding costs, ordering costs and total costs at different levels of activity.

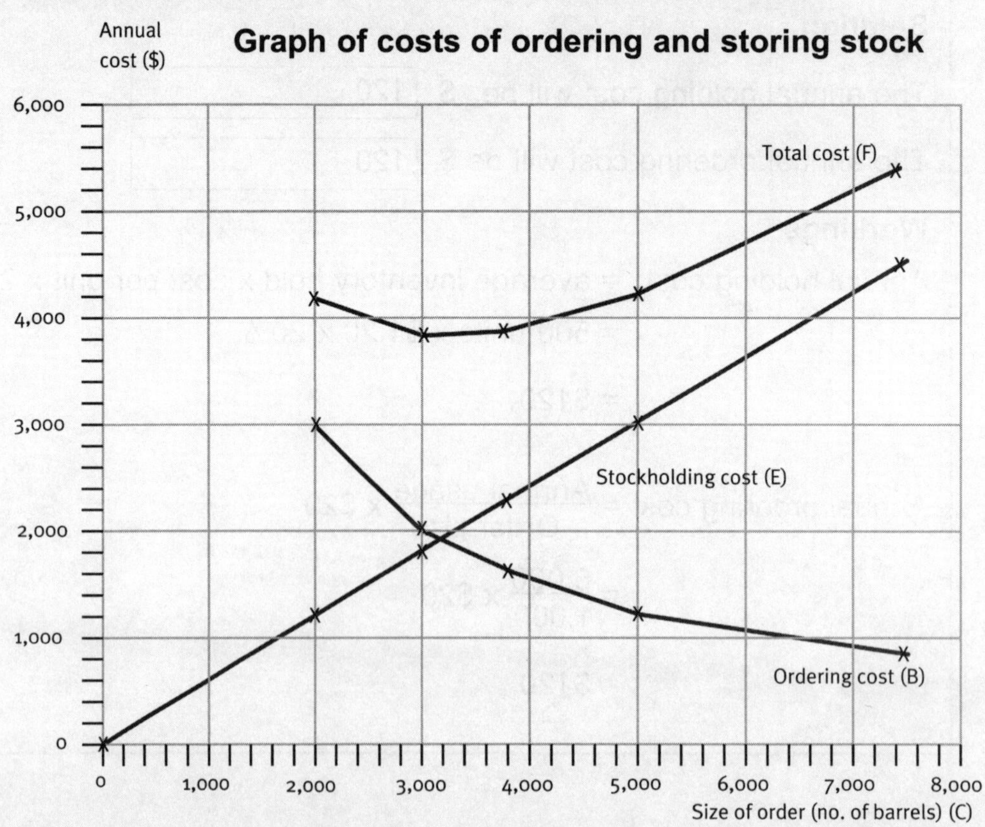

- **Note** that the EOQ is found at the point where total costs (holding + ordering) are at a **minimum**.
- Reading from the graph this is somewhere between 3,000 and 3,200 barrels.
- This is the same point at which holding costs are equal to ordering costs.
- Unfortunately it is only possible to estimate the EOQ by drawing a graph.
- Fortunately there is a formula that allows us to calculate the EOQ more accurately and more speedily.

2.2 EOQ formula

The formula for the EOQ (or Q) is as follows:

$$Q = EOQ = \sqrt{\frac{2C_oD}{C_h}}$$

Where:

D = Demand per annum
C_o = Cost of placing one order
C_h = Cost of holding one unit for one year
Q = Reorder quantity (EOQ)

Note that the formula for the EOQ is provided in your exam. You must make sure that you know what the different symbols represent so that you can use the formula correctly.

2.3 EOQ assumptions

There are a number of important assumptions and formulae related to the EOQ that you should note.

- Average inventory held is equal to half of the EOQ = EOQ/2.
- The number of orders in a year = Expected annual demand/EOQ.
- Total annual holding cost = Average inventory (EOQ/2) x holding cost per unit of inventory.
- Total annual ordering cost = Number of orders x cost of placing an order.
- There is also a formula that allows us to calculate the Total Annual Costs (TAC) i.e. the total of holding costs and ordering costs.

$$TAC = C_o\frac{D}{Q} + C_h\frac{Q}{2}$$

Where:

D = Demand per annum
C_o = Cost of placing one order
C_h = Cost of holding one unit for one year
Q = Reorder quantity (EOQ)

Note that the formula for the TAC is not provided in your exam.

e.g

Illustration 2 – The economic order quantity (EOQ)

A company uses components at the rate of 500 units per month, which are bought in at a cost of $1.20 each from the supplier. It costs $20 each time to place an order, regardless of the quantity ordered.

The total holding cost is 20% per annum of the value of stock held.

The company should order [ ] components

The total annual cost will be $ [ ]

Solution

The company should order [1,000] components

The total annual cost will be $ [240]

Workings

$$\text{Economic order quantity} = \sqrt{\frac{2 \times 20 \times 500 \times 12}{0.2 \times 1.2}} = 1{,}000 \text{ components}$$

$$\text{Total annual cost} = 20 \times \frac{6{,}000}{1{,}000} + 0.24 \times \frac{1{,}000}{2} = \$120 + \$120 = \$240$$

Test your understanding 2

A company is planning to purchase 90,800 units of a particular item in the year ahead. The item is purchased in boxes each containing 10 units of the item, at a price of $200 per box. A safety inventory of 250 boxes is kept.

The cost of holding an item in inventory for a year (including insurance, interest and space costs) is 15% of the purchase price.

The cost of placing and receiving orders is to be estimated from cost data collected relating to similar orders, where costs of $5,910 were incurred on 30 orders. It should be assumed that ordering costs change in proportion to the number of orders placed. 2% should be added to the above ordering costs to allow for inflation. Assume that usage of the item will be even over the year.

The order quantity which minimises total costs is [ ]

This will mean ordering the item every [ ] weeks.

3 The EOQ with discounts

3.1 Quantity discounts

It is often possible to negotiate a quantity discount on the purchase price if bulk orders are placed.

- If a quantity discount is accepted this will have the following effects:
  - The annual purchase price will decrease.
  - The annual holding cost will increase.
  - The annual ordering cost will decrease.
- To establish whether the discount should be accepted or not, the following calculations should be carried out.
  - Calculate TAC with the discount.
  - Compare this with the annual costs without the discount (at the EOQ point).

3.2 EOQ when quantity discounts are available

The steps involved in calculating the EOQ when quantity discounts are available are as follows:

1 Calculate the EOQ, ignoring discounts.

2 If the EOQ is smaller than the minimum purchase quantity to obtain a bulk discount, calculate the total for the EOQ of the annual stockholding costs, stock ordering costs and stock purchase costs.

3 Recalculate the annual stockholding costs, stock ordering costs and stock purchase costs for a purchase order size that is only just large enough to qualify for the bulk discount.

4 Compare the total costs when the order quantity is the EOQ with the total costs when the order quantity is just large enough to obtain the discount. Select the minimum cost alternative.

5 If there is a further discount available for an even larger order size, repeat the same calculations for the higher discount level.

e.g

Illustration 3 – The EOQ with discounts

A company uses components at the rate of 500 units per month, which are bought in at a cost of $1.20 each from the supplier. It costs $20 each time to place an order, regardless of the quantity ordered.

The supplier offers a 5% discount on the purchase price for order quantities of 2,000 items or more. The current EOQ is 1,000 units.

The total holding cost is 20% per annum of the value of stock held.

Required:

Should the discount be accepted?

Solution

	Order quantity = 1,000	**Order quantity = 2,000**
	$	$
Order cost (6,000/1,000 x $20)	120	(6,000/2,000 x $20) = 60
Holding cost (20% x $1.20 x 1,000/2)	120	($0.24 x 0.95 x 2,000/2) = 228
Purchase cost (6,000 x $1.20)	7,200	(6,000 x $1.20 x 0.95) = 6,840
Total annual costs	7,440	7,128

The discount should be accepted because it saves the company $312 ($7,440 – $7,128).

Test your understanding 3

Watton Ltd is a retailer of beer barrels. The company has an annual demand of 36,750 barrels. The barrels cost $12 each. Fresh supplies can be obtained immediately, but ordering costs and the cost of carriage inwards are $200 per order. The annual cost of holding one barrel in stock is estimated to be $1.20. The economic order quantity has been calculated to be 3,500 barrels.

The suppliers introduce a quantity discount of 2% on orders of at least 5,000 barrels and 2.5% on orders of at least 7,500 barrels.

Required:

Determine whether the least-cost order quantity is still the EOQ of 3,500 barrels.

4 Gradual replenishment of inventory

4.1 Gradual replenishment of inventory

The situations we have looked at so far have involved inventory levels being replenished immediately when organisations buy inventory from suppliers. Similar problems are faced by organisations who replenish inventory levels gradually by manufacturing their own products internally.

- The decisions faced by organisations that manufacture and store their own products involve deciding whether to produce large batches at long intervals OR produce small batches at short intervals.
- An amended EOQ model is used to help organisations to decide which course of action to take.
- The amended EOQ model is known as the EBQ (economic batch quantity) model.
- As the items are being produced, there is a machine setup cost. This replaces the ordering cost of the EOQ.
- In the EOQ, inventory is replenished instantaneously whereas here, it is replenished over a period of time.
- Depending on the demand rate, part of the batch will be sold or used while the remainder is still being produced.
- For the same size of batch (Q), the average inventory held in the EOQ model (Q/2) is greater than the average in this situation (see diagram below).
- The EBQ model can be shown graphically as follows.

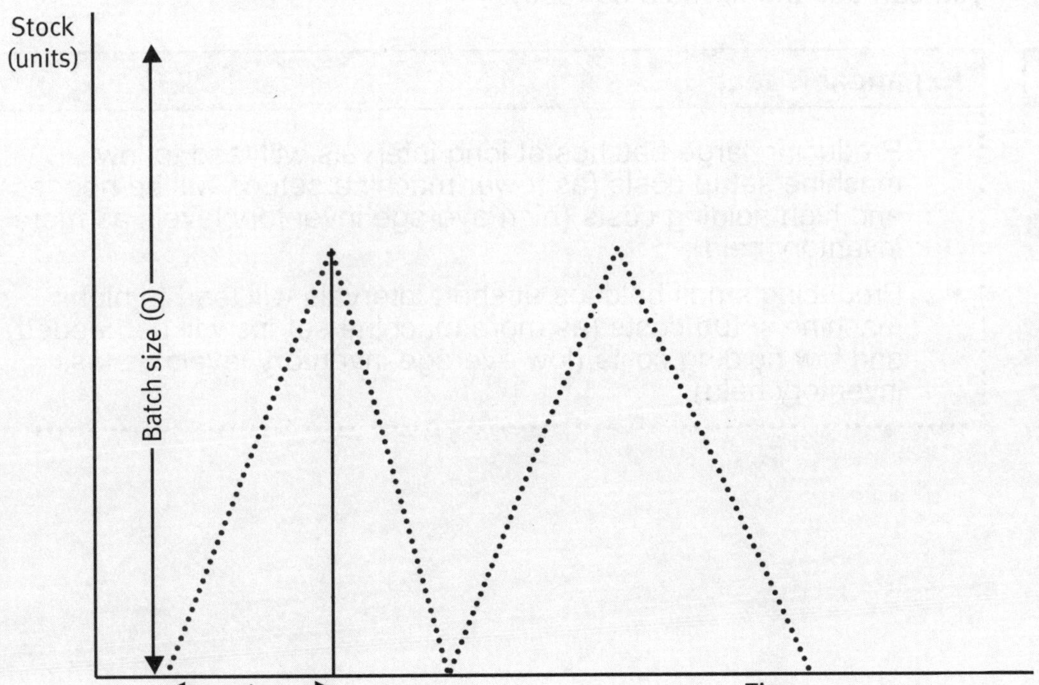

- The maximum stock level will never be as great as the batch size, because some of the batch will be used up while the remainder is being produced.

4.2 The EBQ

The EBQ model is primarily concerned with determining the number of items that should be produced in a batch (compared to the size of an order with the EOQ).

The formula for the EBQ is as follows:

$$\text{Economic batch quantity} = \sqrt{\frac{2C_oD}{C_h(1 - \frac{D}{R})}}$$

Where:

Q = Batch size
D = Demand per annum
C_h = Cost of holding one unit for one year
C_o = Cost of setting up a batch ready to be produced
R = Annual replenishment rate

Note that the formula for the EBQ is provided in your exam. You must make sure that you know what the different symbols represent so that you can use the formula correctly.

Expandable text

- Producing large batches at long intervals will lead to low machine setup costs (as fewer machine setups will be needed) and high holding costs (high average inventory levels as more inventory held).
- Producing small batches at short intervals will lead to high machine setup costs (as more machine setups will be needed) and low holding costs (low average inventory levels as less inventory held).

e.g

Illustration 4 – Gradual replenishment of inventory

The following is relevant for Item X:

- Production is at a rate of 500 units per week.
- Demand is 10,000 units per annum; evenly spread over 50 working weeks.
- Setup cost is $2,700 per batch.
- Storage cost is $2.50 per unit for a year.

Required:

Calculate the economic batch quantity (EBQ) for Item X.

Solution

Annual production rate, R = 500 x 50 = 25,000 units

Annual demand rate = 10,000 units

Cost per setup, C_o = $2,700

Cost of holding one item in stock per year, Ch = $2.50

$$EBQ = \sqrt{\frac{2C_oD}{C_h(1 - \frac{D}{R})}} = \sqrt{\frac{2 \times 2{,}700 \times 10{,}000}{2.5\,(1 - \frac{10{,}000}{25{,}000})}} = 6{,}000 \text{ units}$$

Test your understanding 4

AB Ltd makes a component for one of the engines that it builds. It uses, on average, 2,000 of these components, steadily throughout the year. The component costs $16 per unit to make and it costs an additional $320 to setup the production process each time a batch of components is made. The holding cost per unit is 10% of the unit production cost.

The company makes these components at a rate of 200 per week, and the factory is open for 50 weeks per annum.

Required:

Calculate the EBQ.

5 Reorder levels

5.1 Reorder level

Reorder level – when inventory held reaches the reorder level then a replenishment order should be placed.

- **Lead time** – this is the time expected to elapse between placing an order and receiving an order for inventory.
- **Reorder quantity** – when the reorder level is reached, the quantity of inventory to be ordered is known as the reorder or EOQ.
- **Demand** – this is the rate at which inventory is being used up. It is also known as inventory usage.
- If the demand in the lead time is constant, the reorder level is calculated as follows:

Reorder level (when demand in lead time is constant) = Usage x Lead time

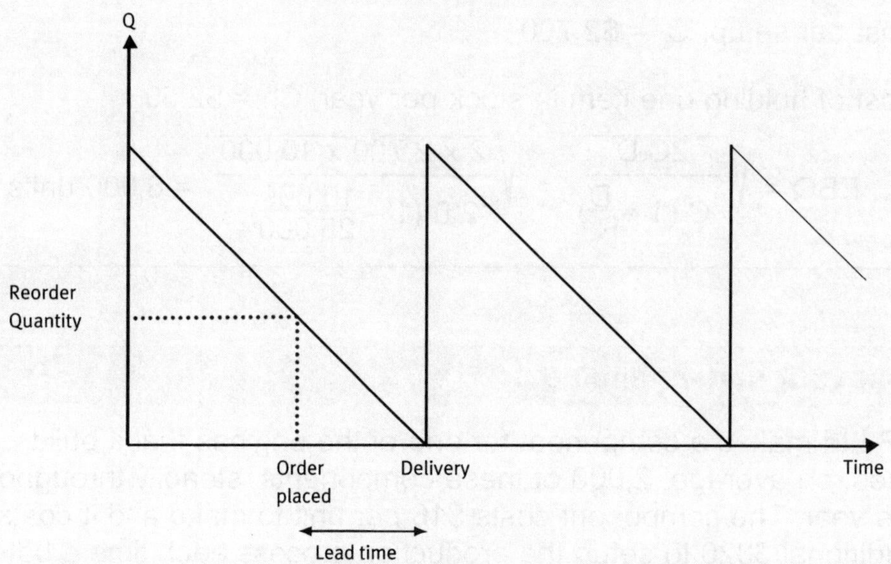

e.g

Illustration 5 – Reorder levels

A company uses Component M at the rate of 1,500 per week. The time between placing an order and receiving the components is five weeks. The reorder quantity is 12,000 units.

Required:

Calculate the reorder level.

Solution

Reorder level	=	Usage x Lead time
	=	1,500 units x 5 weeks = 7,500 units

Test your understanding 5

A national chain of tyre fitters stocks a popular tyre for which the following information is available:

Usage	175 tyres per day
Lead time	16 days
Reorder quantity	3,000 tyres

Based on the data above, at what level of inventory should a replenishment order be issued in order to ensure that there are no stock-outs?

A 2,240
B 2,800
C 3,000
D 5,740

5.2 Other inventory control levels

There are a number of other inventory control levels that are often used.

- The reorder level can also be calculated when demand in the lead time is not constant. In such situations, the maximum demand and lead times are taken into account and the reorder level is calculated as follows:

Reorder level (when demand in lead time is not constant) = Maximum Usage x Maximum Lead time

- **Maximum inventory** – this is a warning level that inventory levels are dangerously high. Inventory should not normally rise above this level.

Maximum inventory level = Reorder level + Reorder quantity – (Minimum usage x Minimum lead time)

- **Minimum inventory** – this is a warning that inventory levels are dangerously low and that stock-outs are a potential threat. Minimum stock is also known as **buffer inventory** or **safety inventory.**

Minimum inventory level = Reorder level – (Average usage x Average lead time)

- **Average inventory** – average inventory has been calculated to be half the reorder quantity. However, if buffer inventory is held by an organisation then the formula for calculating average inventory is as follows.

$$\textbf{Average inventory} = \frac{\textbf{Reorder quantity}}{\textbf{2}} + \textbf{Minimum inventory}$$

Don't forget that minimum inventory is also known as **buffer** or **safety inventory**.

- **Free inventory** – free inventory represents the 'real' quantity of inventory that is available for use by an organisation in the future.

Free inventory = Physical inventory + inventory on order – inventory requisitioned (not yet issued)

e.g

Illustration 6 – Reorder levels

You are given the following information for a component:

	Weekly usage (units)	Lead time (weeks)
Average	800	3
Maximum	1,500	5
Minimum	500	2

Reorder quantity is 12,000 units.

Required:

Calculate the maximum and minimum inventory levels, and the average inventory level.

Solution

Reorder level	= 1,500 x 5	= 7,500
Maximum level of inventory	= 7,500 + 12,000 – (500 x 2)	= 18,500
Minimum level of inventory	= 7,500 – (800 x 3)	= 5,100
Average level of inventory	= 12,000/2 + 5,100	= 11,100

Test your understanding 6

A national chain of tyre fitters stocks a popular tyre for which the following information is available:

Average usage	140 tyres per day
Minimum usage	90 tyres per day
Maximum usage	175 tyres per day
Lead time	10 to 16 days
Reorder quantity	3,000 tyres

Based on the data above, what is the maximum level of inventory possible?

A 2,800

B 3,000

C 4,900

D 5,800

Chapter summary

REORDER LEVELS

Reorder level – Place new order when inventory reaches reorder level = Maximum lead time

Other control levels – maximum inventory and minimum inventory

ORDER QUANITIES AND REORDER LEVELS

THE COSTS OF HOLDING INVENTORY

Interest on captial
Cost of storage
Cost of insurance
Stock-out costs

ECONOMIC ORDER QUANTITY

Reorder quanity that minimises total costs associated with holding inventory

$$EOQ = \sqrt{\frac{2C_oD}{C_n}}$$

THE COSTS OF ORDERING INVENTORY

Administration costs
Machine setup costs

THE ECONOMIC ORDER QUANTITY WITH DISCOUNTS

Compare total annual costs WITH discount to total annual costs WITHOUT discount. Accept discount if total cost lower with discount than without

GRADUAL REPLISHMENT OF INVENTORY

Relevant to organisations that manufacture own products. EOQ modified to produce EBQ

$$EBQ = \sqrt{\frac{2C_oD}{C_n(1-\frac{D}{R})}}$$

Test your understanding answers

Test your understanding 1

Annual holding cost = average inventory held x cost per box x 10%

= 120 x \$20 x 10% = \$240

Annual usage (in boxes) = 1,500/10 x 12 months = 1,800 boxes

Annual ordering cost = $\frac{\text{Annual usage}}{\text{Order size}}$ x \$32

= $\frac{1,800}{240}$ x \$32

= \$240

Test your understanding 2

The order quantity which minimises total costs is 3,487

This will mean ordering the item every 2 weeks

Workings

To avoid confusion this question is best tackled by working in boxes not units

$C_o = \frac{5,910}{30} \times 1.02 = \$200.94$

$C_h = 0.15 \times \$200 = \$30$ per box

$D = 90,800/10 = 9,080$ boxes

$EOQ = \sqrt{\frac{2 \times 200.94 \times 9,080}{30}} = 349$ boxes

Number of orders per year = $\frac{9,080}{349} = 26$

26 orders per annum is equivalent to placing an order every 2 weeks (52 weeks/26 orders).

Test your understanding 3

Order quantity = EOQ of 3,500 barrels	$
Purchase costs (36,750 x $12)	441,000
Annual stockholding costs ($1.20 x 3,500/2)	2,100
Annual ordering costs ($200 x 36,750/3,500)	2,100
Total costs	445,200

Order quantity = 5,000 barrels	$
Purchase costs (36,750 x $12 x 98%)	432,180
Annual stockholding costs ($1.20 x 5,000/2)	3,000
Annual ordering costs ($200 x 36,750/5,000)	1,470
Total costs	436,650

Order quantity = 7,500 barrels	$
Purchase costs (36,750 x $12 x 97.5%)	429,975
Annual stockholding costs ($1.20 x 7,500/2)	4,500
Annual ordering costs ($200 x 36,750/7,500)	980
Total costs	435,455

Total costs are minimised with an order size of 7,500 barrels.

Test your understanding 4

D = 2,000 units

R = 200 x 50 = 10,000 units

C_o = $320

C_h = 10% of $16 = $1.60

$$EBQ = \sqrt{\frac{2C_oD}{C_h(1-\frac{D}{R})}} = \sqrt{\frac{2 \times 320 \times 2,000}{1.60\,(1-\frac{2,000}{10,000})}} = 1,000 \text{ units}$$

Test your understanding 5

B Reorder level = Usage x Lead time

= 175 x 16

= 2,800 units

Test your understanding 6

C Reorder level = 16 x 175 = 2,800

Maximum inventory level = (Reorder level + reorder quantity) – (minimum usage x minimum lead time)

= (2,800 + 3,000) – (90 x 10)

= 4,900 units

chapter

6

Accounting for labour

Chapter learning objectives

Upon completion of this chapter you will be able to:

- calculate direct and indirect costs of labour for both a manufacturing and a service industry
- explain the methods used to relate input labour costs to work done for both a manufacturing and a service industry
- for given data, prepare the journal and ledger entries to record labour costs inputs and outputs, and interpret entries in the labour account
- describe different remuneration methods: time-based systems; piecework systems; individual incentive schemes; group incentive schemes
- calculate the level, and analyse the costs and causes of labour turnover for an organisation in general
- explain and calculate from given data: labour efficiency ratio; capacity ratio; production volume ratios.

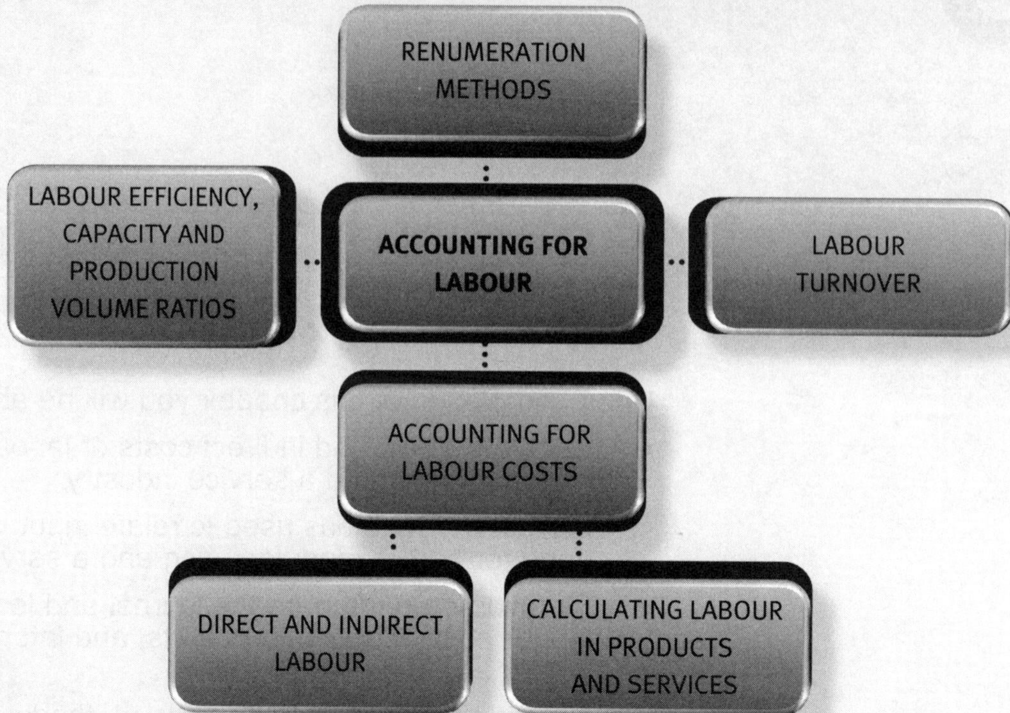

1 Direct and indirect labour

1.1 Direct and indirect labour costs

Labour is often one of the major expenses of a business. One of the most important distinctions of labour is between **direct** and **indirect** costs.

- Direct labour costs make up part of the prime cost of a product and include the basic pay of direct workers.
- Direct workers are those employees who are directly involved in making an organisation's products.
- Indirect labour costs make up part of the overheads (indirect costs) and include the basic pay of indirect workers.
- Indirect workers are those employees who are **not** directly involved in making products, (for example, maintenance staff, factory supervisors and canteen staff.
- Indirect labour costs also include the following.
  - Bonus payments.
  - Employers' National Insurance Contributions.
  - Idle time (when workers are paid but are not making any products, for example when a machine breaks down).
  - Sick pay.
  - Time spent by direct workers doing 'indirect jobs' for example, cleaning or repairing machines.

1.2 Overtime and overtime premiums

When employees work overtime, they receive a **basic pay** element and an **overtime premium**.

- For example, if Fred is paid $8 per hour and overtime is paid at time and a half, when Fred works overtime, he will receive $12 per hour ($8 + $4 (50% x $8)). It is important that his pay is analysed into direct and indirect labour costs.

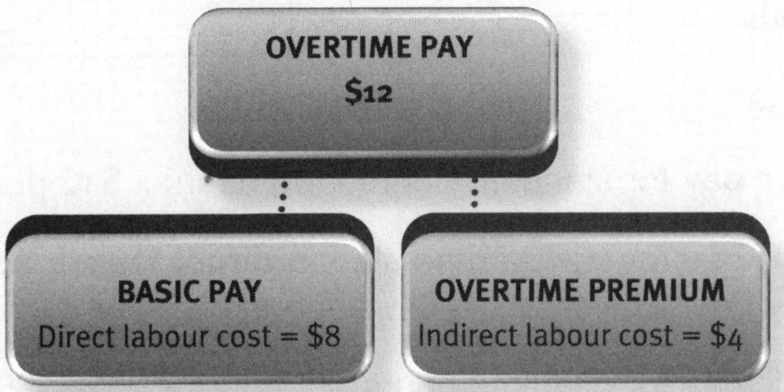

- Overtime premiums are treated as direct labour costs, if at the specific request of a customer because they want a job to be finished as soon as possible.
- Employees who work night shifts, or other anti-social hours may be entitled to a shift allowance or shift premium. Shift premiums are similar to overtime premiums where the extra amount paid above the basic rate is treated as an indirect labour cost.

e.g

Illustration 1 – Direct and indirect labour

Vienna is a direct labour employee who works a standard 35 hours per week and is paid a basic rate of $12 per hour. Overtime is paid at time and a third. In week 8 she worked 42 hours and received a $50 bonus. Complete the following table.

			Direct labour cost	Indirect labour cost
1	Basic pay for standard hours	$		
2	Basic pay for overtime hours	$		
3	Overtime premium	$		
4	Bonus	$		

Solution

			Direct labour cost	Indirect labour cost
1	Basic pay for standard hours	$	420	
2	Basic pay for overtime hours	$	84	
3	Total overtime premium	$		28
4	Bonus	$		50

Workings

1 Basic pay for standard hours = 35 hours x $12 per hour = $420

Basic pay for standard hours is a **direct labour cost** because the work involved is directly attributable to production.

2 Basic pay for overtime hours = 7 hours x $12 = $84

This is also a **direct labour cost** because the **basic rate for overtime** is part of the direct labour cost. It is the **overtime premium** which is usually part of the indirect labour cost.

3 Overtime premium = 1/3 of $12 = $4

Total overtime premium = 7 hours x $4 = $28

Unless overtime is worked at the specific request of a customer, overtime premium is part of the **indirect labour costs** of an organisation.

Test your understanding 1

A company operates a factory which employed 40 direct workers throughout the four-week period just ended. Direct employees were paid at a basic rate of $4.00 per hour for a 38-hour week. Total hours of the direct workers in the four-week period were 6,528. Overtime, which is paid at a premium of 35%, is worked in order to meet general production requirements. Employee deductions total 30% of gross wages. 188 hours of direct workers' time were registered as idle.

Calculate the following for the four-week period just ended.

- Gross wages (earnings) $
- Deductions $

- Net wages $
- Direct labour cost $
- Indirect labour cost $

2 Calculating labour in products and services

2.1 Determining time spent doing jobs

Methods can include:

- time sheets
- time cards
- job sheets.

Expandable text

Time records

It is essential that organisations employ relevant methods in both manufacturing and service industries to relate the labour costs incurred to the work done. One of the ways in which this can be done is to make records of the time spent by employees doing jobs.

- Time recording is required both for payment purposes and also for determining the costs to be charged to specific jobs.
- In manufacturing industries both direct and indirect workers will be supplied with an attendance record on which to record their time of arrival and departure from the factory. Such records are known as time cards (gate or clockcards) and are used to calculate wages and rates of pay.
- The most sophisticated time recorders use plastic 'swipe' cards which are directly linked to a central computer.

Activity time records

Another method of relating work done to costs incurred is by the use of activity time records. Activity time records may be either period related or time related.

- Period-related timesheets are commonly used in service industries, for example in accountancy firms where time spent working for different clients is analysed, often to the nearest 15 minutes.
- Period-related timesheets are records that may cover days, weeks or sometimes longer periods.
- Task-related activity time records are known as job sheets, operations charts or piecework tickets. They are generally more accurate and reliable than time-related activity time records, and are essential when incentive schemes are in use.

An example of a daily timesheet is illustrated below.

Time Sheet

Employee name:	No:
Start date:	Finish date:
Department:	Operation:

Day	Start	Finish	Time	Production	Supervisor's signature
1					
2					
3					
4					
5					
Total					
Time allowed					
Time saved					

	Hours	Rate $	Paid $
Time wages			
Bonus			
Total wages			

2.2 Payroll department

The payroll department is involved in carrying out functions that relate input labour costs to the work done.

- Preparation of the payroll involves calculating gross wages from time and activity records.
- The payroll department also calculates net wages after deductions from payroll (PAYE, Employer's National Insurance Contributions and Employee's National Insurance Contributions).
- The payroll department also carries out an analysis of direct wages, indirect wages, and cash required for payment.

Test your understanding 2

Distinguish between period-related and task-related activity records.

Which are likely to be used in manufacturing industries, and which are likely to be used in service industries?

3 Accounting for labour costs

Labour costs are an expense and are recorded in an organisation's income statement. Accounting transactions relating to labour are recorded in the labour account.

- The labour account is debited with the labour costs incurred by an organisation. The total labour costs are then analysed into direct and indirect labour costs.
- **Direct labour costs** are credited from the labour account and debited in the work-in-progress (WIP) account. Remember, direct labour costs are directly involved in production and are therefore transferred to WIP before being transferred to finished goods and then cost of sales.
- **Indirect labour costs** are also credited 'out of' the labour account and debited to the production overheads account. It is important that total labour costs are analysed into their direct and indirect elements.

Illustration 3 – Accounting for labour costs

Labour account

	$000		$000
Bank (1)	80	WIP (2)	60
		Production overheads (3)	
		Indirect labour	14
		Overtime premium	2
		Shift premium	2
		Sick pay	1
		Idle time	1
	80		80

1 Labour costs incurred are paid out of the bank before they are analysed further in the labour account.

2 The majority of the labour costs incurred by a manufacturing organisation are in respect of direct labour costs. Direct labour costs are directly involved in production and are transferred out

of the labour account via a credit entry to the WIP account as shown above.

3 Indirect labour costs include indirect labour (costs of indirect labour workers), overtime premium (unless overtime is worked at the specific request of a customer), shift premium, sick pay and idle time. All of these indirect labour costs are collected in the production overheads account. They are transferred there via a credit entry out of the labour account and then debited in the production overheads account.

Test your understanding 3

The following information is taken from the payroll records of a company.

	Direct workers	Indirect workers	Total
	$	$	$
Basic pay for basic hours	43,000	17,000	60,000
Overtime – basic pay	10,000	4,500	14,500
Overtime – premium	5,000	2,250	7,250
Training	2,500	1,250	3,750
Sick pay	750	250	1,000
Idle time	1,200	-	1,200

Required:

Using the information given, complete the labour account shown below.

Labour account

	$		$

4 Remuneration methods

There are two basic approaches to remuneration, time-related or output-related. The two basic methods are time-based and piecework systems.

4.1 Time-based systems

We looked at time-based systems, the most common remuneration method, at the beginning of this chapter.

- Employees are paid a basic rate per hour, day, week or month.
- Basic time-based systems do not provide any incentive for employees to improve productivity and close supervision is often necessary.
- The basic formula for a time-based system is as follows.

Total wages = (hours worked x basic rate of pay per hour) + (overtime hours worked x overtime premium per hour)

4.2 Piecework systems

A piecework system pays a fixed amount per unit produced. The basic formula for a piecework system is as follows.

Total wages = (units produced x rate of pay per unit)

- There are two main piecework systems that you need to know about: straight piecework and differential piecework.
- **Straight piecework systems** – these systems are almost extinct today as employees are more likely to be paid a guaranteed minimum wage within a straight piecework system. A variation on the straight piecework system is the differential piecework system.
- **Differential piecework systems** – these systems are the most widely used piecework systems and involve different piece rates for different levels of production.

e.g

Illustration 4 – Remuneration methods

A company operates a differential piecework system and the following weekly rates have been set:

Weekly production	Rate of pay per unit in this band
	$
1 to 500 units	0.20
501 to 600 units	0.25
601 units and above	0.55

Employees are paid a guaranteed minimum wage of $130 per week. How much would be paid to the following employees for the week?

Employee A – output achieved = 800 units
Employee B – output achieved = 570 units

Employee A = $ [ ]

Employee B = $ [ ]

Solution

Employee A = $ 235

Employee B = $ 130

Workings

Employee A = (500 units x $0.20) + (100 units x $0.25) + (200 units x $0.55) = $235

Employee B = (500 units x $0.20) + (70 units x $0.25) = $117.50. This is less than the guaranteed minimum therefore employee B would be paid $130.

Test your understanding 4

The following graph shows the wages earned by an employee during a single day.

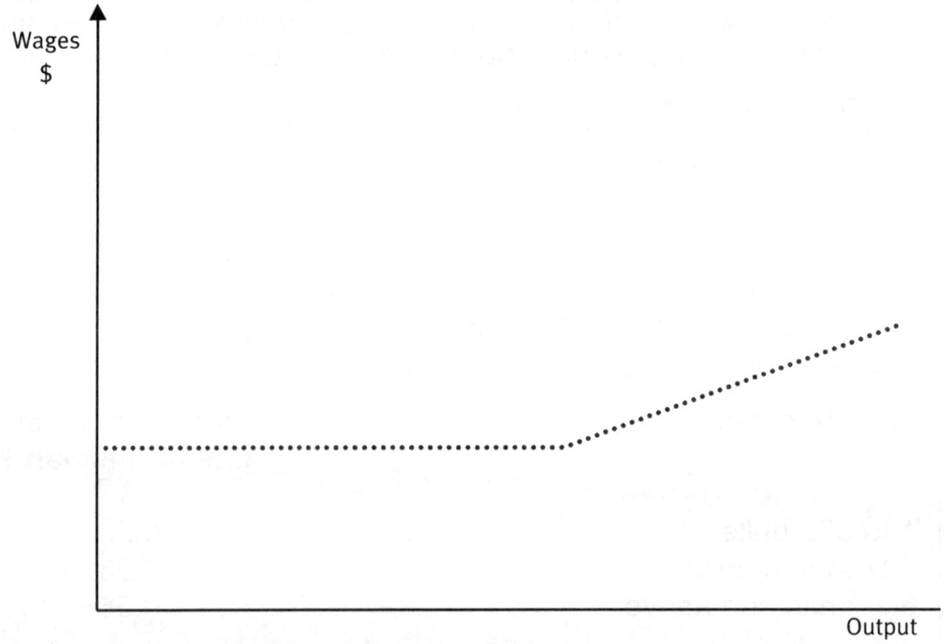

Which one of the following remuneration systems does the graph represent?

A Differential piecework
B A flat rate per hour with a premium for overtime working
C Straight piecework
D Piecework with a guaranteed minimum daily wage

4.3 Incentive schemes

Incentive schemes can be aimed at individuals and/or groups.

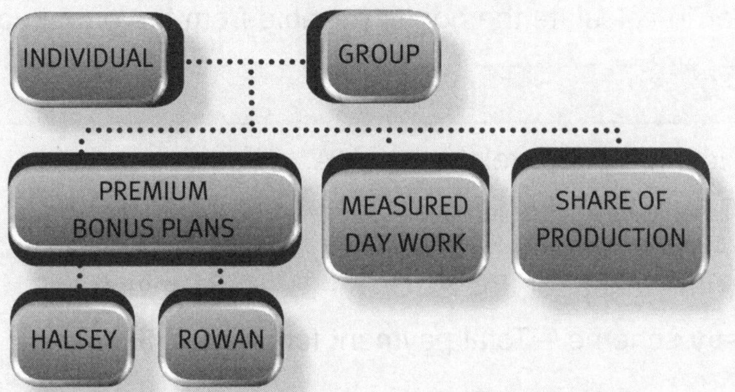

- Many different systems exist in practice for calculating bonus schemes. General rules are as follows:
  - They should be closely related to the effort expended by employees.
  - They should be agreed by employers/employees before being implemented.
  - They should be easy to understand and simple to operate.
  - They must be beneficial to all of those employees taking part in the scheme.
- Most bonus schemes pay a basic time rate, plus a portion of the time saved as compared to some agreed allowed time. These bonus schemes are known premium bonus plans. Examples of such schemes are **Halsey** and **Rowan**.
- **Halsey** – the employee receives 50% of the time saved.

  $$\text{Bonus} = \frac{\text{Time allowed} - \text{Time taken}}{2} \times \text{Time rate}$$

- **Rowan** – the proportion paid to the employee is based on the ratio of time taken to time allowed.

  $$\text{Bonus} = \frac{\text{Time taken}}{\text{Time allowed}} \times \text{Time rate} \times \text{Time saved}$$

- **Measured day work –** the concept of this approach is to pay a high time rate, but this rate is based on an analysis of past performance. Initially, work measurement is used to calculate the allowed time per unit. This allowed time is compared to the time actually taken in the past by the employee, and if this is better than the allowed time an incentive is agreed, e.g. suppose the allowed time is 1 hour per unit and that the average time taken by an employee over the last three months is 50 minutes. If the normal rate is $12/hour, then an agreed incentive rate of (say) $14/hour could be used.

- **Share of production** – share of production plans are based on acceptance by both management and labour representatives of a constant share of value added for payroll. Thus, any gains in value added – whether by improved production performance or cost savings – are shared by employees in this ratio.

In an examination you will be given clear instructions on any bonus scheme in operation. You should follow the instructions given carefully in order to calculate the bonus payable from the data supplied.

e.g

Illustration 5 – Remuneration methods

The following data relate to Job A.

Employee's basic rate	=	$4.80 per hour
Allowed time for Job A	=	1 hour
Time taken for Job A	=	36 minutes

Halsey scheme – Total payment for Job A = $ ______

Rowan scheme – Total payment for Job B = $ ______

Solution

Halsey scheme – Total payment for Job A = $ 3.84

Rowan scheme – Total payment for Job B = $ 4.03

Workings

Halsey

			$
Bonus	=	$\frac{60 - 36}{2} \times \frac{\$4.80}{60}$	0.96
Basic rate	=	$\frac{36}{60} \times \$4.80$	2.88
Total payment for Job A			3.84

Rowan

			$
Bonus	=	$\frac{36}{60} \times \frac{\$4.80}{60} \times 24$	1.15
Basic rate	=	$\frac{36}{60} \times \$4.80$	2.88
Total payment for Job A			4.03

Expandable text

Additional test your understanding

Ten employees work as a group. When production of the group exceeds the standard – 200 pieces per hour – each employee in the group is paid a bonus for the excess production in addition to wages at hourly rates.

The bonus is computed thus: the percentage of production in excess of the standard quantity is found, and one half of the percentage is regarded as the employees' share. Each employee in the group is paid as a bonus this percentage of a wage rate of $5.20 per hour. There is no relationship between the individual worker's hourly rate and the bonus rate.

The following is one week's record:

	Hours worked	Production
Monday	90	24,500
Tuesday	88	20,600
Wednesday	90	24,200
Thursday	84	20,100
Friday	88	20,400
Saturday	40	10,200
	480	120,000

During this week, Jones worked 42 hours and was paid $3 per hour basic.

Complete the following.

1 The bonus rate for the week was $ [ ]

2 The total bonus for the week was $ [ ]

3 The total pay for Jones for the week was $ [ ]

Solution

1 The bonus rate for the week was $ 0.65

2 The total bonus for the week was $ 312

3 The total pay for Jones for the week was $ 153.30

Workings

Standard production for the week = 480 hours x 200 = 96,000 pieces
Actual production for the week = 120,000 pieces
Excess production = 120,000 – 96,000 = 24,000

1. Bonus rate = $\frac{24,000}{96,000}$ x 0.5 x \$5.20
= \$0.65 per hour

2. Total bonus = 480 hours x \$0.65
= \$312

3. Pay for Jones = 42 x (3.00 + 0.65)
= \$153.30

5 Labour turnover

Labour turnover is a measure of the proportion of people leaving relative to the average number of people employed.

- Management might wish to monitor labour turnover, so that control measures might be considered if the rate of turnover seems too high, and the business is losing experienced and valuable staff at too fast a rate.
- Labour turnover is calculated for any given period of time using the following formula:

$$\frac{\textbf{Number of leavers who require replacement}}{\textbf{Average number of employees}} \times 100$$

- The labour turnover percentage calculated can be compared with past figures, targets, and industry averages. It provides an indication of whether an unacceptably high number of people are leaving the organisation.

e.g

Illustration 6 – Labour turnover

At 1 January a company employed 3,641 employees and at 31 December employee numbers were 3,735. During the year 624 employees chose to leave the company. What was the labour turnover rate for the year?

Solution

Labour turnover rate =

$$\frac{\text{Number of leavers who require replacement}}{\text{Average number of employees}} \times 100$$

Average number of employees in the year = (3,641 + 3,735)/2 = 3,688.

Labour turnover rate = (624/3,688) x 100% = 16.9%.

Test your understanding 5

A company had 4,000 staff at the beginning of 20X8. During the year, there was a major restructuring of the company and 1,500 staff were made redundant and 400 staff left the company to work for one of the company's main competitors. 400 new staff joined the company in the year to replace those who went to work for the competitor.

Required:

Calculate the labour turnover rate for 20X8.

Expandable text

Causes of labour turnover

It is important to try to identify why people leave an organisation and to distinguish between avoidable and unavoidable causes of labour turnover.

- Causes of labour turnover – avoidable:
  – poor remuneration
  – poor working conditions
  – lack of training opportunities
  – lack of promotion prospects
  – bullying in the workplace.
- Causes of labour turnover – unavoidable:
  – retirement
  – illness/death
  – family reasons (e.g. pregnancy)
  – relocation.
- Efficient managers will investigate high levels of labour turnover and aim to keep that turnover rate at a minimum.

Costs of labour turnover

Every time an employee leaves, an organisation will incur costs that are associated with replacing the employee. These costs are known as replacement costs.

- Replacement costs include the following:
  – advertising costs
  – cost of selection (time spent interviewing etc.)
  – training new employees

– reduced efficiency until the new employee reaches the required skill.

- A high labour turnover rate tends to lower the performance of employees who remain in the organisation. Such employees may become restless and resentful of the extra burden of training new members and of additional temporary duties imposed upon them.
- In order to keep the labour turnover rate to a minimum, organisations should aim to prevent employees from leaving. Such preventive measures come with their own costs, known as preventive costs.
- Preventive costs include the costs associated with escaping the avoidable causes of labour turnover:
  – pay competitive wages and salaries if remuneration is poor
  – improve poor working conditions
  – offer good training opportunities
  – make sure promotion prospects arise as necessar.
  – stamp out bullying in the workplace
  – investigate high labour turnover rates objectively.

6 Labour efficiency, capacity and production volume ratios

6.1 Labour efficiency ratio

Labour is a significant cost in many organisations and it is important to continually measure the efficiency of labour against pre-set targets.

- The labour efficiency ratio measures the performance of the workforce by comparing the actual time taken to do a job with the expected time.
- The labour efficiency ratio is calculated using the following formula:

$$\frac{\text{Expected hours to produce output}}{\text{Actual hours to produce output}} \times 100\%$$

6.2 Labour capacity ratio

Sometimes the workforce is 'idle' through no fault of its own, and cannot get on with productive work. This sometimes happens if machines break down or need to be reset for a new production run.

- The labour capacity ratio measures the number of hours spent actively working as a percentage of the total hours available for work (full capacity or budgeted hours).
- The labour capacity ratio is calculated using the following formula:

$$\frac{\text{Number of hours spent working (active production)}}{\text{Total hours available (budgeted)}} \times 100\%$$

6.3 Labour production volume ratio

- The labour production volume ratio compares the number of hours expected to be worked to produce actual output with the total hours available for work (full capacity or budgeted hours).
- The labour production volume ratio is calculated using the following formula:

$$\frac{\textbf{Expected hours to produce actual output}}{\textbf{Total hours available (budgeted)}} \times 100\%$$

e.g

Illustration 7 – Labour efficiency, capacity and production volume ratios

Standard hours

A **standard hour** is the number of production units which should be achieved by an experienced worker within a period of one hour.

Standard time allowed per unit	30 minutes
Actual output in period	840 units
Actual hours worked	410
Budgeted hours	400

Expected hours to make actual output = 840 units x 0.5 hours per unit

= 420 standard hours

Standard (std) hours are therefore the expected hours to make actual output.

Labour efficiency ratio =

$$\frac{\text{Expected hours to produce actual output (std hours)}}{\text{Actual hours to produce output}} \times 100\%$$

$$= \frac{420}{410} \times 100\% = 102\%$$

Labour capacity ratio =

$$\frac{\text{Number of hours spent working (active production)}}{\text{Total hours available (budgeted)}} \times 100\%$$

$$= \frac{410}{400} \times 100\% = 102.5\%$$

Production volume ratio =

$$\frac{\text{Expected hours to produce actual output (std hours)}}{\text{Total hours available (budgeted)}} \times 100\%$$

$$= \frac{420}{400} \times 100\% = 105\%$$

Test your understanding 6

A company budgets to make 40,000 units of Product DOY in 4,000 hours (each unit is budgeted to take 0.1 hours each) in a year.

Actual output during the year was 38,000 units which took 4,180 hours to make.

Required:

Calculate the labour efficiency, capacity and production volume ratios.

Chapter summary

ACCOUNTING FOR LABOUR

Renumeration methods

- Time-based systems
- Piecework systems
- Individual incentive schemes
- Group incentive schemes

Labour efficiency capacity and production volume ratios

Labour is significant cost in many organisations – important to use these ratios to continually 'measure' how it is doing by reference to effciency, capacity and production volume ratios

Accounting for labour costs

Debit labour account with labour costs incurred

Credit labour account with direct labour – transfer to WIP

Credit labour account with indirect labour – transfer to production overheads account

Labour turnover

Measure of proportion of employees leaving relative to the average number of people employed

Many causes and costs of labour turnover – both avoidable and unavoidable

Direct and indirect labour

Direct labour – makes up part of prime cost and includes basic pay of direct workers

Inderect labour – makes up part of overheads and includes basic pay of indirect workers

Overtime premiums are treated as overheads unless worked at specific request of customer when treated as direct cost

Calculating labour in prod-ucts and services

Times records

- Time cards
- Clock cards

Activity records

- Period-related

Test your understanding answers

Test your understanding 1

- Gross wages (earnings) $ 26,739.20
- Deductions $ 8,021.76
- Net wages $ 18,717.44
- Direct labour cost $ 25,360
- Indirect labour cost $ 1,379.20

Workings

Basic time	=	40 workers x 38 hrs/week x 4 weeks	=	6,080 hrs
Overtime	=	Total time – Basic time = 6,528 – 6,080	=	448 hrs
Total wages	=	Basic pay + Overtime premium		
	=	6,528 hours at $4.00 per hour	=	$26,112.00
		+ 448 hours at $1.40 per hour	=	$627.20
Gross wages				$26,739.20
Deductions	=	$26,739.20 x 30%	=	$8,021.76
Net pay	=	$26,739.20 x 70%	=	$18,717.44
Productive time	=	Total time – Idle time		
	=	6,528 – 188	=	6,340 hours
Direct labour	=	6,340 hours at $4.00 per hour	=	$25,360
Indirect labour	=	Overtime premium + Idle time costs		
	=	$627.20 + $752 (188 hours x $4.00/hr)	=	$1,379.20
Gross wages				$26,739.20

Test your understanding 2

- Period-related activity records are commonly used to record time spent working in service industries, for example, in law firms where time spent working for different clients is analysed in detail. This ensures that clients are billed for the exact amount of time spent working on their affairs. Period-related activity records include timesheets that may cover days, weeks or sometimes longer periods.
- Task-related activity time records are more commonly used to record time spent working in manufacturing industries. Records which record the amount of time spent carrying out specific tasks or jobs are known as job sheets, operations charts or piecework tickets. They are generally more accurate and reliable than period-related activity time records, and are essential when incentive schemes are in use.

Test your understanding 3

Labour account

	$		$
Bank	87,700	WIP (43,000 + 10,000)	53,000
		Production overheads	
		Indirect labour	
		(17,000 + 4,500)	21,500
		Overtime premium	7,250
		Training	3,750
		Sick pay	1,000
		Idle time	1,200
	87,700		87,700

Test your understanding 4

D The graph represents a piecework system (as shown by the gentle upward-sloping line) with a guaranteed minimum daily wage (as shown by the horizontal line).

Test your understanding 5

Number of staff at beginning of year = 4,000

Number of staff at end of year = 4,000 – 1,500 – 400 + 400 = 2,500

Labour turnover rate =

$$\frac{\text{Number of leavers who require replacement}}{\text{Average number of employees}} \times 100$$

Average number of employees in the year = (4,000 + 2,500)/2 = 3,250

Labour turnover rate = (400/3,250) x 100% = 12.3%.

Test your understanding 6

Expected hours to produce output = 38,000 x 0.1 hours = 3,800 standard hours.

Labour efficiency ratio =

$$\frac{\text{Expected hours to produce actual output (std hours)}}{\text{Actual hours to produce output}} \times 100\%$$

$$= \frac{3{,}800}{4{,}180} \times 100\% = 91\%$$

Labour capacity ratio =

$$\frac{\text{Number of hours spent working (active production)}}{\text{Total hours available (budgeted)}} \times 100\%$$

$$= \frac{4{,}180}{4{,}000} \times 100\% = 104.5\%$$

Production volume ratio =

$$\frac{\text{Expected hours to produce actual output (std hours)}}{\text{Total hours available (budgeted)}} \times 100\%$$

$$= \frac{3{,}800}{4{,}000} \times 100\% = 95\%$$

chapter

7

Accounting for overheads

Chapter learning objectives

Upon completion of this chapter you will be able to:

- explain the different treatment of direct and indirect expenses for a business
- describe, in overview, the steps involved in determining production overhead absorption rates (OARs) and how such rates are used
- explain, for a business in general, the difference between 'allocation' and 'apportionment' of production overheads
- apportion production overheads to cost centres employing appropriate bases, using data supplied
- reapportion service cost centre costs to production cost centres (using the reciprocal method where service cost centres work for each other), using data supplied
- select, apply and discuss appropriate bases for absorption rates, using data supplied
- prepare journal and ledger entries for manufacturing overheads incurred and absorbed, using data supplied
- calculate and explain the under- and over-absorption of overheads, using data supplied
- apply methods of relating non-production overheads to cost units, using data supplied.

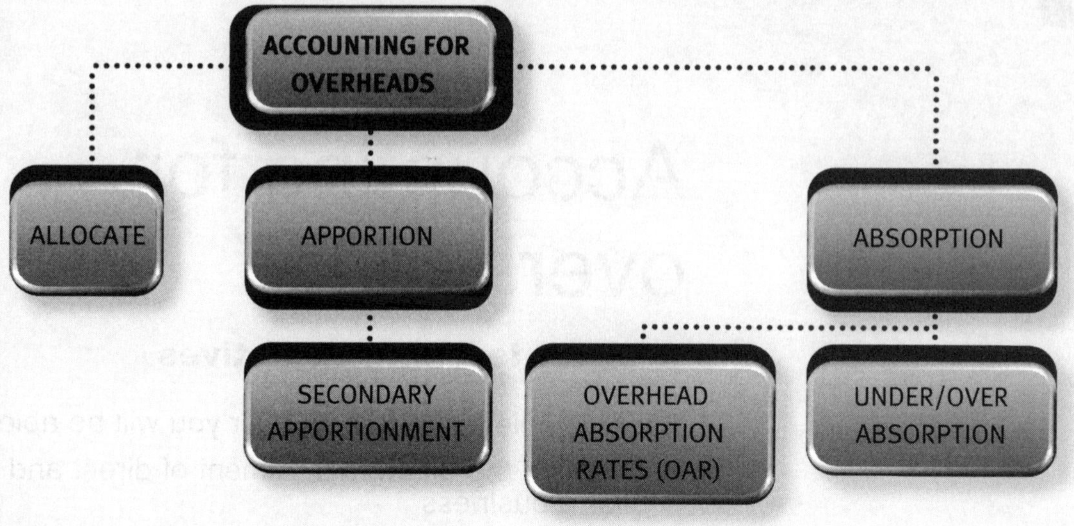

1 Recap of direct and indirect expenses

Direct expenses are expenses that can be directly identified with a specific cost unit or cost centre, for example, the cost of maintaining sewing machines that are used to make shirts. The maintenance expense can be directly related to the cost of producing the shirts.

- Direct expenses are part of the prime cost of a product.

Indirect expenses cannot be directly identified with a specific cost unit or cost centre.

- For example, the cost of renting the factory where shirts are manufactured is classified as an indirect cost because it would be impossible to relate such costs to shirts only, if other clothes, such as dresses and suits were also made in the same factory.
- Indirect expenses are also known as **overheads**.
- Overheads that are associated with production are known as production overheads and those not associated with production are known as non-production overheads (for example, selling overheads, distribution overheads and administration overheads).
- Overheads may be fixed or variable.
- Examples of indirect expenses (overheads) are as follows:
  – factory rent
  – depreciation of equipment
  – heating costs for a factory
  – lighting costs for a factory.
- Production overheads are 'shared out' between units of production under a costing system known as absorption costing.

2 Production overhead absorption

2.1 Fixed production overheads

As we have already seen, production overheads are the total of indirect production costs:

Fixed production overheads = indirect materials + indirect labour + indirect expenses

- Fixed production overheads of a factory will include the following costs:
  - heating the factory
  - lighting the factory
  - renting the factory.
- The total cost of a product also includes a share of the fixed production overheads.
- This is because organisations must recover their fixed production overheads and they do this by absorbing a fixed amount into each product that they make and sell.
- One way of recovering fixed production overheads is on a cost per unit basis.

Illustration 1 – Production overhead absorption

RS Ltd is a manufacturing company producing Product P, which has the following cost card.

		$
Direct labour	2 hrs @ $5 per hour	10
Direct materials	1 kg @ $5 per kg	5
Direct expenses		1
Prime cost		**16**

RS Ltd produces and sells 1,000 units in a month.

Based on past experience, RS Ltd estimates its monthly overheads will be as follows.

	$
Heating	3,000
Power	2,000
Maintenance	500
Total	**5,500**

The overhead cost allocated to each unit of Product P is $ [   ]

The cost per unit of Product P is $ [   ]

Solution

The overhead cost allocated to each unit of Product P is $ 5.50

The cost per unit of Product P is $ 21.50

Workings

The overhead per unit is $\frac{\$5,500}{1,000}$ = $5.50 per unit.

The cost per unit is:

	$
Prime cost	16.00
Overheads	5.50
Total	**21.50**

Test your understanding 1

In addition to producing Product P, RS Ltd now starts to produce another product, Product Q.

RS Ltd plans to make and sell 1,000 units of Product Q in a month, as well as producing 1,000 units of Product P. Due to the increase in production levels, the overheads are likely to increase as follows.

	$
Heating	4,200
Power	2,900
Maintenance	700
Total	7,800

Calculate the overhead cost allocated to each unit of Product P.

Calculate the new cost per unit of Product P.

2.2 Absorption costing

Production overheads are recovered by absorbing them into the cost of a product and this process is therefore called absorption costing.

- The main aim of absorption costing is to recover overheads in a way that fairly reflects the amount of time and effort that has gone into making a product or service.
- Absorption costing involves the following stages:
  - allocation and apportionment of overheads
  - reapportionment of service (non-production) cost centre overheads
  - absorption of overheads.
- **Illustration 1** gave us a brief glimpse at the final stage of absorption costing (absorption of overheads) when we looked at how overheads can be recovered on a cost-per-unit basis.
- However, production overheads are more commonly recovered on the basis of labour hours or machine hours. We will look further at this final stage of absorption of overheads later on in this chapter.
- Before that, we will look at the first stage of absorption costing and explain the differences between 'allocation' and 'apportionment'.

3 'Allocation' and 'apportionment'

3.1 Allocation and apportionment of overheads

The first stage of the absorption costing process involves the allocation and apportionment of overheads.

- Allocation involves charging overheads directly to specific departments (production and service). Examples of overheads that are allocated to specific departments include the following:
  - indirect labour costs for Department A
  - indirect material costs for Department B
  - indirect expenses for Department C.
- If overheads relate to more than one specific department, then they must be apportioned (shared) between these departments using a method known as apportionment.
- The types of fixed production overhead that are usually apportioned are those that are used by many different departments, for example:
  - rent
  - business rates
  - heating costs
  - electricity costs.
- Overheads must be apportioned between different production and service departments on a fair basis.

3.2 Bases of apportionment

There are no hard and fast rules for which basis of apportionment to use except that whichever method is used to apportion overheads, it must be fair. Possible bases of apportionment include the following:

- floor area – for rent and rates overheads
- net book value (NVB) of fixed assets – for depreciation and insurance of machinery
- number of employees – for canteen costs.

e.g

Illustration 2 – 'Allocation' and 'apportionment'

LS Ltd has two production departments (Assembly and Finishing) and two service departments (Maintenance and Canteen).

The following are budgeted costs for the next period:

Indirect materials	$20,000
Rent	$15,000
Electricity	$10,000
Machine depreciation	$5,000
Indirect labour	$16,520
Direct labour	$125,000

The following information is available:

	Assembly	Finishing	Maintenance	Canteen
Area (sq metres)	1,000	2,000	500	500
kW hours consumed	2,750	4,500	1,975	775
Machine value ($)	45,000	35,000	11,000	9,000
Staff	20	30	10	2
Direct labour hours	3,175	3,800	-	-
Indirect materials budget ($)	7,000	8,000	3,000	2,000
Indirect labour budget ($)	1,600	2,220	11,200	1,500

Required:

Complete the extract from the overhead analysis sheet shown below.

Overhead analysis sheet

Overhead	Basis of apportionment	Assembly $	Finishing $	Maintenance $	Canteen $	Total $
Indirect materials						
Rent						
Direct labour						

Solution

Overhead analysis sheet

Overhead	Basis of apportionment	Assembly $	Finishing $	Maintenance $	Canteen $	Total $
Indirect materials	Allocated (W1)	7,000	8,000	3,000	2,000	20,000
Rent	Area (W2)	3,750	7,500	1,875	1,875	15,000
Direct labour	See below (W3)					

Workings

(W1)

Indirect materials are allocated directly to the relevant departments.

(W2)

Rent is apportioned to all departments based on the area occupied.

Total rent cost = $15,000
Total area occupied = (1,000 + 2,000 + 500 + 500) sq metres = 4,000 sq metres

Apportioned to Assembly department = 1,000/4,000 x $15,000 = $3,750

(W3)

Direct labour is not an overhead and is therefore not part of the overhead allocation and apportionment process.

Test your understanding 2

Using the information from **Illustration 2** above, complete the extract of the overhead analysis sheet shown below.

Overhead	Basis of apportionment	Assembly $	Finishing $	Maintenance $	Canteen $	Total $
Electricity						
Machine depreciation						
Indirect labour						

4 Reapportionment of service cost centres costs to production cost centres

4.1 'Reapportionment'

Service cost centres (departments) are not directly involved in making products and therefore the fixed production overheads of service cost centres must be shared out between the production cost centres (departments) using a suitable basis.

- Examples of service cost centres are as follows:
  - stores
  - canteen
  - maintenance department
  - payroll department.
- The basic method of reapportionment (illustrated below) is used when one service department does work for other, but not where services are reciprocated, (e.g. canteen does work for maintenance **and** maintenance does work for the canteen).
- The reciprocal method of reapportionment is used when two service departments do work for each other.

Illustration 3 – Reapportionment of service cost centre costs to production cost centres

The total overheads allocated and apportioned to the production and service departments of LS Ltd are as follows:

Assembly	=	$17,350
Finishing	=	$23,970
Maintenance	=	$18,600
Canteen	=	$6,600

A suitable basis for sharing out the maintenance costs is the time spent servicing equipment. The amount of time spent by the maintenance department servicing equipment in the Assembly and Finishing departments has been analysed as follows:

Assembly 60%
Finishing 40%

The Canteen department's overheads are to be reapportioned on the basis of the number of employees in the other three departments.

	Assembly	Finishing	Maintenance	Canteen
Number of employees	20	30	10	2

Required:

Complete the overhead analysis sheet below. Reapportion the canteen costs first since they DO work for the Maintenance department but the Maintenance department DO NOT do any work for the Canteen.

Overhead	Basis of apportionment	Assembly $	Finishing $	Maintenance $	Canteen $	Total $
Total from above						
Reapportion canteen						
Sub-total						
Reapportion maintenance						
Total						

Solution

Overhead	Basis of apportionment	Assembly $	Finishing $	Maintenance $	Canteen $	Total $
Total from above		17,350	23,970	18,600	6,600	66,520
Reapportion canteen	Employees (W1)	2,200	3,300	1,100	(6,600)	–
Sub-total		19,550	27,270	19,700	0	66,520
Reapportion maintenance	% time (W2)	11,820	7,880	(19,700)	–	–
Total		31,370	35,150	0	0	66,520

Workings:

(W1)

Canteen overheads are reapportioned on the basis of number of employees.

Total employees = 20 + 30 + 10 = 60

Reapportioned to Assembly department = 20/60 x $6,600 = $2,200

(W2)

Assembly = 60% x $19,700 = $11,820
Maintenance = 40% x $19,700 = $7,880

The overhead analysis sheet that you have just completed demonstrates the basic method of service department reapportionment.

4.2 Reciprocal reapportionment

Reciprocal reapportionment (or the repeated distribution method) is used where service cost centres (departments) do work for each other.

- It involves carrying out many reapportionments until all of the service departments' overheads have been reapportioned to the production departments.
- The following illustration will demonstrate the reciprocal method of reapportionment.

e.g

Illustration 4 – Reapportionment of service cost centre costs to production cost centres

The total overheads allocated and apportioned to the production and service departments of LS Ltd are as follows.

Assembly	=	$17,350
Finishing	=	$23,970
Maintenance	=	$18,600
Canteen	=	$6,600

A suitable basis for sharing out the maintenance costs is the time spent servicing equipment. The amount of time spent by the maintenance department servicing equipment in the other three departments has been analysed as follows.

Assembly	50%
Finishing	40%
Canteen	10%

The Canteen department's overheads are to be reapportioned on the basis of the number of employees in the other three departments.

	Assembly	Finishing	Maintenance	Canteen
Number of employees	20	30	10	2

Complete the overhead analysis sheet below and reapportion the service departments' overheads to the production departments.

Overhead	Assembly $	Finishing $	Maintenance $	Canteen $	Total $
Total from above	20	30	10	2	
Reapportion canteen					
Reapportion maintenance					
Reapportion canteen					
Reapportion maintenance					
Reapportion canteen					
Reapportion maintenance					
Total					

Solution

Overhead	Assembly $	Finishing $	Maintenance $	Canteen $	Total $
Total from above	17,350	23,970	18,600	6,600	66,520
Reapportion canteen	2,200	3,300	1,100	(6,600)	–
Reapportion maintenance	9,850	7,880	(19,700)	1,970	–
Reapportion canteen	657	985	328	(1,970)	–
Reapportion maintenance	164	131	(328)	33	–
Reapportion canteen	11	17	5	(33)	–
Reapportion maintenance	3	2	(5)	0	–
Total	30,235	36,285	0	0	66,520

Test your understanding 3

A company has three production departments, Alpha, Beta and Gamma, and two service departments, Maintenance (M) and Payroll (P). The following table shows how costs have been allocated and the relative usage of each service department by other departments.

	Production			Service	
Department	**Alpha**	**Beta**	**Gamma**	**M**	**P**
Costs	$3,000	$4,000	$2,000	$2,500	$2,700
Proportion M (%)	20	30	25	–	25
Proportion P (%)	25	25	30	20	–

Required

Complete the overhead analysis sheet below and reapportion the service department overheads to the production departments using the reciprocal method.

Overhead	Alpha $	Beta $	Gamma $	M $	P $
Total overheads					
Reapportion M					
Reapportion P					
Reapportion M					
Reapportion P					
Reapportion M					
Reapportion P					
Total					

5 Appropriate bases for absorption rates

5.1 Bases of absorption

You will remember that the main aim of absorption costing is to recover production overheads by absorbing a fixed amount of overhead into each unit of product that is produced. We looked at absorbing overheads on a cost-per-unit basis at the beginning of this chapter.

- Overheads can also be absorbed into cost units using the following absorption bases:
  - – machine-hour rate (when production is machine intensive)
  - – labour-hour rate (when production is labour intensive)
  - – percentage of prime cost
  - – percentage of direct wages.
- The overhead absorption rate (OAR) may be calculated as follows:

$$\text{OAR} = \frac{\textbf{Total production overhead}}{\textbf{Total of absorption basis}}$$

- The absorption basis is most commonly units of a product, labour hours, or machine hours.

5.2 Departmental OARs

It is usual for a product to pass through more than one department during the production process. Each department will normally have a separate departmental OAR.

- For example, a machining department will probably use a machine-hour OAR.
- Similarly, a labour-intensive department will probably use a labour-hour OAR.
- An alternative to a departmental OAR is what is termed a blanket OAR.
- With blanket OARs, only one absorption rate is calculated for the entire factory regardless of the departments involved in production.
- Blanket OARs are also known as single factory-wide OARs.

5.3 Predetermined OARs

Production overheads are usually calculated at the beginning of an accounting period in order to determine an OAR for products before they are sold to customers.

- This means that budgeted (or expected) figures must be used for production overheads and activity levels (machine hours, labour hours).
- This means that the OARs calculated at the beginning of an accounting period are 'predetermined'.
- The predetermined OAR is calculated as follows.

$$\text{OAR} = \frac{\textbf{Budgeted overheads}}{\textbf{Budgeted level of activity}}$$

- Predetermined OARs illustrate the difference between cost and financial accounting very nicely.
- In financial accounting we would wait until the end of the period to calculate the actual overheads; in cost accounting we need to

inform customers of prices NOW, so we use budgets (estimates) to show what we think future costs will be.

e.g

Illustration 5 – Appropriate bases for absorption rates

Ballard Ltd makes three products A, B and C. Each passes through two departments: Machining and Assembly.

Labour hours used in each department by each product

	Machining	Assembly
Product A	1 hr	1 hr
Product B	2 hrs	½ hr
Product C	None	4 hrs

Production is expected to be as follows:

Product A	1,000 units
Product B	2,000 units
Product C	500 units

Overheads are budgeted as follows:

Machining	Assembly
$100,000	$150,000

Complete the following.

Machining department OAR per hour = $ ______

Assembly department OAR per hour = $ ______

Blanket OAR per hour = $ ______

Overhead absorbed by Product B using a separate departmental overhead rate = $ ______

Solution

Machining department OAR per hour = $ 20

Assembly department OAR per hour = $ 37.50

Blanket OAR per hour = $ 27.78

Overhead absorbed by Product B using a separate departmental overhead rate = $ 58.75

Workings

	Machining	Assembly
Budgeted overheads	$100,000	$150,000
Budgeted labour	(1 x 1,000) + (2 x 2,000) = 5,000	(1 x 1,000) + (½ x 2,000) + (4 x 500) = 4,000
OAR	$20 per hour	$37.50 per hour

Using a blanket OAR:

	Company wide
Overheads	$250,000
Hours	5,000 + 4,000 = 9,000
OAR	$27.78 per hour

Apply to Product:	Machining	Assembly	Total
B	$40	$18.75	$58.75

Product B – Machining department overhead = 2 hours x$20 = $40

Product B – Assembly department overhead = 0.5 hours x$37.50 = $18.75

Test your understanding 4

The Major Gnome Manufacturing Company has two departments – Moulding and Painting – and uses a single production OAR based on direct labour hours. The budget and actual data for Period 6 are given below:

	Direct wages hours $	Labour hours	Machine	Production overhead $
Budget				
Moulding	24,000	4,000	12,000	180,000
Painting	70,000	10,000	1,000	100,000
	94,000	14,000	13,000	280,000
Actual				
Moulding	30,000	5,000	14,000	200,000
Painting	59,500	8,500	800	95,000
	89,500	13,500	14,800	295,000

During Period 6, a batch of Pixie Gnomes was made, with the following costs and times:

	Direct wages hours $	Labour hours	Machine
Moulding	726	120	460
Painting	2,490	415	38
	3,216	535	498

The direct material cost of the batch was $890.

Complete the following.

(a) Using a single blanket OAR based on labour hours, the cost of the batch of Pixie Gnomes is $ ______

It has been suggested that appropriate departmental OARs may be more realistic.

(b) The OAR in:

(i) the moulding department is $ ______

(ii) the painting department is $ ______

(c) Using departmental OARs, the cost of the batch of Pixie Gnomes is $ [ ]

6 Journal and ledger entries for manufacturing overheads

6.1 Production overheads account

The direct costs of production (materials, labour and expenses) are debited in the work-in-progress (WIP) account. Indirect production costs are collected in the production overheads account.

- Non-production overheads are debited to one of the following:
  - administration overheads account
  - selling overheads account
  - distribution overheads account
  - finance overheads account.
- Production overheads, as you will remember, include rent and rates, indirect materials and indirect labour costs.
- Absorbed production overheads are credited to the production overheads account.
- Any difference between the actual and absorbed overheads is known as the under- or over-absorbed overhead and is transferred to the income statement at the end of an accounting period.

e.g

Illustration 6 – Journal and ledger entries for manufacturing overheads

Production overheads

	$000		$000
Labour	20	WIP (1)	108
Expenses	92	Under absorption	
		(Bal. figure) (2)	9
Stores	5		
	117		117

Over/under-absorption of overheads

	$000		$000
Production overheads (2)	9	Income statement (3)	9
	9		9

1 Production overheads are usually absorbed on the basis of a percentage of the cost of direct labour or some other basis. The absorbed overheads are 'credited out' of the production overheads account and transferred to the WIP account where they are added to the cost of production, and hence the cost of sales.

2 The production overheads account acts as a collecting place for all the indirect costs of a production process. All the costs are debited to this account. Once the amount of overheads absorbed has been calculated, they are transferred to the WIP account. The difference between the overheads absorbed and the overheads actually incurred is known as the under- or over-absorbed overhead. This is a balancing figure and is transferred to the Over/under-absorption of overheads account.

3 At the end of an accounting period, the balance on the Over/under-absorption account is transferred to the income statement where it is written off (under-absorbed overhead) or increases profit (over-absorbed overhead).

Test your understanding 5

Transaction	Debit which account?	Credit which account?
Indirect materials issued from stores		
Indirect wages analysed in the labour account		
Indirect expenses purchased (cash)		
Production overheads absorbed into the cost of production		
Direct materials issued from stores		

7 Under- and over-absorption of overheads

7.1 Under- and over-absorption of overheads

You will remember that the predetermined OAR is calculated using budgeted (estimated) figures as follows:

$$\text{OAR} = \frac{\text{Budgeted overheads}}{\text{Budgeted level of activity}}$$

- Remember also that the budgeted level of activity can relate to machine hours, labour hours and so on.
- If either or both of the estimates for the budgeted overheads or the budgeted level of activity are different from the actual results for the year then this will lead to one of the following:
  - under-absorption (recovery) of overheads
  - over-absorption (recovery) of overheads.

7.2 Absorption of overheads

At the end of an accounting period, the overheads absorbed will be calculated as follows.

Overheads absorbed = predetermined OAR x actual level of activity

- If at the end of this period, the overheads absorbed are greater than the actual overheads, then there has been an over-absorption of overheads.
- If, on the otherhand, the overheads absorbed are less than the actual overheads, then there has been an under-absorption of overheads.
- Under-absorption is sometimes referred to as under-recovery of overheads and over-absorption is sometimes referred to as over-recovery of overheads.

e.g

Illustration 7 – Under- and over-absorption of overheads

The following data relate to Lola Ltd for Period 8.

	Budget	Actual
Overheads	$80,000	$90,000
Labour hours worked	20,000	22,000

Overheads were under/over-absorbed by (delete as appropriate) $ [ ]

Solution

Overheads were under-absorbed by $ [ ]

Workings

$$OAR = \frac{\$80,000}{20,000} = \$4 \text{ per labour hour worked}$$

Overhead absorbed = 22,000 x $4	= $88,000
Actual overhead	= $90,000
Under-absorbed overhead	= $2,000

Test your understanding 6

The following data relate to Lola Ltd for Period 9.

	Budget	Actual
Overheads	$148,750	$146,200
Machine hours	8,500	7,928

Overheads were under-absorbed by $ ______

7.3 Working backwards

Sometimes you may be given information relating to the actual under- or over-absorption in a period and be expected to calculate the budgeted overheads or the actual number of hours worked.

- As long as you remember the basic formula involved in calculating under/over-absorption, you shouldn't have any problems.
- The main thing to remember is that if actual overheads are greater than absorbed overheads then we have under-absorption and any under-absorbed overheads need to be deducted from actual overheads incurred in order to calculate the actual overheads absorbed.
- Similarly, if over-absorption occurs, the over-absorbed overhead needs to be added to actual overhead in order to calculate the actual overheads absorbed.

Illustration 8 – Under- and over-absorption of overheads

A business absorbs its fixed production overhead on the basis of direct labour hours. The budgeted direct labour hours for week 24 were 4,200. During that week 4,050 direct labour hours were worked and the production overhead incurred was $16,700. The overhead was under-absorbed by $1,310.

The budgeted fixed overhead for the week (to the nearest $10) was $ [ ]

Solution

The budgeted fixed overhead for the week (to the nearest $10) was $ 15,960

Working

Actual overhead	$16,700
Under-absorbed	$(1,310)
Overhead absorbed	$15,390

$$OAR = \frac{15,390}{4,050} = \$3.80 \text{ per hour}$$

Budgeted fixed overhead = 4,200 x $3.80 = $15,960

Test your understanding 7

A business absorbs its fixed overheads on the basis of machine hours worked. The following figures are available for the month of June:

Budgeted fixed overhead	$45,000
Budgeted machine hours	30,000
Actual fixed overhead	$49,000

If there was an over-absorption of overhead of $3,500 how many machine hours were worked in the month?

Expandable text

If you want to consolidate the material covered so far in this chapter, have a go at the following additional Test your understanding.

Additional Test your understanding

ABC Limited is preparing its departmental budgets and product cost estimates for the year ending 31 December 20X5. The company has three manufacturing departments – Machining, Assembly, and Finishing – together with a production maintenance department. The following costs and related data have been estimated for the year to 31 December 20X5:

	Machining $000	Assembly $000	Finishing $000	Maintenance $000	Total $000
Costs:					
Direct wages	60	32	72	0	164
Indirect wages	10	6	8	30	54
Direct materials	80	10	4	0	94
Indirect materials	15	4	8	20	47
Power					102
Light and heat					10
Depreciation					7
Rent and rates					25
Personnel					63
Other data:					
Direct labour hours	12,000	8,000	16,000	6,000	42,000
Machine hours	40,000	5,000	6,000	0	51,000
Employees	6	4	8	3	21
Floor area (m2)	1,000	400	300	300	2,000
Net book value of fixed assets ($)	20,000	8,000	3,000	4,000	35,000

The maintenance department is expected to spend 60% of its time working for the Machining department, with the remainder of its time being shared equally between Assembly and Finishing.

(a) Calculate the total overhead in the:
   (i) Machining department
   (ii) Assembly department
   (iii) Finishing department

(b) Calculate an appropriate OAR in the:
   (i) Machining department
   (ii) Assembly department
   (iii) Finishing department

(c) Assuming that all the actual fixed overhead costs incurred amounted to $128,000, and the actual direct labour and machine hours were 10,500 and 39,000 respectively, calculate the amount of overheads over/under-absorbed in the Machining department.

Solution

Workings

(a)

Item	Basis	Machining $000	Assembly $000	Finishing $000	Maintenance $000	Total $000
Indirect wages	Allocated	10	6	8	30	54
Indirect materials	Allocated	15	4	8	20	47
Power	Machine hours	80	10	12	-	102
Light and heat	Floor area	5	2	1.50	1.50	10
Depreciation	NBV of assets	4	1.60	0.60	0.80	7
Rent and rates	Floor area	12.50	5	3.75	3.75	25
Personnel	Employees	18	12	24	9	63
		144.50	40.60	57.85	65.05	308
Apportion maintenance (6:2:2)		39.03	13.01	13.01	(65.05)	-
		(i) 183.53	(ii) 53.61	(iii) 70.86	Nil	308

(b) Comparing the labour and machine hours for each department shows that the Machining department is machine intensive and the other departments are labour intensive.

Absorption rates

(i) Machine department – rate per machine hour

$$\frac{\text{Overhead cost}}{\text{Machine hours}} = \frac{\$183{,}530}{40{,}000} = \$4.58825 \text{ per machine hour}$$

(ii) Assembly department – rate per labour hour

$$\frac{\text{Overhead cost}}{\text{Labour hours}} = \frac{\$53{,}600}{8{,}000} = \$6.70125 \text{ per labour hour}$$

(iii) Finishing department – rate per labour hour

$$\frac{\text{Overhead cost}}{\text{Labour hours}} = \frac{\$70{,}860}{16{,}000} = \$4.42875 \text{ per labour hour}$$

(c) Overhead absorbed = 39,000 x $4.58825 = $178,942

Overhead incurred = $128,000

Over-absorption = $50,942

8 Relating non-production overheads to cost units

8.1 Non-production overheads

We have already seen how non-production overheads can be included in the total cost of a product.

- Non-production overheads include administration, distribution and selling overheads.
- Some companies may wish to relate non-production overheads to cost units in the same way that production overheads are allocated and apportioned to cost units.
- Relating non-production overheads to cost units is important in the calculation of a 'fair' profit for a product.
- The cost card below shows how the total cost of a unit of product is built up from direct and indirect costs.

COST CARD – statement of the total cost of one unit of a product

	$
Direct materials	X
Direct labour	X
Direct expenses	X
PRIME COST	XX
Variable production overheads	X
MARGINAL PRODUCTION COST	XX
Fixed production overheads	X

TOTAL PRODUCTION COST	XX
Non-production overheads:	
Administration	X
Selling	X
Distribution	X
TOTAL COST	XX
Profit	X
Sales price	XXX

8.2 Relating non-production overheads to cost units

There are two main methods of relating non-production overheads to cost units:

- **Method 1:** Find a basis of apportioning the non-production overheads to cost units that closely corresponds to the non-manufacturing overhead, for example, direct labour hours or direct machine hours.
- **Method 2:** Allocate non-production overheads on the basis of the abililty that the product has to carry the cost, for example, as a proportion of production cost. This is the most commonly used method.

e.g

Illustration 9 – Relating non-production overheads to cost units

A company manufactures Product X which has a production cost of $25 per unit. The company has budgeted production costs of $400,000 for the manufacture of Product X and budgeted non-production overheads of $80,000 associated with the production of Product X.

Required:

Calculate the total cost of Product X if non-production overheads are related to cost units on the basis of a proportion of production costs of Product X.

Solution

$$\text{Non-production overhead per unit} = \frac{\text{Budgeted non-production cost}}{\text{Budgeted production cost}} = \frac{\$80,000}{\$400,000}$$

= 20% of production cost

Therefore, total cost of Product X = Production cost + non-production overhead

= \$(25 + (20% x \$25)) = \$25 + \$5 = \$30

Test your understanding 8

A company makes two products for which the following information for a period is relevant:

Budgeted production and sales – Product X	10,000 units
Budgeted production and sales – Product Y	10,000 units
Selling overheads	$100,000
Distribution overheads	$80,000
Budgeted sales revenue – Product X	$450,000
Budgeted sales revenue – Product Y	$550,000
Budgeted cost of production – Product X	$300,000
Budgeted cost of production – Product Y	$100,000

Selling overheads are absorbed on the basis of sales value and distribution overheads are absorbed as a percentage of production costs.

Calculate the non-production overheads to be absorbed by Product X.

There is no hard and fast rule as to how to relate non-production overheads to cost units. It is usually a matter of using the information given in the question and your common sense. For example, if you are given information regarding sales value or sales revenue, then this may be a good basis on which to apportion selling overheads.

Chapter summary

Recap of direct and indirect expenses

- **Direct expenses are part of the prime cost of a product**
- **Indirect expenses are known as overheads**

Journal and ledger entries for manufacturing overheads

ACCOUNTING FOR OVERHEADS

Relating non-production overheads to cost units

Allocation and apportionment

- Allocation charges overheads directly to specific departments
- If overheads relate to more than one specific department they must be apportioned (shared) between departments
- Apportioned fixed production overheads include: rent, rates, heating and electricity costs

Reappointionment of service cost centre costs to production cost centres

Reapportionment involves sharing out the fixed production overheads of service cost centres between production cost centres

Basic method – one service department does work for another, but not vice versa

PRODUCTION OVERHEAD ABSORPTION

Reciprocal method – both service departments do work for each other

Appropriate bases for absorption

- Machine-hour rate
- Labour-hour rate
- Percentage of prime cost
- Percentage of direct wages

Under- and over-absorption of overheads

If either or both of the estimates for budgeted overheads or budgeted level of activity are different from actual results then this will lead to under- or over-absorption (recovery) of overheads

Test your understanding answers

Test your understanding 1

The overhead cost allocated to each unit of Product P is $ 3.90

The cost per unit of Product P is now $ 19.90

Workings

The overhead cost per unit is now $\frac{\$7,800}{2,000}$ = $3.90 per unit.

The cost per unit of Product P is now:

	$
Prime cost	16.00
Overheads	3.90
Total	**19.90**

Test your understanding 2

Overhead	Basis of apportionment	Assembly $	Finishing $	Maintenance $	Canteen $	Total $
Electricity	kW Hours (W1)	2,750	4,500	1,975	775	10,000
Machine depreciation	Machine value (W2)	2,250	1,750	550	450	5,000
Indirect labour	Allocated (W3)	1,600	2,220	11,200	1,500	16,520

Workings

(W1)

Electricity is apportioned to all departments on the basis of kW hours.

Total electricity costs = $10,000

Total kW hours consumed = (2,750 + 4,500 + 1,975 + 775)
= 10,000 kW hours

Apportioned to Finishing department = 4,500/10,000 x $10,000 = $4,500

(W2)

Machine depreciation is apportioned to all departments on the basis of machine value.

Total machine depreciation costs = $5,000

Total machine value = $(45,000 + 35,000 + 11,000 + 9,000)
= $100,000

Apportioned to Maintenance department = 11,000/100,000 x $5,000 = $550

(W3)

Indirect labour costs are allocated directly to all departments based on the indirect labour budget for each department.

Test your understanding 3

Overhead	Alpha $	Beta $	Gamma $	M $	P $
Total overheads	3,000	4,000	2,000	2,500	2,700
Reapportion M	500 (20%)	750 (30%)	625 (25%)	(2,500)	625 (25%)
					3,325
Reapportion P	831 (25%)	831 (25%)	998 (30%)	665 (20%)	(3,325)
Reapportion M	133 (20%)	200 (30%)	166 (25%)	(665)	166 (25%)
Reapportion P	41 (25%)	42 (25%)	50 (30%)	33 (20%)	(166)
Reapportion M	7 (20%)	10 (30%)	8 (25%)	(33)	8 (25%)
Reapportion P	3 (25%)	2 (25%)	3 (30%)		(8)
Total	4,515	5,835	3,850		

Test your understanding 4

(a) Using a single blanket OAR based on labour hours, the cost of the batch of Pixie Gnomes is $ 14,806

It has been suggested that appropriate departmental OARs may be more realistic.

(b) The OAR in:

(i) the moulding department is $ 15

(ii) the painting department is $ 10

(c) Using departmental absorption rates, the cost of the batch of Pixie Gnomes is $ 15,156

Workings

$$\text{Blanket OAR} = \frac{\$280,000}{14,000} = \$20 \text{ per labour hour}$$

(a) Cost of batch of Pixie Gnomes

	$
Direct materials	890
Direct labour	3,216
Overheads (535 hours @ $20 per hour)	10,700
TOTAL COST	14,806

(b)

	(i) Moulding	(ii) Painting
Budgeted overheads	$180,000	$100,000
Budgeted hours	12,000 machine hours	10,000 labour hours
OAR	$15 per machine hour	$10 per labour hour

(c) Cost of a batch of Pixie Gnomes using separate departmental OARs

	$
Direct materials	890
Direct labour	3,216
Moulding overheads (460 x $15)	6,900
Painting overheads (415 x $10)	4,150
TOTAL COST	15,156

Test your understanding 5

Transaction	Debit which account?	Credit which account?
Indirect materials issued from stores	Production overheads account	Material inventory account
Indirect wages analysed in the labour account	Production overheads account	Labour account
Indirect expenses purchased (cash)	Production overheads account	Bank
Production overheads absorbed into the cost of production	WIP account	Production overheads account
Direct materials issued from stores	WIP account	Material inventory account

Test your understanding 6

Overheads were under-absorbed by $ 7,460

OAR = $\frac{\$148,750}{8,500}$ = $17.50 per machine hour

Overhead absorbed = 7,928 x $17.50	=	$138,740
Actual overhead	=	$146,200
Under-absorbed overhead	=	$7,460

Test your understanding 7

35,000 machine hours were worked in the month.

Workings

$$\text{OAR} = \frac{\$45{,}000}{30{,}000} = \$1.50 \text{ per hour}$$

Actual overhead	$49,000
Over-absorbed overhead	$3,500
Absorbed overhead	$52,500

$$\text{Machine hours worked} = \frac{\text{Overheads absorbed}}{\text{Overhead absorption rate}}$$

$$= \frac{\$52{,}000}{\$1.50}$$

$$= 35{,}000 \text{ hours}$$

Test your understanding 8

$$\text{Selling overheads – Product X} = \frac{\text{Budgeted sales revenue Product X}}{\text{Total budgeted sales revenue}} = \frac{\$450{,}000}{\$1{,}000{,}000}$$

= 45% of selling overheads

= 45% of $100,000 = $45,000

Budgeted production = 10,000 units, therefore budgeted selling overhead per unit = $45,000/10,000 = $4.50 per unit.

Distribution overheads are absorbed as a percentage of production costs.

Total production costs = $(300,000 + 100,000) = $400,000

$$\text{Distribution overheads related to Product X} = \frac{\$300{,}000}{\$400{,}000} \times \$80{,}000 = \$60{,}000$$

Budgeted production = 10,000 units, therefore budgeted selling overhead per unit = $60,000/10,000 = $6.00 per unit.

chapter

8

Marginal and absorption costing

Chapter learning objectives

Upon completion of this chapter you will be able to:

- explain the importance of, and apply the concept of, contribution using data supplied
- calculate and discuss the effect of absorption and marginal costing on inventory valuation and profit determination using data supplied
- describe the advantages and disadvantages of absorption and marginal costing for a manufacturing business
- understand and use the concept of a contribution to sales ratio, carrying out calculations using supplied data
- calculate and interpret a breakeven point from information supplied
- calculate and interpret a margin of safety from information supplied
- understand and use the concepts of target profit or revenue calculating, from supplied data, the volumes of sales needed to reach the targets
- identify, on supplied charts the elements in: traditional breakeven charts; contribution breakeven charts; profit/volume (P/V) charts
- apply cost/volume/profit (CVP) analysis to single product situations using supplied data.

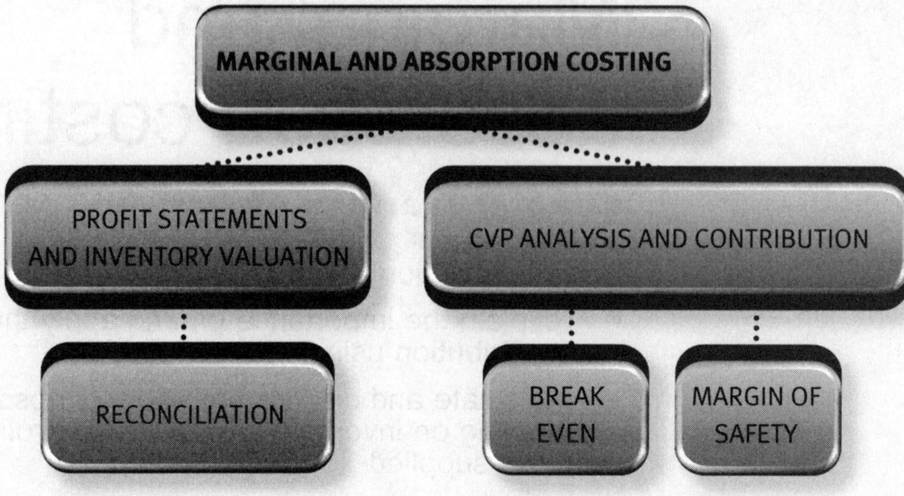

1 The concept of contribution

1.1 Marginal costing

Marginal costing is an accounting system in which variable costs are charged to cost units and fixed costs for the period are written off in full to the income statement.

- Marginal costing is an alternative costing system to absorption costing.
- The marginal cost of a unit of product is the total of the variable costs of the product (i.e. direct materials, direct labour and variable overheads).
- The marginal cost of a product is therefore the additional cost of producing an extra unit of that product.

1.2 The contribution concept

The contribution concept lies at the heart of marginal costing. Contribution can be calculated as follows.

1.3 Contribution and profit

Contribution = Sales price – Variable costs

e.g

Illustration 1 – The concept of contribution

The following information relates to a company that makes a single product, a specialist lamp, which is used in the diamond-cutting business.

The cost card for the lamp is as follows.

	$	$
Sales price		600
Direct materials	200	
Direct labour	150	
Direct expenses	Nil	
Prime cost	350	
Variable production overheads	50	
Fixed production overheads	100	
Total cost	500	

Fixed costs have been estimated to be $120,000 based on a production level of 1,200 lamps.

Let us look at the costs and revenues involved when different volumes of lamps are sold.

		Sales of 1,200 lamps		**Sales of 1,500 lamps**
		$		$
Sales revenue		720,000		900,000
Direct materials	240,000		300,000	
Direct labour	180,000		225,000	
Direct expenses	Nil		Nil	
Prime cost	420,000		525,000	
Variable production overheads	60,000		75,000	
Marginal cost of production		**480,000**		**600,000**
CONTRIBUTION		**240,000**		**300,000**
Fixed production overheads		120,000		120,000
Total profit		120,000		180,000
Contribution per unit		**200**		**200**
Profit per unit		100		120

- We can see that the profit per lamp has increased from **$100** when 1,200 lamps are sold to **$120** when 1,500 lamps are sold.
- This is because all of the variable costs (direct materials, direct labour, direct expenses and variable overheads) have increased but the fixed costs have remained constant at $120,000.

Based on what we have seen above, the idea of profit is not a particularly useful one as it depends on how many units are sold. For this reason, the contribution concept is frequently employed by management accountants.

- Contribution gives an idea of how much 'money' there is available to 'contribute' towards paying for the overheads of the organisation.
- At varying levels of output and sales, contribution per unit is constant.
- At varying levels of output and sales, profit per unit varies.
- **Total contribution = Contribution per unit x Sales volume.**
- **Profit = Total contribution – Fixed overheads.**

1.4 Marginal costing and the decision-making process

Marginal costing (and therefore the contribution concept) is widely used in the decision-making process.

- The study of marginal costing and decision making is very important in management accounting. It involves the following topics which are relevant to your study of this paper:
  – CVP analysis
  – relevant costing
  – limiting factor analysis.
- Whilst studying these topics you must keep 'the contribution concept' at the front of your mind.

Expandable text

A diagram showing the decision-making process is shown below.

Decision-making process

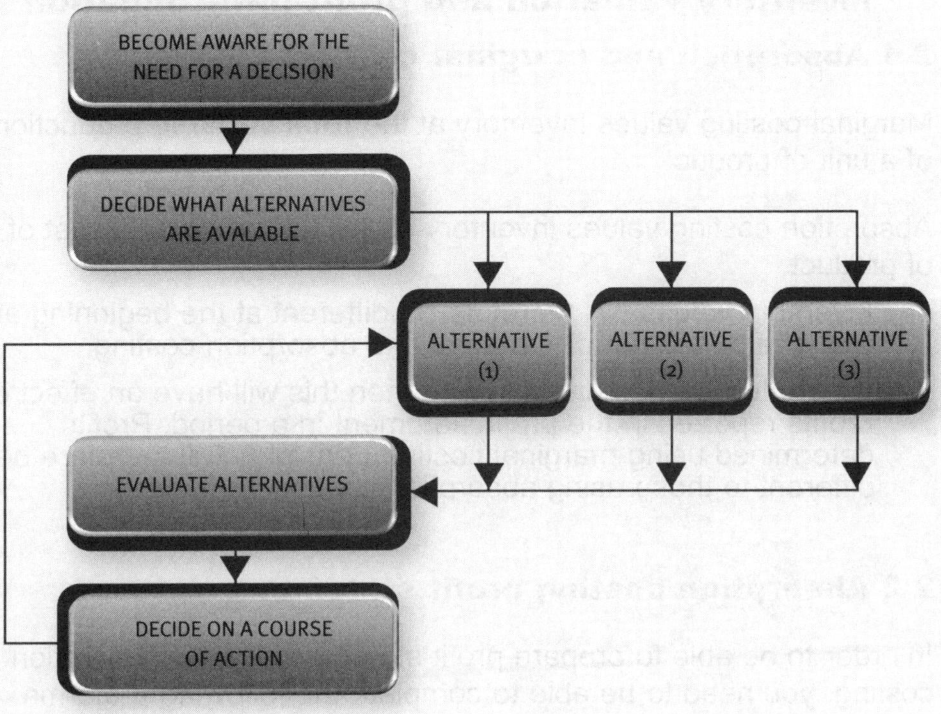

Test your understanding 1

Buhner Ltd makes only one product, the cost card of which is:

	$
Direct materials	3
Direct labour	6
Variable production overhead	2
Fixed production overhead	4
Variable selling cost	5

The selling price of one unit is $21.

Budgeted fixed overheads are based on budgeted production of 5,000 units. Opening inventory was 1,000 units and closing inventory was 4,000 units.

Sales during the period were 3,000 units and actual fixed production overheads incurred were $25,000.

(a) Calculate the total contribution earned during the period.

(b) Calculate the total profit or loss for the period.

2 The effect of absorption and marginal costing on inventory valuation and profit determination

2.1 Absorption and marginal costing

Marginal costing values inventory at the **total variable** production cost of a unit of product.

Absorption costing values inventory at the **full** production cost of a unit of product.

- Inventory values will therefore be different at the beginning and end of a period under marginal and absorption costing.
- If inventory values are different, then this will have an effect on profits reported in the profit statement in a period. Profits determined using marginal costing principles will therefore be different to those using absorption costing principles.

2.2 Absorption costing profit statement

In order to be able to prepare profit statements under absorption costing, you need to be able to complete the following proforma.

Absorption costing profit statement

	$	$
Sales		X
Less Cost of sales:		
(valued at full production cost)		
Opening inventory	X	
Variable cost of production	X	
Fixed overhead absorbed	X	
	X	
less closing inventory	(X)	
		(X)
		X
(under)/over-absorption		(X) / X
Gross profit		X
Less Non-production costs		(X)
Profit/loss		X

- **Valuation of inventory** – opening and closing inventory are valued at full production cost under absorption costing.
- Under/over-absorbed overhead – an adjustment for under or over absorption of overheads is necessary in absorption costing profit statements.

2.3 Marginal costing profit statement

In order to be able to prepare profit statements under marginal costing, you need to be able to complete the following proforma.

Marginal costing profit statement

	$	$
Sales		X
Less Cost of sales: (marginal production costs only)		
Opening inventory	X	
Variable cost of production	X	
less Closing inventory	(X)	
		(X)
		X
Less Other variable costs		(X)
Contribution		X
Less fixed costs (actually incurred)		(X)
Profit/loss		X

- Valuation of inventory – opening and closing inventory are valued at full marginal cost under marginal costing.
- Under/over-absorbed overhead – no adjustment for under or over absorption of overheads is needed in marginal costing profit statements. The fixed costs actually incurred are deducted from contribution earned in order to determine the profit for the period.

e.g

Illustration 2 – Effects of absorption and marginal costing

A company commenced business on 1 March making one product only, the cost card of which is as follows.

	$
Direct labour	5
Direct material	8
Variable production overhead	2
Fixed production overhead	5
Standard production cost	$20

Variable cost of production

The fixed production overhead figure has been calculated on the basis of a budgeted normal output of 36,000 units per annum. The fixed production overhead incurred in March was $15,000 each month.

Selling, distribution and administration expenses are:

Fixed	$10,000 per month
Variable	15% of the sales value

The selling price per unit is $35 and the number of units produced and sold were:

	March (units)
Production	2,000
Sales	1,500

Prepare the absorption costing and marginal costing profit statements for March by filling in the proformas below.

Solution

Absorption costing profit statement – March

	$	$
Sales		
Less Cost of sales: (valued at full production cost)		
Opening inventory		
Variable cost of production		
Fixed overhead absorbed		
Closing inventory		
(under)/over-absorption		
Gross profit		
Less non-production costs		
Profit/loss		

Value of closing inventory at the end of March (using absorption costing) = $

Marginal costing profit statement – March

	$	$
Sales		
Less Cost of sales: (marginal production costs only)		
Opening inventory		
Variable cost of production		
less Closing inventory		
less Other variable costs		
Contribution		
Less Fixed costs (actually incurred)		
Profit/loss		

Value of closing inventory at the end of March (using marginal costing) = $

Solution

Absorption costing profit statement – March

	$	$
Sales		52,500
Less Cost of sales: (valued at full production cost)		
Opening inventory	-	
Variable cost of production (2,000 x $15)	30,000	
Fixed overhead absorbed (2,000 x $5)	10,000	
less Closing inventory (500 x $20)	(10,000)	
		(30,000)
		22,500
(under)/over-absorption (W1)		(5,000)
Gross profit		17,500
Less Non-Production Costs (W2)		(17,875)
Profit/loss		(375)

Value of closing inventory at the end of March (using absorption costing) = $ 10,000

Workings

(W1)

March	$
Overheads absorbed (2,000 x $5)	10,000
Overheads incurred	15,000
Under-absorption on overheads	5,000

(W2)

Non-production costs

Fixed = $10,000
Variable = 15% x $52,500 = $7,875
Total = $(10,000 + 7,875) = $17,875

Marginal costing profit statement – March

		$	$
Sales			52,500
Less Cost of sales: (marginal production costs only)			
	Opening inventory	–	
	Variable cost of production (2,000 x $15)	30,000	
	less Closing inventory (500 x $15)	(7,500)	
			(22,500)
			30,000
Less other variable costs (15% x $52,500)			(7,875)
Contribution			22,125
Less Fixed costs (actually incurred) $(15,000 + 10,000)			(25,000)
Profit /(loss)			**(2,875)**

Value of closing inventory at the end of March (using marginal costing) = $ 7,500

Test your understanding 2

Duo Ltd makes and sells two products, Alpha and Beta. The following information is available for period 3:

	Alpha	Beta
Production (units)	2,500	1,750
Sales (units)	2,300	1,600
Opening stock (units)	0	0

Financial data:

	Alpha $	Beta $
Unit selling price	90	75
Unit cost:		
direct materials	15	12
direct labour	18	12
variable production overheads	12	8
fixed production overheads	30	20
variable selling overheads	1	1

Fixed production overheads for the period were $105,000 and fixed administration overheads were $27,000.

Required:

(a) Prepare a profit statement for period 3 based on marginal costing principles.

(b) Prepare a profit statement for period 3 based on absorption costing principles.

2.4 Reconciling profits reported under the different methods

We have now seen how profits differ under absorption and marginal costing when inventory increases or decreases in a period.

- If inventory levels increase, absorption costing gives the higher profit.
- If inventory levels decrease, marginal costing gives the higher profit.
- If inventory levels are constant, both methods give the same profit.

Expandable text

- If inventory increases during a period then absorption costing will show the higher profit figure. This is because fixed overheads held in closing inventory are carried forward (thereby reducing cost of sales) to the next accounting period instead of being written off in the current accounting period (as a period cost, as in marginal costing).
- If inventory decreases during a period, then absorption costing profits will be lower than marginal costing profits. This is because fixed overhead brought forward in opening inventory is released, thereby increasing cost of sales and reducing profits.
- If inventory levels remain the same (i.e. if production levels are the same as sales levels) during a period (i.e. there is no increase or decrease) then absorption costing profits will be the same as marginal costing profits.

- We can illustrate how the different profit figures can be reconciled by revisiting **Illustration 2** above.

Illustration 3 – Effects of absorption and marginal costing

A company commenced business on 1 March making one product only, the cost card of which is as follows.

	$
Direct labour	5
Direct material	8
Variable production overhead	2
Fixed production overhead	5
Full production cost	$20

- Marginal cost of production = $(5 + 8 + 2) = $15
- Full cost of production = $20 (as above)
- Difference in cost of production = $5 which is the fixed production overhead element of the full production cost.

- This means that each unit of opening and closing inventory will be valued at $5 more under absorption costing.

The number of units produced and sold was as follows.

	March (units)
Production	2,000
Sales	1,500

- Closing inventory at the end of March is the difference between the number of units produced and the number of units sold, i.e. 500 units (2,000 – 1,500).
- Loss for March under absorption costing = $375 (as calculated in **Illustration 2**).
- Loss for March under marginal costing = $2,875 (as calculated in **Illustration 2**).
- Difference in loss (profits) = $2,875 – $375 = $2,500.
- This difference can be analysed as being due to the fixed overhead held in inventory, i.e. 500 units of inventory 'holding' $5 fixed overhead per unit.
- 500 x $5 = $2,500 which is the difference between the profit in the profit statements under the different costing methods for March.

Test your understanding 3

(a) In a period where opening inventory was 5,000 units and closing inventory was 3,000 units, a company had a profit of $92,000 using absorption costing. If the fixed overhead absorption rate was $9 per unit, calculate the profit using marginal costing.

(b) When opening inventory was 8,500 litres and closing inventory was 6,750 litres, a company had a profit of $62,100 using marginal costing. The fixed overhead absorption rate was $3 per litre. Calculate the profit using absorption costing.

3 The advantages and disadvantages of absorption and marginal costing

3.1 Absorption costing versus marginal costing

The main differences between absorption costing and marginal costing are as follows.

- Inventory valuations (and hence profit).
- Profit statement layout.

Expandable text

- Profit statement layout – with absorption costing fixed production overheads are included in cost of sales and a gross profit is calculated. With marginal costing, only variable costs are included in cost of sales and a contribution is calculated (fixed overheads are treated as a period cost and are deducted in full in the period to which they relate).
- Absorption costing profit statements include an adjustment for under/over absorption of overheads. This is not necessary in marginal costing profit statements because the fixed production overheads are deducted in full in the period to which they relate.
- Absorption and marginal costing give rise to different profit figures during periods in which inventory levels increase or decrease. Remember that if inventory levels remain the same (or if production levels are the same as sales levels) then marginal costing and absorption costing profits will be the same.

3.2 Advantages and disadvantages of absorption and marginal costing

Advantages of marginal costing	Advantages of absorption costing
• Contribution per unit is constant unlike profit per unit which varies with changes in sales volumes. • There is no under or over absorption of overheads (and hence no adjustment is required in the income statement). • Fixed costs are a period cost and are charged in full to the period under consideration. • Marginal costing is useful in the decision-making process. • It is simple to operate.	• Absorption costing includes an element of fixed overheads in inventory values (in accordance with SSAP 9). • Analysing under/over absorption of overheads is a useful exercise in controlling costs of an organisation. • In small organisations, absorbing overheads into the costs of products is the best way of estimating job costs and profits on jobs.

Expandable text

Disadvantages of Marginal & Absorption costing

- (1) The main disadvantages of marginal costing are that closing inventory is not valued in accordance with SSAP 9 principles and that fixed production overheads are not 'shared' out between units of production, but written off in full instead.
- (1) The main disadvantages of absorption costing are that it is more complex to operate than marginal costing and it does not provide any useful information for decision making (like marginal costing does).

4 Contribution to sales ratios and breakeven points

4.1 CVP analysis

CVP analysis makes use of the contribution concept in order to assess the following measures for a single product:

- contribution to sales (C/S) ratio
- breakeven point
- margin of safety
- target profit.

4.2 C/S ratio

The C/S ratio of a product is the proportion of the selling price that contributes to fixed overheads and profits. It is comparable to the gross profit margin. The formula for calculating the C/S ratio of a product is as follows:

$$\textbf{C/S ratio} = \frac{\textbf{Contribution per unit}}{\textbf{Selling price per unit}} \textbf{ or } \frac{\textbf{Total contribution}}{\textbf{Total sales revenue}}$$

The C/S ratio is sometimes referred to as the P/V ratio.

Illustration 4 – Contribution to sales ratios and breakeven points

The following information relates to Product J.

Selling price per unit	$20
Variable cost per unit	$12
Fixed costs	$100,000

Calculate the contribution to sales ratio.

Solution

Contribution per unit = $(20 -12) = $8

$$\text{C/S ratio} = \frac{\text{Contribution per unit}}{\text{Selling price per unit}} = \frac{\$8}{\$20} = 0.4 \text{ or } 40\%$$

4.3 Breakeven point

The breakeven point is the point at which neither a profit nor a loss is made.

- At the breakeven point the following situations occur.

  Total sales revenue = Total costs, i.e. Profit = 0

  or

  Total contribution = Fixed costs, i.e. Profit = 0

- The following formula is used to calculate the breakeven point in terms of numbers of units sold.

$$\textbf{Breakeven point (in terms of numbers of units sold)} = \frac{\textbf{Fixed costs}}{\textbf{Contribution per unit}}$$

- It is also possible to calculate the breakeven point in terms of sales revenue using the C/S ratio. The equation is as follows:

$$\textbf{Breakeven point (in terms of sales revenue)} = \frac{\textbf{Fixed costs}}{\textbf{C/S ratio}}$$

e.g

Illustration 5 – Contribution to sales ratios and breakeven points

The following information relates to Product K.

Selling price per unit	$20
Variable cost per unit	$12
Fixed costs	$100,000

Required:

(a) Calculate the breakeven point in terms of numbers of units sold.
(b) Calculate the breakeven point in terms of sales revenue.

Solution

(a) Breakeven point in terms of numbers of units sold $= \frac{\text{Fixed costs}}{\text{Contribution per unit}}$

$$= \frac{\$100{,}000}{\$(20 - 12)} = 12{,}500 \text{ units}$$

(b) C/S ratio = 8/20 = 0.4

Breakeven point (in terms of sales revenue) $= \frac{\text{Fixed costs}}{\text{Contribution per unit}}$

$$= \frac{\$100{,}000}{0.4} = \$250{,}000$$

(Proof: breakeven point in terms of units = 12,500 units @ $20 each = $250,000)

5 Margin of safety and target profits

5.1 Margin of safety

The margin of safety is the amount by which anticipated sales (in units) can fall below budget before a business makes a loss. It can be calculated in terms of numbers of units or as a percentage of budgeted sales.

The following formulae are used to calculate the margin of safety:

Margin of safety (in terms of units) = Budgeted sales – Breakeven point sales

$$\textbf{Margin of safety (as a \% of budgeted sales)} = \frac{\textbf{Budgeted sales – Breakeven sales}}{\textbf{Budgeted sales}} \times 100\%$$

e.g

Illustration 6 – Margin of safety and target profits

Arrow Ltd manufactures Product L to which the following information relates.

Selling price per unit	\$20
Variable cost per unit	\$12
Fixed costs	\$100,000

Budgeted sales for the period are 16,000 units.

Required:

(a) Calculate the margin of safety in terms of units.
(b) Calculate the margin of safety as a % of budgeted sales.

Solution

(a) Breakeven point in terms of numbers of units sold $= \frac{\text{Fixed costs}}{\text{Contribution per unit}}$

$= \frac{\$100,000}{\$(20 - 12)} = 12,500$ units

Margin of safety (in terms of units) = Budgeted sales – Breakeven point sales

= 16,000 – 12,500 = 3,500 units

(b) Margin of safety (as a % of budgeted sales) $= \frac{\text{Budgeted sales – Breakeven sales}}{\text{Budgeted sales}} \times 100\%$

$= \frac{16,000 - 12,500}{16,000} \times 100\%$

= 21.88%

5.2 Target profit

Sometimes an organisation might wish to know how many units of a product it needs to sell in order to earn a certain level of profit (or target profit). This can be calculated by using the following formula.

$$\textbf{Sales volume to achieve a target profit} = \frac{\textbf{Fixed costs + Required profit}}{\textbf{Contribution per unit}} = \frac{\textbf{Target contribution}}{\textbf{Contribution per unit}}$$

e.g

Illustration 7 – Margin of safety and target profits

Arrow Ltd manufactures Product L and wishes to achieve a profit of $20,000. The following information relates to Product L.

Selling price per unit	$20
Variable cost per unit	$12
Fixed costs	$100,000

Required:

Calculate the sales volume required to achieve a profit of $20,000.

Solution

Contribution per unit = $(20 – 12) = $8

Sales volume to achieve a target profit = $\frac{\text{Fixed costs + Required profit}}{\text{Contribution per unit}}$

= $\frac{\$(100{,}000 + 20{,}000)}{\$8}$

= 15,000 units

Test your understanding 4

The following information relates to Product Alpha.

Selling price per unit	$100
Variable cost per unit	$56
Fixed costs	$220,000

Budgeted sales are 7,500 units.

Required:

(a) Calculate the C/S ratio.
(b) Calculate the breakeven point in terms of units sold.
(c) Calculate the breakeven point in terms of sales revenue.
(d) Calculate the unit sales required to achieve a target profit of $550,000.
(e) Calculate the margin of safety (expressed as a percentage of budgeted sales).

6 Breakeven charts and P/V charts

6.1 Breakeven charts and P/V charts

The measures that we have calculated above (breakeven point, margin of safety and so on) can also be determined by drawing and interpreting the following graphs:

- traditional breakeven charts
- contribution breakeven charts
- P/V charts.

It is important that you are able to identify the points that represent the margin of safety, breakeven point, total contribution, fixed costs, variable costs, total costs and budgeted sales on the graphs that we are going to study in this chapter.

6.2 Traditional breakeven charts

The traditional breakeven chart plots total costs and total revenues at different levels of output.

e.g

Illustration 8 – Breakeven charts and P/V charts

Traditional breakeven chart

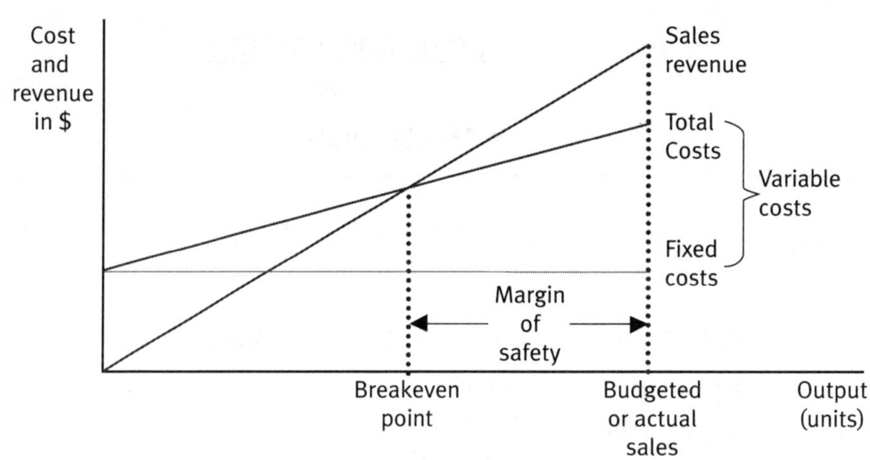

- The traditional breakeven chart is constructed as follows:
  - plotting the fixed costs line as a straight line parallel to the horizontal axis
  - plotting the sales revenue line from the origin
  - the total costs line is represented by fixed costs plus variable costs.
- Note the points at which the breakeven point and the margin of safety occur.

- Breakeven point is the point where the sales revenue is equal to the total costs.
- Margin of safety is the area between the breakeven point and the budgeted or actual sales.

6.3 Contribution breakeven charts

A variation on the traditional breakeven chart is the contribution breakeven chart. The main differences between the two charts are as follows.

- The traditional breakeven chart shows the fixed cost line whereas the contribution chart shows the variable cost line.
- Contribution can be read more easily from the contribution breakeven chart than the traditional breakeven chart.

e.g

Illustration 9 – Breakeven charts and P/V charts

Contribution breakeven chart

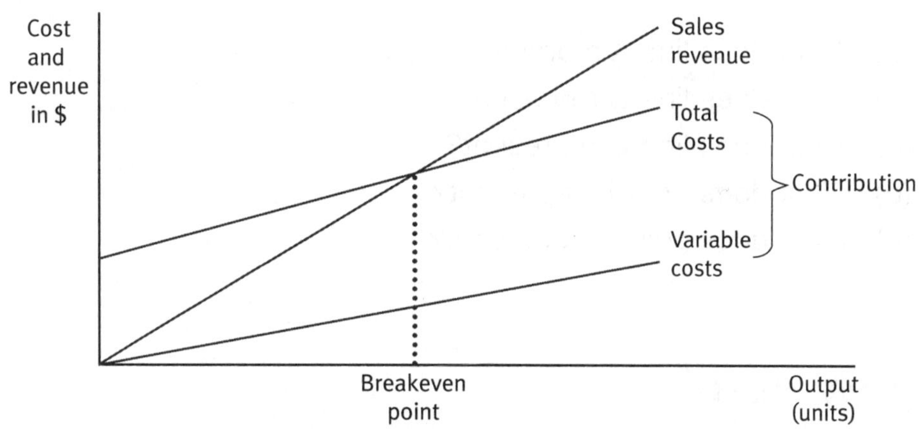

Test your understanding 5

Study the traditional breakeven chart shown below.

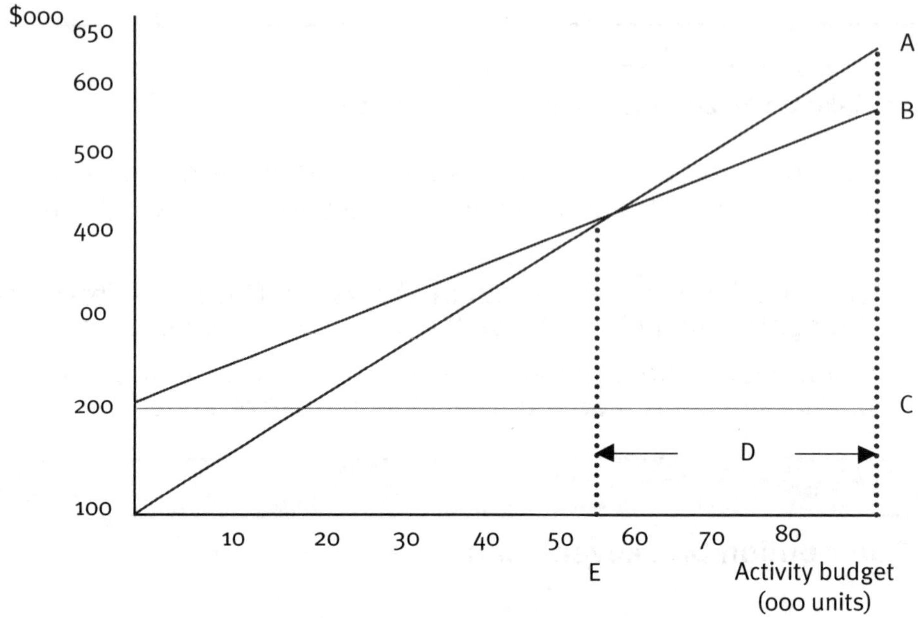

(a) What does line A represent?

(b) What does line B represent?

(c) What does line C represent?

(d) What does area D represent?

(e) What does point E represent?

6.4 P/V charts

Breakeven charts usually show both costs and revenues over a certain level of activity. They do not highlight directly the amounts of profits or losses at the various levels of activity. However, a P/V chart clearly identifies the net profit or loss at different levels of activity.

e.g

Illustration 10 – Breakeven charts and P/V charts

P/V chart

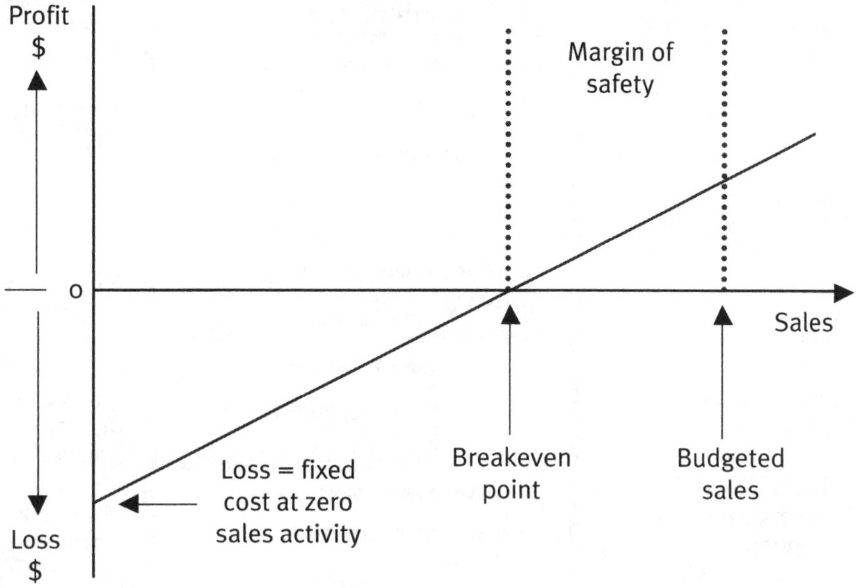

The chart above shows the amount of net profit or loss at different levels of (sales) activity. Make sure that you are able to identify the points shown on the graph above in an examination.

Test your understanding 6

Study the P/V chart shown below.

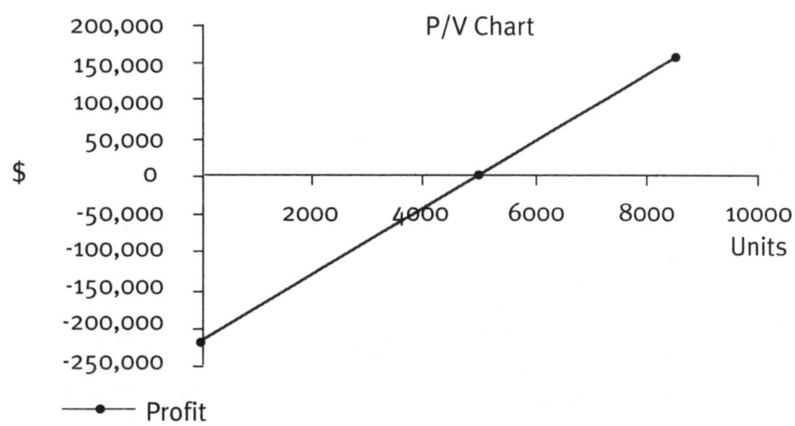

(a) Estimate the number of units required to break even.

(b) Estimate the fixed costs.

Chapter summary

MARGINAL AND ABSORPTION COSTING

The effect of absorption and marginal costing on inventory value and profit determination

Inventory up:
AC→MC profits

Inventory down:
AC←MC profits

The conception of contribution

Contribution = Sales Price – Variable costs

Widely used in decision-making process, e.g. CVP analysis

The advantages and disadvantages of absorption and marginal costing

Each costing method has a number of advantages and disadvantages

C/V/P ANALYSIS

Contribution to sales ratios and breakeven points

Breakeven point (units)

$$\frac{\text{Fixed cost}}{\text{Contribution per unit}}$$

Breakeven point (revenue)

$$\frac{\text{Fixed cost}}{\text{C/S ratio}}$$

C/S ratio

$$\frac{\text{Contribution per unit}}{\text{Selling price per unit}} \text{ or } \frac{\text{Total contribution}}{\text{Total sales revenue}}$$

Breakeven charts and P/V charts

Traditional breakeven charts

Contribution breakeven charts

P/V charts

Margin of safety and target profits

Marging of safety (in terms of units):
Budgeted sales - Breakeven point sales

MOS may also be stated as a percentage of budgeted sales.

Target profit:

$$\frac{\text{Fixed costs+Required profit}}{\text{Contribution per unit}}$$

Test your understanding answers

Test your understanding 1

(a) Total variable costs = $(3 + 6 + 2 + 5) = $16

Contribution per unit (selling price less total variable costs) = $21 – $16 = $5

Total contribution earned = 3,000 x $5 = $15,000

(b) Total profit/(loss) = Total contribution – Fixed production overheads incurred

= $(15,000 – 25,000)

= $(10,000)

Test your understanding 2

(a)

	Alpha		Beta		Total
	$000	$000	$000	$000	$000
Sales		207		120	
Opening inventory	–		–		
Variable production cost (2500 x 45; 1750 x 32)	112.5		56		
Closing inventory (200 x 45; 150 x 32)	(9)		(4.8)		
		(103.5)		(51.2)	
		103.5		68.8	
Variable selling costs		(2.3)		(1.6)	
Contribution		101.2		67.2	168.4
Fixed production costs					(105)
Fixed administration costs					(27)
Profit					36.4

(b)

	Alpha		Beta		Total
	$000	$000	$000	$000	$000
Sales		207		120	
Opening inventory	–		–		
Full production costs (2500 x 75; 1750 x 52)	187.5		91		
Closing inventory (200 x 75; 150 x 52)	(15)		(7.8)		
		(172.5)		(83.2)	
		34.5		36.8	71.3
Over-absorbed overhead (working)					5

Gross profit	76.3
Less: non-production overheads	
variable selling overheads	(3.9)
fixed administration overheads	(27.0)
	45.4

Working

	$
Overhead absorbed = (2,500 x $30) + (1,750 x $20)	110,000
Overheads incurred =	105,000
Over-absorbed overhead	5,000

Test your understanding 3

(a)	Absorption costing profit =	$92,000
	Difference in profit = change in inventory x fixed cost per unit = 2,000 x $9 =	$18,000
	Marginal costing profit =	$110,000

Since inventory levels have fallen in the period, marginal costing shows the higher profit figure, therefore marginal costing profit will be $18,000 higher than the absorption costing profit, i.e. $110,000.

(b)	Marginal costing profit	$62,100
	Difference in profit = change in inventory x fixed cost per unit = (8,500 – 6,750) x $3	$(5,250)
	Absorption costing profit	$56,850

Inventory levels have fallen in the period and therefore marginal costing profits will be higher than absorption costing profits. Absorption costing profit is therefore $5,250 less than the marginal costing profit.

Test your understanding 4

(a) Contribution per unit = $(100 – 56) = $44

$$\text{C/S ratio} = \frac{\text{Contribution per unit}}{\text{Selling price per unit}} = \frac{\$44}{\$100} = 0.44$$

(b) Breakeven point in terms of numbers of units sold

$$= \frac{\text{Fixed costs}}{\text{Contribution per unit}}$$

$$= \frac{\$220,000}{\$44} = 5,000 \text{ units}$$

(c) Breakeven point in terms of sales revenue

$$= \frac{\text{Fixed costs}}{\text{C/S ratio}}$$

$$= \frac{\$220,000}{0.44} = \$500,000$$

(Proof: breakeven units x selling price per unit = 5,000 x $100 = $500,000)

(d) Unit sales to achieve a target profit

$$= \frac{\text{Fixed costs + Required profit}}{\text{Contribution per unit}}$$

$$= \frac{\$(220,000 + 550,000)}{\$44}$$

= 17,500 units

(e) Margin of safety (as a % of budgeted sales)

$$= \frac{\text{Budgeted sales – Break – even sales}}{\text{Budgeted sales}} \times 100\%$$

$$= \frac{7,500 - 5,000}{7,500} \times 100\%$$

= 33.33%

Test your understanding 5

(a) Line A represents total revenue earned (the total revenue line).

(b) Line B represents total costs (total costs line).

(c) Line C represents fixed costs (fixed cost line).

(d) Area D represents the margin of safety.

(e) Point E represents the breakeven point.

Test your understanding 6

(a) Reading from the graph, the number of units required to breakeven can be estimated as 5,000 units. The breakeven point on a P/V chart is the point at which the profit line cuts the x-axis, i.e. the point at which profit is zero.

(b) The fixed costs can be estimated to be $225,000, i.e. the point at which the profit line cuts the y-axis. This is the point at which costs are incurred even when there is zero sales activity.

chapter

9

Relevant costing

Chapter learning objectives

Upon completion of this chapter you will be able to:

- explain the concept, giving suitable examples, of relevant costing
- calculate, using supplied data, the relevant cost for materials, labour, overheads
- calculate, using supplied data, the relevant costs associated with non-current assets
- explain and apply, using supplied data, the concept of opportunity cost.

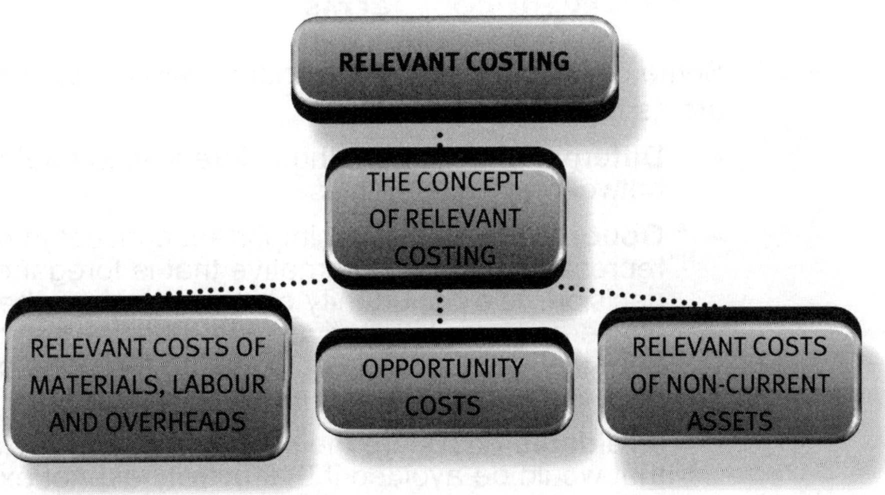

1 Relevant costing

1.1 The concept of relevant costing

As you already know, the decision-making process involves making a choice between two or more alternatives. Decisions will generally be based on taking the decision that maximises shareholder value, so all decisions will be taken using relevant costs and revenues.

- Relevant costs and revenues are those costs and revenues that change as a direct result of a decision taken.
- Relevant costs and revenues have the following features:
  - They are future costs and revenues.
  - They are cash flows.
  - They are incremental costs and revenues.

Expandable text

- Future costs and revenues – as it is not possible to change what has happened in the past, then relevant costs and revenues must be future costs and revenues.
- Cash flows – in addition, future costs and revenues must be cash flows arising as a direct consequence of the decision taken. Relevant costs do not include items which do not involve cash flows (depreciation and notional costs for example).
- Incremental costs and revenues – relevant costs are incremental costs and it is the increase in costs and revenues that occurs as a direct result of a decision taken that is relevant. Common costs can be ignored for the purposes of decision making.

1.2 Relevant cost terms

Some of the other terms associated with relevant costs and revenues are as follows:

- **Differential costs** are the differences in total costs or revenues between two alternatives.
- **Opportunity cost** is an important concept in decision making. It represents the best alternative that is foregone in taking the decision. The opportunity cost emphasises that decision making is concerned with alternatives and that the cost of taking one decision is the profit or contribution foregone by not taking the next best alternative.
- **Avoidable costs** are the specific costs associated with an activity that would be avoided if that activity did not exist.

In an examination, unless told otherwise, assume that variable costs are relevant costs.

1.3 Non-relevant costs

Costs which are not relevant to a decision are known as non-relevant costs and include: sunk costs; committed costs; non-cash flow costs; general fixed overheads; and net book values.

- **Sunk costs** are past costs or historical costs which are not directly relevant in decision making, for example, development costs or market research costs.
- **Committed costs** are future costs that cannot be avoided, whatever decision is taken.
- **Non-cash flow costs** are costs which do not involve the flow of cash, for example, depreciation and notional costs. A notional cost is a cost that will not result in an outflow of cash either now or in the future, for example, sometimes the head office of an organisation may charge a 'notional' rent to its branches. This cost will only appear in the accounts of the organisation but will not result in a 'real' cash expenditure.
- **General fixed overheads** are usually not relevant to a decision. However, some fixed overheads may be relevant to a decision, for example, stepped fixed costs may be relevant if fixed costs increase as a direct result of a decision being taken.
- **Net book values** are not relevant costs because like depreciation, they are determined by accounting conventions rather than by future cash flows.

e.g

Illustration 1 – The concept of relevant costing

A decision has to be made whether to use production method A or B.

The cost figures are as follows.

	Method A		Method B	
	Costs last year	Expected costs next year	Costs last year	Expected costs next year
	$	$	$	$
Fixed costs	5,000	7,000	5,000	7,000
Variable costs per unit:				
Labour	2	6	4	12
Materials	12	8	15	10

Relevant cost of Method A = $ ______

Relevant cost of Method B = $ ______

Solution

Relevant cost of Method A = $ 14

Relevant cost of Method B = $ 22

First we can reject all of the costs last year (fixed costs and variable costs) as they are sunk costs and therefore irrelevant costs. Note that past costs can be used as a guide to what future costs might be, but they are still not relevant to the decision under consideration here.

Secondly we can reject expected fixed costs since they are the same ($7,000) for both methods and can therefore be ignored. Note that fixed costs are not always irrelevant. If fixed costs were to vary between decision alternatives they would be of some relevance since there would be a differential cost to consider.

The only relevant costs in this situation are the expected (future) variable costs for materials and labour as shown below.

	Method A	Method B
	$	$
Expected future variable costs per unit:		
Labour	6	12
Materials	8	10
	14	22

Test your understanding 1

A sunk cost is:

A a cost committed to be spent in the current period
B a past cost which is irrelevant for decision making
C a cost connected with oil exploration in the North Sea
D a cost unaffected by fluctuations in the level of activity.

2 Relevant costs for materials, labour and overheads

2.1 Relevant cost for materials

The relevant cost of materials can be determined by the following decision tree.

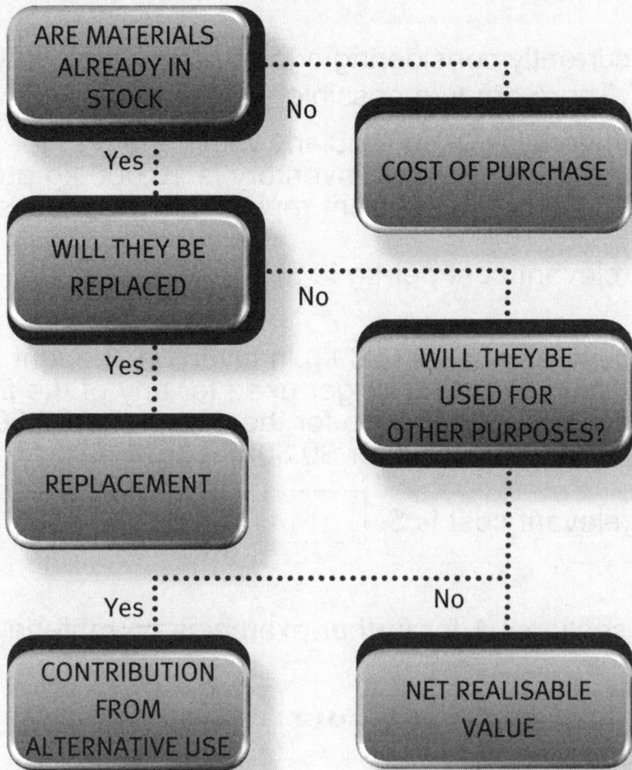

Use the diagram shown above when attempting questions on the relevant cost of materials.

e.g

Illustration 2 – Relevant costs for materials, labour and overheads

Z Ltd has 50 kg of material P in inventory that was bought five years ago for $70. It is no longer used but could be sold for $3/kg.

Z Ltd is currently pricing a job that could use 40 kg of material P.

The relevant cost of material P that should be included in the contract is $ ______

Solution

The relevant cost of material P that should be included in the contract is $ ______

Materials in inventory? – Yes
Will they be replaced? – No (no longer used)
Used for other purposes? – No
Net realisable value – 40 kg @ $3/kg = $120

Test your understanding 2

A firm is currently considering a job that requires 1,000 kg of raw material. There are two possible situations.

(a) The material is used regularly within the firm for various products. The present inventory is 10,000 kg purchased at $1.80 per kg. The current replenishment price is $2.00 per kg.

The relevant cost per kg is $ ______

(b) The company has 2,000 kg in inventory, bought 2 years ago for $1.50 per kg, but no longer used for any of the firm's products. The current market price for the material is $2.00, but the company could sell it for $0.80 per kg.

The relevant cost is $ ______

Note: See section 4.1 for further examples on materials.

2.2 Relevant cost for labour

A similar problem exists in determining the relevant costs of labour. In this case the key question is whether spare capacity exists and on this basis a decision tree as shown below can be used to identify the relevant cost.

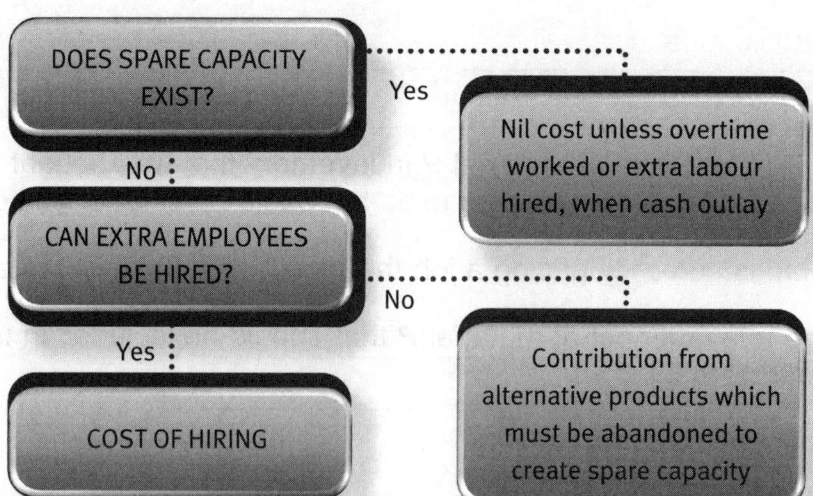

Use the diagram shown above when doing the following questions on the relevant cost of labour.

e.g

Illustration 3 – Relevant costs for materials, labour and overheads

(a) 100 hours of unskilled labour are needed for a contract. The company has no surplus capacity at the moment, but additional temporary staff could be hired at $4.50 per hour.

The relevant cost of the unskilled labour on the contract is

$ [ ]

(b) 100 hours of semi-skilled labour are needed for a contract. There is at the moment roughly 300 hours worth of spare capacity. There is a union agreement that there are no lay-offs. The workers are paid $6.50 per hour.

The relevant cost of the semi-skilled labour on the contract is

$ [ ]

Solution

(a) The relevant cost of the unskilled labour on the contract is

$ [450]

The relevant cost is the cost of hiring temporary staff at $4.50 per hour = 100 x $4.50 = $450

(b) The relevant cost of the semi-skilled labour on the contract is

$ [0]

Spare capacity exists and therefore the relevant cost of the semi-skilled labour is $0.

Test your understanding 3

Z Ltd is pricing a job that involves the use of 20 hours of skilled labour and 50 hours of semi-skilled labour.

The four existing skilled workers are paid $15 per hour with a minimum weekly wage of $450. They are currently working 24 hours a week.

The semi-skilled workforce is currently fully utilised. They are each paid $10 per hour, with overtime payable at time and a half. Additional workers may be hired for $12 per hour.

The relevant labour cost for Z Ltd's job = $ [ ]

2.3 Relevant cost for overheads

In addition to calculating the relevant cost of materials and labour, you may also be required to calculate the relevant cost of overheads.

RELEVANT COST OF OVERHEADS

Only those overheads that vary as a direct result of a decision taken are relevant overheads

Illustration 4 – Relevant costs for materials, labour and overheads

JB Ltd absorbs overheads on a machine hour rate, currently $20/hour, of which $7 is for variable overheads and $13 for fixed overheads. The company is deciding whether to undertake a contract in the coming year. If the contract is undertaken, it is estimated that fixed costs will increase for the duration of the contract by $3,200.

Required:

Identify the relevant costs of the overheads for the contract.

Solution

- The variable cost per hour of overhead is relevant since this cost would be avoidable if the contract were not undertaken. The relevant cost of variable overheads is therefore $7 per machine hour.
- The fixed cost per hour is an absorption rate. Actual fixed costs would not increase by $13 per hour for any component made. Actual fixed costs would increase by $3,200 in total. The relevant cost of fixed overheads is therefore $3,200.

Test your understanding 4

Explain why fixed overhead absorption rates are assumed to be irrelevant to a decision and variable overhead absorption rates are assumed to be relevant to the same decision.

3 Relevant costs for non-current assets

3.1 Relevant costs of non-current assets

The relevant costs associated with non-current assets, such as plant and machinery, are determined in a similar way to the relevant costs of materials.

- If plant and machinery is to be replaced at the end of its useful life, then the relevant cost is the current replacement cost.
- If plant and machinery is not to be replaced, then the relevant cost is the higher of the sale proceeds (if sold) and the net cash inflows arising from the use of the asset (if not sold).

e.g

Illustration 5 – Relevant costs for non-current assets

A machine which cost $10,000 four years ago has a written-down value of $6,000 and the depreciation to be charged this year is $1,000. It has no alternative use, but it could be sold now for $3,000. In one year's time it will be unsaleable.

Relevant cost of the machine = $ [ ]

Solution

Relevant cost of the machine = $ [3,000]

- $10,000 (the cost of the machine four years ago) is a sunk cost and is not relevant to the decision.
- $6,000 (written-down value of the machine) is not relevant because it is determined by accounting conventions and not by future cash flows.
- $1,000 (depreciation charge this year) is not relevant because this is a non-cash flow cost.
- $3,000 (sale proceeds if the machine were sold now) is a relevant cost (future cash flow).

The cost of keeping the machine and selling it in a year's time is $3,000 because this is the amount that you will miss out on if you don't sell it now.

Test your understanding 5

A machine which originally cost $80,000 has an estimated useful life of 10 years and is depreciated at the rate of $8,000 per annum. The net book value of the machine is currently $40,000 and the net sale proceeds if it were to be sold today are $25,000.

Required:

Identify whether the costs associated with the machine are relevant or not. If you think they are not relevant, give reasons.

4 Opportunity costs

4.1 The concept of opportunity cost

Opportunity cost represents the best alternative that is foregone in taking a decision. The concept of opportunity cost emphasises that decision making is concerned with alternatives and that the cost of taking one decision is the profit or contribution foregone by not taking the next best alternative.

- If resources to be used on projects are scarce (e.g. labour, materials, machines), then consideration must be given to profits or contribution which could have been earned from alternative uses of the resources.
- For example, the skilled labour which may be needed on a new project might have to be withdrawn from normal production. This withdrawal would cause a loss in contribution which is obviously relevant to the project appraisal.
- The cash flows of a single department or division cannot be looked at in isolation. It is always the effects on cash flows of the whole organisation which must be considered.

Illustration 6 – Opportunity costs

A new contract requires the use of 50 tons of metal ZX 81. This metal is used regularly on all the firm's projects. There are 100 tons of ZX 81 in inventory at the moment, which were bought for $200 per ton. The current purchase price is $210 per ton, and the metal could be disposed of for net scrap proceeds of $150 per ton. What cost should be charged to the new contract for metal ZX 81?

Solution

The use of the material in inventory for the new contract means that more ZX 81 must be bought for normal workings. The cost to the organisation is therefore the money spent on purchase, no matter whether existing inventory or new inventory is used on the contract.

Assuming that the additional purchases are made in the near future, the relevant cost to the organisation is current purchase price:

50 tons x $210 = $10,500

Test your understanding 6

A new contract requires the use of 50 tons of metal ZX 81. There are 25 tons of ZX 81 in inventory at the moment, which were bought for $200 per ton. The company no longer has any use for metal ZX 81. The current purchase price is $210 per ton, and the metal could be disposed of for net scrap proceeds of $150 per ton. What cost should be charged to the new contract for metal ZX 81?

e.g

Illustration 7 – Opportunity costs

A mining operation uses skilled labour costing $4 per hour, which generates a contribution, after deducting these labour costs, of $3 per hour.

A new project is now being considered which requires 5,000 hours of skilled labour. There is a shortage of the required labour. Any used on the new project must be transferred from normal working. What is the relevant cost of using the skilled labour on the project?

Solution

How much contribution cash flow is lost if the labour is transferred from normal working?

	$
Contribution per hour lost from normal working	3
Add back: labour cost per hour which is not saved	4
Cash lost per labour hour as a result of the labour transfer	7
The contract should be charged with 5,000 x $7	$35,000

Test your understanding 7

A mining operation uses skilled labour costing $4 per hour, which generates a contribution, after deducting these labour costs, of $3 per hour.

A new project is now being considered which requires 5,000 hours of skilled labour. There is a surplus of the required labour which is sufficient to cope with the new project. The workers who are currently idle are being paid full wages. What is the relevant cost of using the skilled labour on the project?

Test your understanding 8

100 hours of skilled labour are needed for a contract. The skilled labour force is working at full capacity at the moment and the workers would have to be taken off production of a different product in order to work on the client's contract. The details of the other product are shown below.

	$/unit
Selling price	60
Direct materials	10
Direct labour	1 hour @ $10/hour
Variable overheads	15
Fixed overheads	15

The skilled workers' pay rate would not change, regardless of which product they worked on.

The relevant cost of the skilled labour on the contract is $ ______

Chapter summary

RELEVANT COSTING

The concept of relevant costing

Relevant costs and revenue are:

- Future costs and revenues
- Cash flows
- Incremental costs are revenues

Assume variable costs are relevant unless told otherwise

Relevant costs of materials, labour and overheads

Materials: In stock/replaced/other purpose?

Labour: Spare capacity/extra employees hired? (lost contribution or cost of hiring)

Overheads: Only those that vary as a drect result of a decision taken are relevant overheads

Relevant costs non-current assets

Replaced? – Replacement cost

Not replaced – higher of sale proceeds or net cash inflows

Opportunity cost

Opportunity cost represents the best alternative that is foregone in taking a decision. Concept of opportunity cost emphasises that decision making is concerned with alternatives and that the cost of taking one decision is the profit or contribution foregone by not taking the next best.

Test your understanding answers

Test your understanding 1

B A sunk cost is a past cost and is therefore not relevant for future decisions.

Test your understanding 2

(a) The relevant cost per kg is $ 2.00

The material is in inventory and is used regularly by the company. It will therefore be replaced at the current replenishment price of $2.00. The relevant cost per kg is therefore the current replenishment cost of $2.00.

(b) The relevant cost is $ 800

After using the material for the job that it is considering, the next best alternative is to sell the material for $0.80 per kg. The relevant cost in this situation is therefore the benefit foregone, i.e. the net realisable value (sale proceeds) of the material in inventory = 1,000 kg x $0.80 = $800.

Note: see section 4.1 for further examples on materials.

Test your understanding 3

The relevant labour cost for Z Ltd's job = $ 600

- Skilled workers: Minimum weekly wage covers $450/$15 = 30 hours work. Each worker therefore has 6 hours per week spare capacity which is already paid for: 6 x 4 = 24 hours which is sufficient for the job. Relevant cost = $0.
- Semi-skilled workers: Overtime cost = $10 x 1½ = $15 per hour. It is therefore cheaper to hire additional workers. Relevant cost = 50 hours x $12 = $600.

Note: see section 4.1 for further examples on labour costs.

Test your understanding 4

Fixed overhead absorption rates are not considered to be relevant costs in decision making because fixed overhead absorption is not a cash flow and does not represent 'real' spending.

Variable overheads, on the other hand, will increase as activity levels increase and will result in additional expenditure being incurred. Such expenditure will represent 'real' cash spending.

Test your understanding 5

		Relevant?	Not relevant – reason
1	$80,000 – original cost	No	Sunk cost
2	$8,000 – annual depreciation	No	Not a cash flow
3	$40,000 – net book value	No	Not a cash flow
4	$25,000 – net sale proceeds	Yes	

Test your understanding 6

The only alternative use for the material held in inventory is to sell it for scrap. To use 25 tons on the contract is to give up the opportunity of selling it for:

25 x $150 = $3,750

The organisation must then purchase a further 25 tons, and assuming this is in the near future, it will cost $210 per ton.

The contract must be charged with:

	$
25 tons @ $150	3,750
25 tons @ $210	5,250
	9,000

Test your understanding 7

How much contribution cash flow is lost if the labour is transferred from doing nothing to the project? Answer: nothing.

The relevant cost is therefore zero.

Test your understanding 8

The relevant cost of the skilled labour on the contract is $ 3,500

How much contribution cash flow is lost if the labour is transferred from normal to working?

Contribution earned from other product per hour = $(60 – 10 – 10 – 15) = $25

	$
Contribution per hour lost from normal working	25
Add back: labour cost per hour which is not saved	10
Cash lost per labour hour as a result of the labour transfer	35
The contract should be charged with 100 x $35	3,500

chapter

10

Dealing with limiting factors

Chapter learning objectives

Upon completion of this chapter you will be able to:

- identify an organisation's single limiting factor using data supplied
- determine the optimal production plan where an organisation is restricted by a single limiting factor using data supplied
- formulate a linear programming problem involving two variables using data supplied
- determine the optimal solution to a linear programming problem using a graphical approach from a supplied or derived linear programming formulation
- for two supplied simple linear equations, use simultaneous equations to determine where the two lines cross
- use simultaneous equations, where appropriate, in the solution of a linear programming problem.

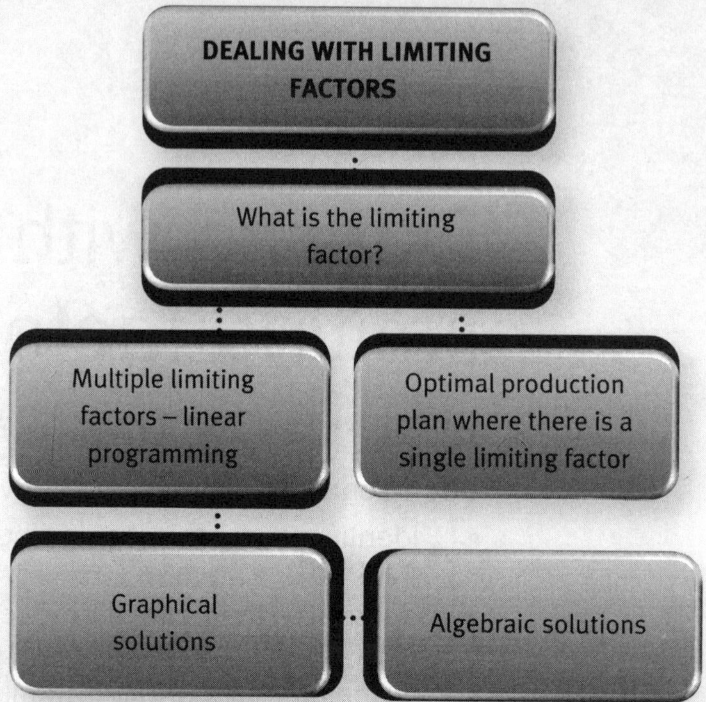

1 What is a limiting factor?

A **limiting factor** is a factor that prevents a company from achieving the level of activity that it would like to.

- Limiting factor analysis looks at using the contribution concept to address the problem of scarce resources.
- Scarce resources are where one or more of the manufacturing inputs (materials, labour, machine time) needed to make a product is in short supply.
- Production can also be affected by the number of units of a product that is likely to be demanded in a period (the sales demand).

e.g

Illustration 1 – What is a limiting factor?

Suppose A Ltd makes two products, X and Y. Both products use the same machine and the same raw material that are limited to 200 hours and $500 per week respectively. Individual product details are as follows.

	Product X per unit	Product Y per unit
Machine hours	5.0	2.5
Materials	$10	$5
Contribution	$20	$15
Maximum weekly demand	50 units	100 units

We can identify the limiting factor by calculating the number of products that can be made with the resources available.

Machine hours	200/5	=	40 units of X, or
	200/2.5	=	80 units of Y
Materials	$500/$10	=	50 units of X, or
	$500/$5	=	100 units of Y

Therefore, machine hours is the limiting factor because it limits the production of Products X (40 units) and Y (80 units). The materials constraint does not prevent the firm making enough units to meet demand.

Test your understanding 1

Two products, Alpha and Gamma are made of Material X and require skilled labour in the production process. The product details are as follows:

	Alpha	Gamma
	$	$
Selling price	10.00	15.00
Variable cost	6.00	7.50
Contribution	4.00	7.50
Material X required per unit	2 kg	4 kg
Skilled labour time required per unit	1 hour	3 hours

The maximum demand per week is 30 units of Alpha and 10 units of Gamma.

The company can sell all the Alphas and Gammas that it can make, but there is a restriction on the availability of both Material X and skilled labour. There are 150 kg of material, and 45 hours of skilled labour, available per week.

Identify the limiting factor.

2 Optimal production plan where there is a single limiting factor

2.1 Contribution per unit of limiting factor

In order to decide which products should be made in which order, it is necessary to calculate the contribution per unit of limiting factor (or scarce resource).

- Suppose A Ltd makes two products, X and Y. Both products use the same machine and the same raw material that are limited to 200 hours and $500 per week respectively. Individual product details are as follows.

	Product X per unit	**Product Y per unit**
Machine hours	5.0	2.5
Materials	$10	$5
Contribution	$20	$15

- It has already been established that the limiting factor is machine hours. Product X requires five machine hours and Product Y requires two and a half machine hours. The contribution per machine hour (limiting factor) is therefore as follows.

  Contribution per machine hour = Contribution per unit/Machine hours per unit

  Product X $20/5 hours = $4 per machine hour
  Product Y $15/2.5 hours = $6 per machine hour

- Product Y earns a higher contribution per unit of limiting factor (machine hours) and therefore Product Y should be made in preference to Product X.

Contribution per unit of limiting factor = **Contribtion per unit / Units of limiting factor required per unit**

2.2 Optimal production plan

When limiting factors are present, contribution (and therefore profits) are maximised when products earning the highest amount of contribution per unit of limiting factor are manufactured first. The profit-maximising production mix is known as the optimal production plan.

- The optimal production plan is established as follows.

Step 1 Calculate the contribution per unit of product.

Step 2 Calculate the contribution per unit of scarce resource.

Step 3 Rank products.

Step 4 Allocate the scarce resource to the highest-ranking product.

Step 5 Once the demand for the highest-ranking product is satisfied, move on to the next highest-ranking product and so on until the scarce resource (limiting factor) is used up.

e.g

Illustration 2 – Optimal production plan where there is a single limiting factor

A company is able to produce four products and is planning its production mix for the following period. Relevant data is given below:

	A	B	C	D
Selling price ($) per unit	19	25	40	50
Labour cost per unit ($)	6	12	18	24
Material cost per unit ($)	9	9	15	16
Maximum demand (units)	1,000	5,000	4,000	2,000

Labour is paid $6 per hour and labour hours are limited to 12,000 hours in the period.

Required:

Determine the optimal production plan and calculate the total contribution it earns for the company.

Solution

	A	B	C	D
	$	$	$	$
Selling price	19	25	40	50
Variable costs:				
Direct labour	(6)	(12)	(18)	(24)
Direct material	(9)	(9)	(15)	(16)
Contribution per unit	4	4	7	10
	A	B	C	D
Hours per unit (labour cost/$6)	1	2	3	4
Contribution per hour	$4	$2	$2.33	$2.50
Rank	1	4	3	2

Remember to allocate the scarce resource (labour hours) to the highest-ranking product first (A). Once the demand for the highest-ranking product is satisfied, move on to the next highest-ranking product (D) and then the next (C) until the scarce resource (labour hours) is used up.

Optimal production plan

Product	Units	Hours used	Hours left	Contribution per unit ($)	Total contribution ($)
A	1,000	1,000	11,000	4	4,000
D	2,000	8,000	3,000	10	20,000
C	1,000	3,000	0	7	7,000
					31,000

Test your understanding 2

The following data relates to Products Able and Baker.

		Product	
		Able	**Baker**
Direct materials per unit		$10	$30
Direct labour:			
Grinding	$5 per hour	7 hours per unit	5 hours per unit
Finishing	$7.50 per hour	15 hours per unit	9 hours per unit
Selling price per unit		$206.50	$168.00
Budgeted production		1,200 units	600 units
Maximum sales for the period		1,500 units	800 units

Notes:

1 No opening or closing inventory is anticipated.

2 The skilled labour used for the grinding processes is highly specialised and in short supply, although there is just sufficient to meet the budgeted production. However, it will not be possible to increase the supply for the budget period.

Determine the optimal production plan and calculate the total contribution it earns for the company.

3 Multiple limiting factors – linear programming

3.1 Linear programming

As we have seen, when there is only one resource that limits the activities of an organisation (other than sales demand), products are ranked in order of contribution per unit of limiting factor in order to establish the optimal production plan.

- When there is more than one limiting factor (apart from sales demand) the optimal production plan cannot be established by ranking products.
- In such situations, a technique known is linear programming is used.

3.2 Formulating a linear programming problem

The first stage in solving a linear programming problem is to 'formulate' the problem, i.e. translate the problem into a mathematical formula.

- The steps involved in this stage are as follows.
  - **Step 1** Define the unknowns, i.e. the variables (that need to be determined).
  - **Step 2** Formulate the constraints, i.e. the limitations that must be placed on the variables.
  - **Step 3** Formulate the objective function (that needs to be maximised or minimised).

Expandable text

- The constraints are determined by the scarce resources, for example, if labour or materials are restricted. There is also a constraint known as the non-negativity constraint.
- The non-negativity constraint fulfils the requirement of linear programming that there should be no negative values in a linear programming solution. You cannot make a negative amount of a product. Each variable in a linear programming problem must therefore be greater than or equal to 0.
- The objective function of a linear programming problem must also be formulated.
- The objective of a linear programming problem is usually to maximise or minimise something. Most organisations will wish to maximise profit or contribution. Sometimes organisations may wish to minimise costs.

e.g

Illustration 3 – Multiple factors – linear programming

A company makes two products, X and Y, and wishes to maximise profit. Information on X and Y is as follows:

	Product X	Product Y
Material kg per unit	1	1
Labour hours per unit	5	10
	$	$
Selling price per unit	80	100
Variable cost per unit	50	50
Contribution per unit	30	50

The company can sell any number of product X, but expects the maximum annual demand for Y to be 1,500 units. Labour is limited to 20,000 hours and materials to 3,000 kg per annum.

Required:

Using the information given, formulate the linear programming problem.

Solution

Step 1 Define the unknowns, i.e. the variables that need to be determined

Let x = number of units of X produced and sold each year

Let y = number of units of Y produced and sold each year

Step 2 Formulate the constraints, i.e. the limitations that must be placed on the variables

Constraint			
Materials	x + y	≤	3,000
Labour hours	5x + 10y	≤	20,000
Maximum sales	y	≤	1,500
Non-negativity	x	≥	0
	y	≥	0

Step 3 Formulate the objective function that needs to be maximised or minimised

The objective is to maximise contribution.

So objective: maximise 30x + 50y.

Test your understanding 3

A builder has purchased 21,000 square metres of land on which it is planned to build two types of dwelling, detached and town houses, within an overall budget of $2.1 million.

A detached costs $35,000 to build and requires 600 square metres of land.

A town house costs $60,000 to build and requires 300 square metres of land.

To comply with local planning regulations, not more than 40 buildings may be constructed on this land, but there must be at least 5 of each type.

From past experience the builder estimates the contribution on the detached house to be about $10,000 and on the town house to be about $6,000. Contribution is to be maximised.

Using the information given, formulate the linear programming problem.

4 Graphical solutions

It is possible to solve linear programming problems with two variables by drawing a graph of the constraints and the objective function.

- The steps involved in the graphical approach are as follows:
  - **Step 1** Define the unknowns, i.e. the variables (that need to be determined).
  - **Step 2** Formulate the constraints, i.e. the limitations that must be placed on the variables.
  - **Step 3** Formulate the objective function (that needs to be maximised or minimised).
  - **Step 4** Graph the constraints and objective function.
  - **Step 5** Determine the optimal solution to the problem by reading from the graph.

e.g

Illustration 4 – Graphical solutions

The constraints and the objective function of a linear programming problem concerning how many units of products X and Y to be produced and sold each year have been formulated to be as follows:

Constraint

Materials	x + y	≤	3,000
Labour hours	5x + 10y	≤	20,000
Maximum sales	y	≤	1,500
Non-negativity	x	≥	0
	y	≥	0

The objective function is to maximise 30x + 50y.

Where:

x = number of units of X produced and sold each year
y = number of units of Y produced and sold each year

Required:

Determine the optimal solution to this linear programming problem using a graphical approach.

Solution

Step 4 Graph the constraints and objective function

Constraints represent regions on the graph. To show these it is best to draw the straight line representing equality and then deciding which side is feasible. To draw a straight line, we need just two points on the line, which can then be joined up.

1 **Materials constraint: x + y ≤ 3,000**

- Draw the line x + y = 3,000 and choose the region below it ('≤')
- End points:

If x = 0, y = 3,000
If y = 0, x = 3,000

2 **Labour constraint: 5x + 10y ≤ 20,000**

- We draw the line 5x + 10y = 20,000 and then select the area below the line ('≤') as feasible.
- If x = 0, then y = $\frac{20,000}{10}$ = 2,000
- If y = 0, then x = $\frac{20,000}{5}$ = 4,000

3 **Maximum sales constraint: y ≤ 1,500**

- Draw the line y = 1,500 and then select the region below it.

4 **Non-negativity constraints:** these are the vertical and horizontal axes.

5 **To graph the objective function**

Take any reasonable value for maximum contribution, e.g. let maximum contribution be, say, $75,000, so: 30x + 50y = 75,000

- If x = 0, then y = $\frac{75,000}{50}$ = 1,500
- If y = 0, then x = $\frac{75,000}{30}$ = 2,500
- To draw 30x + 50y = 75,000, mark x = 0, y = 1,500 and x = 2,500, y = 0, and join them up.

Note: Any contribution line can be drawn. The purpose of drawing the line is merely to establish the **slope** of the line. Starting with a higher contribution will give an iso-contribution line that is parallel to the first but further out. To maximise contribution we thus want to push the line as far out as is feasible.

We can now graph the constraints and identify the feasible region, i.e. all production possibilities given the constraints. If we then draw the objective function we can determine the optimal solution to this linear programming problem, i.e. the point at which optimum production takes place.

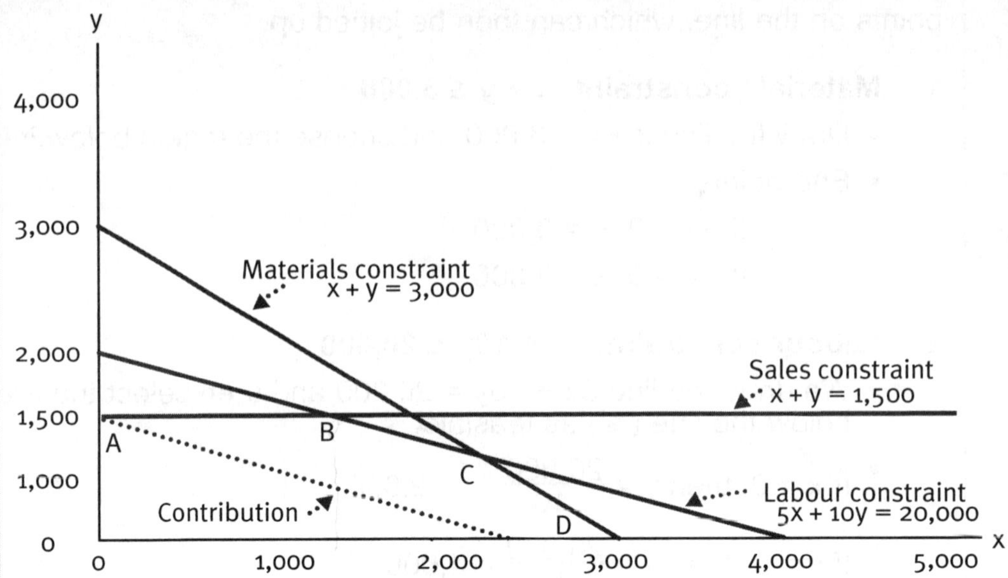

- The feasible region is shown as OABCD. These are combinations of values for x and y that satisfy all the constraints. Therefore the area on the graph above these lines is 'out of bounds' or more technically 'not feasible'.
- To show that feasible solutions are, as in this case, all below the constraint lines, it is normal practice to shade or hatch above the line indicating that anything above is outside the feasible region. Some questions can be minimising problems, e.g. the objective function will be to minimise costs subject to minimum output levels. The constraints will be minimum output levels, therefore the feasible region will be on or above the line and will be hatched under the line.

Step 5 Determine the optimal solution to the problem

We now need to establish which feasible values for x and y give the maximum contribution achievable. There are two ways in which this can be done.

- **Method 1**: Calculate the contribution earned at each of the points A, B C and D (point o can be eliminated at this point since contribution earned here will be zero).
- **Method 2**: Manipulate the objective function to find the point of the optimal feasible solution (by reading from the graph).

Method 1: Calculate the contribution earned at each of the points A, B and C.

Reading from the graph, we can see:

Point A is at x = 0 and y = 1,500
Point B is at x = 1,000 and y = 1,500
Point C is at x = 2,000 and y = 1,000
Point D is at x = 3,000 and y = 0

The contribution earned at each of these points is as follows:

Point	x	y	Contribution (30x + 50y)
A	0	1,500	$75,000
B	1,000	1,500	$105,000
C	2,000	1,000	$110,000
D	3,000	0	$90,000

The point at which the highest contribution is earned represents the optimal solution.

Maximum contribution is therefore earned at Point C ($110,000) where x = 2,000 and y = 1,000.

The optimal solution to this linear programming problem is therefore to poduce and sell 2,000 units of Product X and 1,000 units of Product Y.

Method 2: Manipulate the objective function to find the point of the optimal feasible solution (by reading from the graph).

To find the optimal production using this method, we need to draw the objective function and 'slide' it as far away from the origin as possible without leaving the feasible region.

- The dotted line on the graph shows the objective function with a contribution of $75,000, but any convenient number will do since all such lines will be parallel with each other. Such a line is called an iso-contribution line.
- Place a ruler against the iso-contribution line, then, by moving the ruler away from the origin (in the case of a maximisation problem) or towards the origin (in the case of a minimisation problem) but keeping it parallel to the iso-contribution line, the last corner of the feasible solution space which is met represents the optimal solution.The optimal solution is at C.
- Reading from the graph we can see that Point C is at x = 2,000 and y = 1,000. This represents the optimal solution, i.e. produce and sell 2,000 units of product X and 1,000 units of product Y.
- At the optimal solution, Point C, the contribution earned is 30x + 50y = [(30 x 2,000) + (50 x 1,000)] = 60,000 + 50,000 = $110,000

Test your understanding 4

The constraints and the objective function of a linear programming problem concerning how many detached houses and town houses to be built have been formulated to be as follows:

Constraints:

Area:	$600x + 300y$	$\leq$ 21,000
Cost:	$35x + 60y$	$\leq$ 2,100 (in $000)
Number:	$x + y$	$\leq$ 40
Minimum:	x	$\geq$ 5
	y	$\geq$ 5
Non-negativity :	x	$\geq$ 0
	y	$\geq$ 0

The objective function is to maximise $10x + 6y$

Where:

x = the number of detached houses
y = the number of town houses.

Determine the optimal solution to this linear programming problem using a graphical approach. (Note: do not draw the iso-contribution line in order to determine the optimal solution.)

5 Algebraic solutions

5.1 Using equations to solve linear programming problems

Equations can be used to determine where two lines cross.

- For example, in **Illustration 4**, we established that the optimal solution was at Point C using the graphical method.
- Point C represents the point at which the sales constraint intersects the labour constraint.

Labour constraint $5x + 10y = 20{,}000$ (1)

Materials constraint $x + y = 3{,}000$ (2)

- The basic method is to eliminate one of the two unknowns between the equations.
- This is achieved by adding or subtracting the equations.
- This process is known as solving simultaneous equations.

e.g

Illustration 5 – Algebraic solutions

Solve the following simultaneous equations.

$$5x + 10y = 20{,}000 \quad (1)$$
$$x + y = 3{,}000 \quad (2)$$

Solution

Step 1

- By multiplying equation (2) by 10, the coefficients of y become equal:

$$(1):\quad 5x + 10y = 20{,}000$$
$$10 \times (2):\quad 10x + 10y = 30{,}000 \ldots \text{ Equation (3)}$$

Step 2

- Equation (2) when multiplied is called equation (3). You can deduct equation (1) from equation (3) to eliminate y.

$$(3)\quad 10x + 10y = 30{,}000$$
$$(1)\quad 5x + 10y = 20{,}000$$
$$5x \qquad 10{,}000$$

Step 3

- Obtain a value for x by rearranging the equation:

$$5x = 10{,}000$$
$$x = \frac{10{,}000}{5}$$
$$x = 2{,}000$$

Step 4

- Substitution into any of (1), (2) or (3) is possible but in this case (2) is most convenient giving:

$$2{,}000 + y = 3{,}000$$
$$\therefore y = 1{,}000$$

- So the solution is x = 2,000 y = 1,000 as before.

Test your understanding 5

Suppose that the optimal solution to a linear programming problem is at the intersection of the following two constraint lines:

(1) $2x + 3y = 1{,}700$
(2) $5x + 2y = 2{,}600$

Determine the values of x and y using simultaneous equations.

5.2 Establishing the optimal solution using simultaneous equations

You may consider that the whole process of linear programming would be easier by solving the constraints as sets of simultaneous equations and not bothering with a graph. This is possible and you may get the right answer, but such a technique should be used with caution!

- It is not recommended that you solve sets of simultaneous equations until you have determined graphically which constraints are effective in determining the optimal solution.
- The solutions obtained for linear programming problems using the graphical method rely on the graphs being drawn very clearly so that accurate readings may be taken.
- If it is not easy to read the co-ordinates of the required points from a linear programming graph then the use of simultaneous equations provides a reliable check.

Test your understanding 6

Alfred Ltd is preparing its plan for the coming month. It manufactures two products, the Flaktrap and the Saptrap. Details are as follows.

	Product		
Amount per unit	Flaktrap	Saptrap	Price/wage rate
Selling price ($)	125	165	
Raw material (kg)	6	4	$5/kg
Labour hours			
Skilled	10	10	$3/hour
Semi-skilled	5	25	$3/hour

The company's variable overhead rate is $1 per labour hour (for both skilled and semi-skilled labour). The supply of skilled labour is limited to 2,000 hours per month and the supply of semi-skilled labour is limited to 2,500 hours per month. At the selling prices indicated, maximum demand for Flaktraps is expected to be 150 units per month and the maximum demand for Saptraps is expected to be 80 units per month.

Use simultaneous equations to solve the linear programming problem given above.

Chapter summary

DEALING WITH LIMITING FACTORS

What is the limiting factor?

A limiting factor is a factor that prevents a company from achieving the level of activity that it would like to. It is usually sales demand but it might be material, labour, machine capacity and so on

Multiple limiting factors – linear programming

Step 1 Define the unknowns, i.e. the variables (that need to be declared).
Step 2 Formulate the constraints, i.e. the limitations that must be placed on the variables.
Step 3 Formulate the objective function (that needs to be maximised or minimised).

Optimal production plan where there is a single limiting factor

Make products in order of contribution earned per unit of limiting factor (start with the highest earner)

Contribution per unit of limiting factor =

$$\frac{\text{Contribution per unit}}{\text{Units of limiting factor required per unit}}$$

Graphical solutions

Step 4 Graph the constraints and objective function.
Step 5 Determine the optimal solution to the problem by manipulating the iso-contibution line and reading from the graph or calculating the contribution earned at each point of feasible area.

Algebraic solutions

When it is difficult to read the required points from a linear programming graph, the optimal solution to the problem can be established (or confirmed) by solving the relevant simultaneous equations. Simultaneous equations are used in conjunction with the graphical method in solving linear programming problems, and not on their own.

Test your understanding answers

Test your understanding 1

	Alpha	Gamma	Total
Maximum demand per week (units)	30	10	
Material X required per unit (kg) (W1)	2	4	
Material X required for maximum demand (kg)	60	40	**100**
Labour time per unit (hours) (W2)	1	3	
Skilled labour time required for maximum demand (hours)	30	30	**60**

Material X requirement (100 kg) is less than the amount of Material X available in a week (150 kg). Material X does not, therefore, limit the activities of the organisation.

60 hours of skilled labour are required in order to produce the maximum number of units of each product demanded each week. However, only 45 hours of skilled labour are available and so skilled labour is the limiting factor in this situation because it limits the organisation's activities.

Workings

(W1) Alpha = 30 x 2 kg = 60 kg
Gamma = 10 x 4 kg = 40 kg

(W2) Alpha = 30 x 1 hour = 30 hours
Gamma = 10 x 3 hours = 30 hours

Test your understanding 2

	Product			
	Able		Baker	
	$	$	$	$
Selling price		206.50		168.00
Variable costs:				
Direct material	10.00		30.00	
Direct labour: Grinding	35.00		25.00	
Finishing	112.50		67.50	
		(157.50)		(122.50)
Contribution per unit		49.00		45.50

Calculate the contribution per grinding hour (resource that is in short supply) and rank products.

	Able	**Baker**
Contribution per unit	$49.00	$45.50
Grinding hours per unit	7	5
Contribution per grinding hour	$7.00	$9.10
Ranking	2	1

Optimal production plan

Product	Units	Hours used	Hours left (W)	Contribution per unit ($)	Total contribution ($)
Baker	800 (x5)	4,000	7,400	45.50	36,400
Able	1,057 (x7)	7,399	1	49.00	51,793
					88,193

(W) Hours available = 1200 x 7 + 600 x 5 = 11,400

After making 800 Bakers there will be 11,400 – 4000 = 7,400 left.

Test your understanding 3

Step 1 Define the unknowns, i.e. the variables that need to be determined

Let x = the number of detached houses
Let y = the number of town houses

Step 2 Formulate the constraints, i.e. the limitations that must be placed on the variables

Constraint:

Area:	600x + 300y	≤	21,000
Cost:	35x + 60y	≤	2,100 (in $000)
Number:	x + y	≤	40
Minimum:	x	≥	5
	y	≥	5
Non-negativity :	x	≥	0
	y	≥	0

Step 3 Formulate the objective function that needs to be maximised or minimised

The objective is to maximise contribution.

So objective: maximise 10x + 6y (in $000).

Test your understanding 4

The graph of the linear programming problem can be constructed by drawing the following lines:

				End points
Area constraint:	600x + 300y	=	21,000	(0,70), (35,0)
Cost constraint:	35x + 60y	=	2,100 (in $000)	(60,0), (0,35)
Number constraint:	x + y	=	40	(0,40), (40,0)
Minimum constraint:	x	=	5	
	y	=	5	
Non-negativity constraints:	x	=	0	
	y	=	0	

Graph of linear programming problem

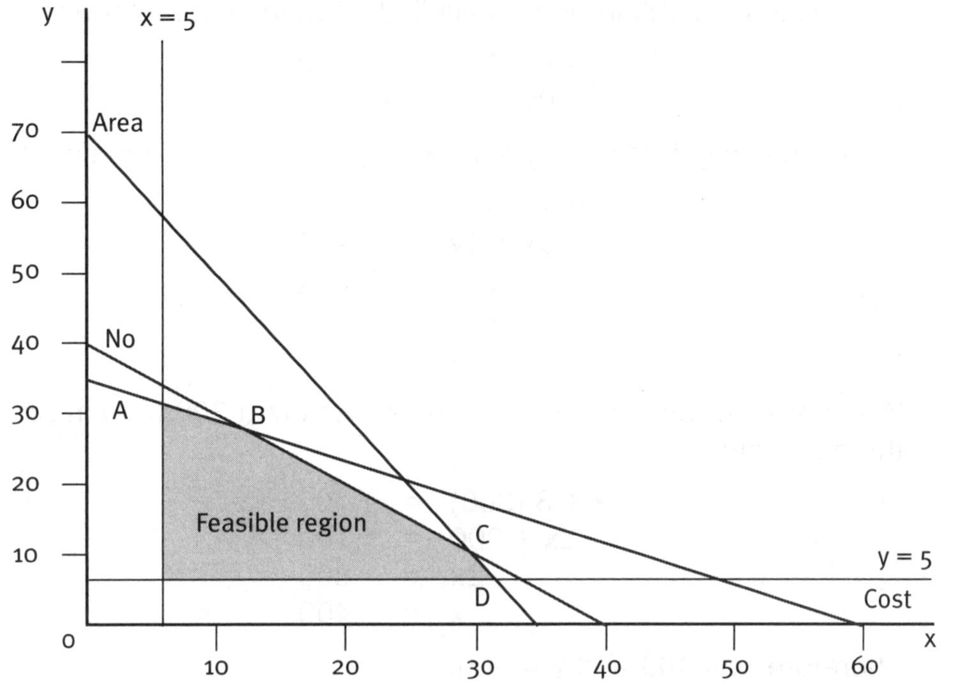

The feasible region is shown by the shaded area.

Reading from the graph, Point A is at (5,32), Point B is at (12,28), Point C is at (30,10) and Point D is at (32,5). We can calculate the contributions earned at each of these points as follows:

Point	x	y	Contribution($000) (10x + 6y)
A	5	32	242
B	12	28	288
C	30	10	360
D	32	5	350

Maximum contribution is earned at Point C ($360,000) where x = 30 and y = 10.

The objective function is to maximise 10x + 6y.

At Point C, x = 30 and y = 10. If we insert these values into our objective function, maximum contribution is $360,000 [(10 x 30) + (6 x 10) = $360,000].

The optimal solution to this linear programming problem is therefore: build 30 detached houses, and 10 town houses.

Test your understanding 5

In this example, if we multiply equation (1) by 5 and equation (2) by 2, we will have 10x in both multiplied equations, as follows:

(3)	10x + 15y	=	8,500
(4)	10x + 4y	=	5,200

Next, we can get rid of x by subtracting equation (4) from equation (3).

(3)	10x + 15y	=	8,500
(4)	10x + 4y	=	5,200
Subtract	11y	=	3,300
	y	=	300

We can establish the value of x by substituting 300 for y in any of the equations.

(1)	2x + 3 (300)	=	1,700
	2x + 900	=	1,700
	2x	=	800
	x	=	400

Therefore x = 400 and y = 300.

Test your understanding 6

Let x be the number of Flaktraps to be produced each month and y be the number of Saptraps to be produced each month.

The constraints are as follows:

Skilled labour	10x + 10y	≤	2,000
Semi-skilled labour	5x + 25y	≤	2,500
Flaktrap demand	x	≤	150
Saptrap demand	y	≤	80
Non-negativity constraints	x	≥	0
	y	≥	0

The possible production combinations of Flaktraps (x) and Saptraps (y) are shown in the graph below. This gives a feasibility region of OABCDE.

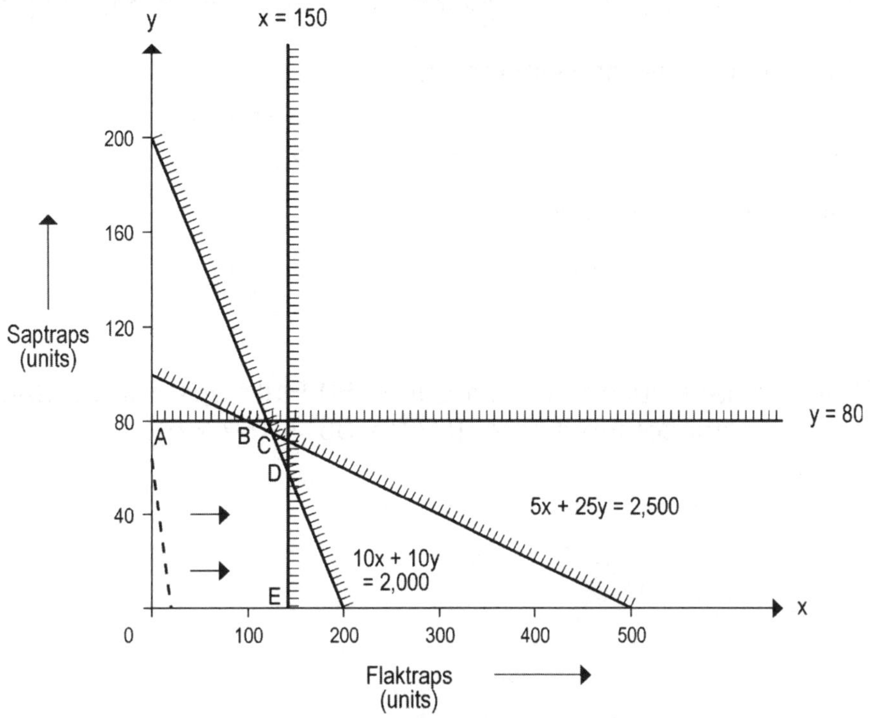

Determining the optimal solution

Having identified the feasible region we must find the optimal solution within this feasible region. We can do this by drawing the objective function, which is to maximise contribution. We are not given the contribution for each product so we must therefore calculate it.

	Flaktrap	Saptrap
	$	$
Selling price	125	165
Raw materials	30	20
Labour: skilled	30	30
semi-skilled	15	75
Variable overheads	15	35
Contribution	35	5

The objective function is therefore to maximise contribution = 35x + 5y

Let 350 = 35x + 5y

When x = 0, $y = \frac{350}{5} = 70$

When y = 0, $x = \frac{350}{35} = 10$

Plotting and 'sliding' the objective function gives an optimal point at D.

Point D is at the intersection of:

$$x = 150 \text{ and}$$
$$10x + 10y = 2{,}000$$

Substituting for x gives:

$$10(150) + 10y = 2{,}000$$
$$10y = 500$$
$$y = 50$$

The optimal solution is to produce 150 Flaktraps and 50 Saptraps giving a total contribution of [(150 x 35) + (50 x 5)] = $5,500.

chapter

11

Job, batch and process costing

Chapter learning objectives

Upon completion of this chapter you will be able to:

- describe the characteristics of: job costing, batch costing, process costing and describe situations in which each would be appropriate using suitable examples
- prepare cost records and accounts in job and batch costing situations from information supplied
- for process costing, using a simple numerical example, explain the concepts of normal and abnormal losses and abnormal gains
- calculate the cost per unit of process outputs from data supplied
- prepare process accounts involving normal and abnormal losses and abnormal gains from data supplied
- calculate and explain the concept of equivalent units from data supplied
- apportion process costs between work remaining in process and transfers out of a process using the weighted average method from data supplied (Note: situations involving work-in-progress (WIP) and losses in the same process are excluded)
- apportion process costs between work remaining in process and transfers out of a process using the FIFO method from data supplied
- prepare process accounts in situations where work remains incomplete, from data supplied
- prepare process accounts where losses and gains are identified at different stages of the process, from data supplied
- distinguish between by-products and joint products using appropriate examples
- value by-products and joint products at the point of separation using a variety of ways of splitting pre-separation costs, from data supplied

- show how post-separation costs are treated to value final joint products from data supplied
- prepare process accounts in situations where by-products and/or joint products occur, from data supplied.

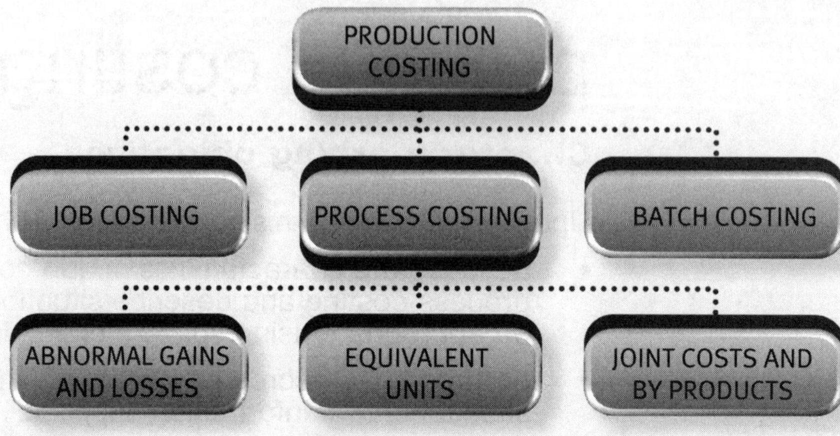

1. Different types of production

1.1 Costing systems

- Specific order costing is the costing system used when the work done by an organisation consists of separately identifiable jobs or batches.
- Continuous operation costing is the costing method used when goods or services are produced as a direct result of a sequence of continuous operations or processes, for example process and service costing.

1.2 Job costing

Job costing is a form of specific order costing and it is used when a customer orders a specific job to be done. Each job is priced separately and each job is unique.

- The main aim of job costing is to identify the costs associated with completing the order and to record them carefully.
- Individual jobs are given a unique job number and the costs involved in completing the job are recorded on a job cost sheet or job card.
- The selling prices of jobs are calculated by adding a certain amount of profit to the cost of the job.

e.g

Illustration 1 – Different types of production

Individual job costs are recorded on a job card similar to the one shown below.

JOB CARD

Customer:	Green & Co Ltd	Job No:	342
Description:	Transfer machine	Promised delivery date:	3.11.X1
Date commenced:	25.9.X1	Actual delivery date:	13.11.X1
Price quoted:	$2,400		
Despatch note no:	7147		

	Materials estimate $1,250		Labour estimate $100		Overhead estimate $176		Other charges estimate $25	
Date Ref					Hourly rate $11			
	Cost	Cum $	Hrs	Cum $	Cost $	Cum $	Cost $	Cum $
20X1 b/f		1,200	17	110		187		13
6 Nov MR 1714	182	1,382						
7 Nov Consultant's test fee								10
8 Nov MR 1937	19	1,401						
9 Nov MRN	(26)	1,375						
10 Nov Labour analysis			5	138		55	242	

Summary	$	**Comments**
Materials	1,375	
Labour	138	
Overhead	242	
Other charges	23	
	1,778	
Invoice price (invoice number 7147 dated 12.12.X1)	2,400	
Profit	622	

The flow of documents in a job costing system is shown as follows.

Documentation in a job costing system

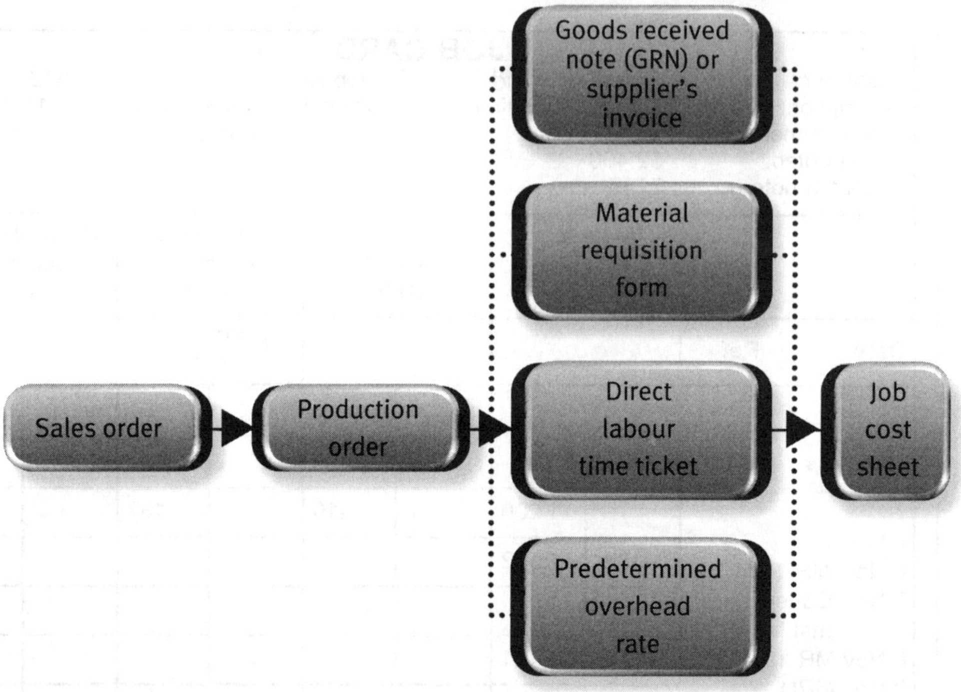

1.3 Batch costing

Batch costing is a form of specific order costing which is very similar to job costing.

- Within each batch are a number of identical units but each batch will be different.
- Each batch is a separately identifiable cost unit which is given a batch number in the same way that each job is given a job number.
- Costs can then be identified against each batch number. For example materials requisitions will be coded to a batch number to ensure that the cost of materials used is charged to the correct batch.
- When the batch is completed the unit cost of individual items in the batch is found by dividing the total batch cost by the number of items in the batch.

$$\textbf{Cost per unit in batch} = \frac{\textbf{Total production cost of batch}}{\textbf{Number of units in batch}}$$

- Batch costing is very common in the engineering component industry, footwear and clothing manufacturing industries.
- The selling prices of batches are calculated in the same ways as the selling prices of jobs, i.e. by adding a profit to the cost of the batch.

1.4 Process costing

Process costing is a costing method used when mass production of many identical products takes place, for example, the production of bars of chocolate, cans of soup or tins of paint.

- One of the distinguishing features of process costing is that all the products in a process are identical and indistinguishable from each other.
- For this reason, an average cost per unit is calculated for each process.

$$\textbf{Average cost per unit} = \frac{\textbf{Costs of production}}{\textbf{Expected or normal output}}$$

- Another main feature of process costing is that the output of one process forms the material input of the next process.

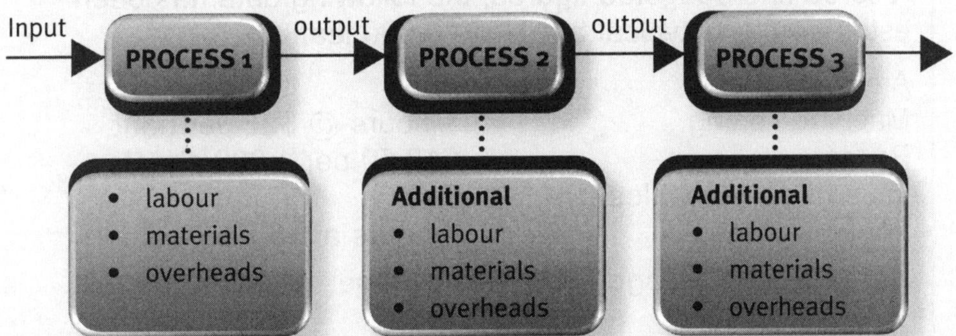

- Also, where there is closing work-in-progress (WIP) at the end of one period, this forms the opening WIP at the beginning of the next period.

Test your understanding 1

Which of the following are characteristics of job costing?

(i) Homogenous products.
(ii) Customer-driven production.
(iii) Production can be completed within a single accounting period.

A (i) only
B (i) and (ii) only
C (ii) and (iii) only
D (i) and (iii) only

2 Profit calculations for job and batch costing

As we have already seen, the costs of jobs and batches are built up from the cost of materials purchased, cost of wages needed to complete the job or batch production and any direct expenses and overheads.

Once the total production costs of the job or batch have been established, a profit can be calculated and added to the total production costs. There are two main methods of calculating job and batch profits.

- Profit mark-up (or profit on total cost) expresses profit as a percentage of the total production cost of a product.
- Profit margin (or profit on sales), on the other hand, expresses profit as a percentage of the selling price of a product.

e.g

Illustration 2 – Costing for job and batch costing

Jetprint Ltd specialises in printing advertising leaflets and is in the process of preparing its price list. The most popular requirement is for a folded leaflet made from a single sheet of A4 paper. From past records and budgeted figures, the following data has been estimated for a typical batch of 10,000 leaflets:

Artwork	$65
Machine setting	4 hours @ $22 per hour
Paper	$12.50 per 1,000 sheets
Ink and consumables	$40
Printer's wages	4 hours at $8 per hour

Note: Printer's wages vary with volume.

General fixed overheads are $15,000 per period during which a total of 600 labour hours are expected to be worked.

The firm wishes to achieve 30% profit mark-up when 10,000 leaflets are produced and 30% profit margin when 20,000 leaflets are produced.

Required:

(a) Calculate the selling price for 10,000 leaflets.
(b) Calculate the selling price for 20,000 leaflets.

Solution

	(a) Producing 10,000 leaflets	**(b) Producing 20,000 leaflets**
	$	**$**
Artwork	65	65
Machine setting (4 hours @ $22)	88	88
Paper	125	250
Ink and consumables	40	80
Printer's wages ($8 per hour)	32	64
Marginal cost of sales	350	547
General fixed overheads (W1)	100	200

	$	$
Absorption cost of sales	450	747
Profit (W2) – to nearest $	135	320
Selling price	585	1,067

Workings:

(W1) Overhead absorption rate = $\frac{\$15,000}{600}$ = $25 per hour

For 10,000 leaflets, general fixed overheads = 4 hours x $25 = $100

For 20,000 leaflets, general fixed overheads = 8 hours x $25 = $200

(W2) If profit is 30% mark-up, profit = 30% x $450 = $135.

Therefore sales price = $450 + $135 = $585 for 10,000 leaflets.

If profit is 30% of sales **(30% profit margin)**, cost is 70% of sales. Profit is the difference between sales and cost of sales.

Therefore sales = $\frac{\text{Cost}}{0.7} = \frac{\$747}{0.7}$ = $1,067 for 20,000 leaflets.

Profit = $(1,067 x 747) = $320 for 20,000 leaflets.

Test your understanding 2

A business has a job costing system and its aim is to make a net profit of 25% on sales. The cost estimates for Job 264 are as follows:

Direct materials	50 kg @ $4 per kg
Direct labour	30 hours @ $9 per hour
Variable production overhead	$6 per direct labour hour

Fixed production overheads are budgeted as $80,000 and are absorbed on the basis of direct labour hours. The total budgeted direct labour hours for the period are 20,000.

Other overheads are recovered at the rate of $40 per job.

Calculate the price that should be quoted for Job 264.

3 Simple process costing

The details of process costs and units are recorded in a process account which shows (in very general terms) the materials, labour and overheads input to the process and the materials output at the end of the process.

e.g

Illustration 3 – Simple process costing

The details relating to Process 1 are shown in the Process 1 Account as follows.

Process 1 Account

	Units	$		Units	$
Raw materials	1,000	10,000			
Direct labour		8,000			
Departmental overheads		6,000	Output transferred to Process 2	1,000	24,000
	1,000	24,000		1,000	24,000

$$\text{Average cost per unit} = \frac{\text{Cost of production}}{\text{Expected or normal output}}$$

Costs of production = $24,000

Expected or normal output = 1,000 units

Average cost per unit in Process 1 = $\frac{24,000}{1,000}$ = $24 per unit

Test your understanding 3

Process 2 Account

	Units	$		Units	$
Input transferred from Process 1	1,000				
Additional raw materials		5,000			
Direct labour		4,000			
Departmental overheads		3,000	Output transferred to Process 3	1,000	
	1,000			1,000	

Calculate the average cost per unit in Process 2 and complete the Process 2 Account shown above.

4 Process costing with losses and gains

4.1 Normal losses

Sometimes in a process, the total of the input units may differ from the total of the output units. This is quite normal and usually happens when there are losses or gains in the process.

- Losses may occur due to the evaporation or wastage of materials and this may be an expected part of the process.
- Losses may sometimes be sold and generate a revenue which is generally referred to as scrap proceeds or scrap value.
- Normal loss is the loss that is expected in a process and it is often expressed as a percentage of the materials input to the process.

e.g

Illustration 4 – Process costing with normal losses

If 1,000 units are input into a process at a cost of $1,800 and normal loss is 10% of input, the average cost per unit is calculated as follows.

$$\textbf{Average cost per unit} = \frac{\textbf{Total cost of inputs}}{\textbf{Units input – Normal loss}}$$

Where:

Total cost of inputs = $1,800

Units input = 1,000 units

Normal loss = 10% of 1,000 units = 100 units

$$\text{Average cost per unit} = \frac{\$1{,}800}{1{,}000 - 100}$$

$$= \frac{\$1{,}800}{900} = \$2 \text{ per unit}$$

4.2 Normal loss and scrap value

If normal loss is sold as scrap it is not given a cost but the revenue is used to reduce the input costs of the process.

- If normal loss is sold as scrap then the formula for calculating the average cost of the units output from a process is modified as follows.

$$\textbf{Average cost per unit} = \frac{\textbf{Total cost of inputs – Scrap value of normal loss}}{\textbf{Units input – Normal loss}}$$

- If normal loss has a scrap value, it is valued in the process account at this value.

- If normal loss does not have a scrap value, it is valued in the process account as $Nil.

e.g

Illustration 5 – Process costing with normal losses and scrap

1,000 units are input into a process at a cost of $1,800 and normal loss is 10% of input. Scrap units are sold for $0.90 each.

The scrap proceeds of the 100 normal loss units will be $90. The average cost per unit is calculated as follows.

$$\text{Average cost per unit} = \frac{\$1,800 - \$90}{1000 - 100}$$

$$= \frac{\$1,710}{900} = \$1.90 \text{ per unit}$$

You can see how the average cost per unit falls from $2 to $1.90 when the normal loss units are sold as scrap.

e.g

Illustration 6 – Process costing with normal losses and scrap

The following data relates to Process 1.

Materials input – 1,000 units costing $10,000
Labour costs – $8,000
Departmental overheads – $6,000
Normal loss is 4% of input and is sold as scrap for $12 per unit.

Required:

Calculate the average cost per unit in Process 1 and complete the process account and the scrap account.

Process 1 Account

	Units	$		Units	$
Raw materials			Normal loss		
Direct labour					
Departmental overheads			Transfer to Finished goods		

Average cost per unit in Process 1 = $ ______

Scrap account

	$		$
Process 1		Cash	
	______		______
	______		______

Solution

Process 1 Account

	Units	$		Units	$
Raw materials	1,000	10,000	Normal loss (W1)	40	480
Direct labour		8,000			
Departmental overheads		6,000	Transfer to Finished goods (W3)	960	23,520
	1,000	24,000		1,000	24,000

Average cost per unit in Process 1 (W2) = $ [ ]

Scrap account

	$		$
Process 1 (W1)	480	Cash	480
	480		480

Workings

(W1)
Normal loss = 4% x 1,000 = 40 units
Scrap value of normal loss = 40 x $12 = $480
This amount is debited to the scrap account and credited to the process account.

(W2)

$$\text{Average cost per unit} = \frac{\text{Total cost of inputs} - \text{Scrap value of normal loss}}{\text{Units input} - \text{Normal loss}}$$

$$\text{Average cost per unit} = \frac{\$24{,}000 - \$480}{1{,}000 - 40}$$

$$= \frac{\$23{,}520}{960} = \$24.50 \text{ per unit}$$

(W3)

Units transferred to finished goods are valued at the average cost per unit, $24.50.

Value of goods transferred = 960 x $24.50 = $23,520

4.3 Abnormal losses and gains

Normal loss is the expected loss in a process. Normal gain is the expected gain in a process. If the loss or the gain in a process is different to what we are expecting (i.e. differs from the normal loss or gain), then we have an abnormal loss or an abnormal gain in the process.

- The costs of abnormal losses and gains are not absorbed into the cost of good output but are shown as losses and gains in the process account.
- Abnormal loss and gain units are valued at the same cost as units of good output.

e.g

Illustration 7 – Process costing with losses and gains

(i) If 1,000 units are input into a process at a cost of $1,800 and normal loss is 10% of input and actual output is 860 units, we can calculate the abnormal loss or gain as follows.

Input = 1,000 units

Expected output = 90% of 1,000 units = 900 units

Actual output = 860 units

Therefore, abnormal loss = expected output – actual output = 900 units – 860 units = 40 units.

Input = actual output + normal loss + abnormal loss

1,000 = 860 + 100 + 40 (Bal.fig)

(ii) However, if actual output had been 960 units then we would have had an abnormal gain.

Abnormal gain = actual output – expected output = 960 units – 900 units = 60 units.

Input = actual output + normal loss + abnormal gain

1,000 = 960 + 100 + (60)

Whenever you start a process-costing question you should begin by calculating the normal loss or gain and then any abnormal loss or gain.

e.g

Illustration 8 – Process costing with losses and gains

The following data relates to Process 1.

Materials input – 1,000 units costing $10,000
Labour costs – $8,000
Departmental overheads – $6,000
Normal loss is 4% of input and is sold as scrap for $12 per unit.
Actual output = 944 units

Required:

Calculate the average cost per unit in Process 1 and complete the process account, abnormal gains and losses account and the scrap account shown below.

Process 1 Account

	Units	$		Units	$
Raw materials			Normal loss		
Direct labour					
Departmental overheads			Transfer to Finished goods		

Average cost per unit in Process 1 = $ ______

Abnormal gains and losses account

	$		$
	____		____
	____		____

Scrap account

	$		$
Process 1		Cash	
	____		____
	____		____

Solution

Process 1 Account

	Units	$		Units	$
Raw materials	1,000	10,000	Normal loss (W1)	40	480
Direct labour		8,000	Abnormal loss (W3)	16	392
Departmental overheads		6,000	Transfer to Finished goods (W4)	944	23,128
	1,000	24,000		1,000	24,000

Average cost per unit in Process 1 (W2) = $ 24.50

Abnormal gains and losses account

	$		$
Process 1(w3)	392	Scrap (16 x $12)	192
		Income statement	200
	392	1,000	392

Scrap account

	$		$
Process 1 (W3) (normal loss)	480	Cash (56 x $12)	672
Abnormal gain and loss	192		
	672		672

Workings:

(W1)

Normal loss = 4% x 1,000 = 40 units
Scrap value of normal loss = 40 x $12 = $480

(W2)

Expected output = 1,000 – 40 = 960 units
Actual output = 944 units
Abnormal loss = exected output – actual output = 960 – 944 = 16 units

Abnormal loss is valued at the same cost as good output, i.e. $24.50 per unit.

(W3)

Abnormal loss value = 16 x $24.50 = $392

(W4)

Value of units transferred to finished goods = 944 x $24.50 = $23,128

4.4 Suggested approach for answering normal loss, abnormal loss/gain questions

1 Draw the process account, and enter the inputs – units and values.

2 Enter the normal loss – units and value (if any).

3 Enter the good output – units only.

4 Balance the units. Balancing figure is abnormal loss or gain.

5 Calculate the average cost per unit:

$$\frac{\text{Total cost of inputs – Scrap value of normal loss}}{\text{Units input – Normal loss}}$$

6 Value normal loss at scrap value (or at $0 if it does not have a scrap value).

7 Value the good output and abnormal loss or gain at this average cost per unit.

Test your understanding 4

W&B Ltd produce a breakfast cereal that involves several processes. At each stage in the process, ingredients are added, until the final stage of production when the cereal is boxed up ready to be sold.

In Process 2, W&B Ltd have initiated a quality control inspection. This inspection takes place BEFORE any new ingredients are added in to Process 2. The inspection is expected to yield a normal loss of 5% of the input from Process 1. These losses are sold as animal fodder for $1 per kg.

The following information is for Process 2 for the period just ended:

	Units	$
Transfer from Process 1	500 kg	750
Material added in Process 2	300 kg	300
Labour	200 hrs	800
Overheads	–	500
Actual output	755 kg	–

Prepare the process account, abnormal loss and gain account, and scrap account for Process 2 for the period just ended.

5 Work-in-progress (WIP) and equivalent units (EUs)

5.1 WIP

At the end of an accounting period there may be some units that have entered a production process but the process has not been completed. These units are called closing WIP (or WIP) units.

- If we assume that there is no opening WIP, then the output at the end of a period will consist of the following:
  - fully-processed units
  - part-processed units (closing WIP).
- Closing WIP units become the opening WIP units in the next accounting period.
- It would not be fair to allocate a full unit cost to part-processed units and so we need to use the concept of EUs which spreads out the process costs of a period fairly between the fully- processed and part-processed units.

5.2 Concept of EUs

Process costs are allocated to units of production on the basis of EUs.

- The idea behind this concept is that a part-processed unit can be expressed as a proportion of a fully-completed unit.
- For example, if 100 units are exactly half-way through the production process, they are effectively equal to 50 fully-completed units. Therefore the 100 part-processed units can be regarded as being equivalent to 50 fully-completed units or 50 EUs.

e.g

Illustration 9 – WIP and EUs

Department X worked on only 2 units last month. The first unit was started and completed during the month but the second unit was only 50% complete at the end of the month. The total cost incurred during the month was $30.

If we apply the concept of EUs, we have one fully-processed unit and one half-processed unit. We therefore have one-and-a-half EUs. The total process costs for the period must therefore be shared out between one-and-a-half EUs as follows.

Average cost per EU = $30/1.5EU = $20 per EU

The fully processed unit is therefore valued at $20 and the part-processed unit is consequently valued at $10 (50% of $20).

e.g

Illustration 10 – WIP and EUs

For process 1 in ABC Co the following is relevant for the latest period:

Period costs	$4,440
Input	800 units
Output	600 fully-worked units and 200 units only 70% complete

There were no process losses.

Statement of EUs			
	Output	**%**	**EUs**
Fully-worked units	600	100%	600
Closing WIP	200	70%	140
Total	800		740
Costs			$4,440
Cost per EU			$6

Cost per EU = $4,440/740 units = $6 per unit

The Process 1 account can be completed as follows:

Process 1 Account					
	Units	$		Units	$
Input	800	4,440	Transferred to next process (600 x $6)	600	3,600
			WIP(140 EUs x $6)	200	840
	800	4,440		800	4,440

5.3 Different degrees of completion

For most processes the material is input at the start of the process, so it is only the addition of labour and overheads that will be incomplete at the end of the period.

- This means that the material cost should be spread over all units, but conversion costs should be spread over the EUs.
- This can be achieved using an expanded Statement of EUs which separates out the materials and labour costs.
- Note that the term conversion costs is often used to describe the addition of labour and overheads in a process.

e.g

Illustration 11 – WIP and EUs

For Process 1 in LJK Ltd the following is relevant for the latest period:

Material costs	500 units @ $8 per unit
Labour	$2,112
Overheads	150% of labour cost
Output:	400 fully-worked units, transferred to Process 2. 100 units only 40% complete with respect to conversion, but 100% complete with respect to materials.

There were no process losses.

The value of fully-worked units and WIP are calculated as follows:

Statement of EUs					
	Output	Materials		Conversion	
		%	EUs	%	EUs
Fully-worked units	400	100%	400	100%	400
WIP	100	100%	100	40%	40
Total	500		500		440
Costs			$4,000		$(2,112 + 3,168) = $5,280
Cost per EU			$8		$12

The value of fully-worked units is (W1) $ 8,000

The value of WIP is (W2) $ 1,280

Workings

(W1)

Fully-worked units are valued at $20 per unit ($8 + $12).

400 x $20 = $8,000

(W2)

WIP is valued as follows:

Materials	100 units x $8 =	$800
Conversion	40 units x $12 =	$480
Total WIP value	=	$800 + $480 = $1,280

Test your understanding 5

A firm operates a process costing system. Details of Process 2 for Period 1 are as follows.

During the period 8,250 units were received from the previous process at a value of $453,750, labour and overheads were $350,060 and material introduced was $24,750.

At the end of the period the closing WIP was 1,600 units which were 100% complete in respect of materials, and 60% complete in respect of labour and overheads. The balance of units was transferred to Finished goods.

There was no opening WIP.

Calculate the cost per EU, the value of finished goods and closing WIP.

Statement of EUs					
	Output	Materials		Conversion	
		%	EUs	%	EUs
Fully-worked					
Closing WIP					
Total units					
Costs:					
Total cost					
Cost per EU					

The value of finished goods is $

The value of WIP is $

6 Weighted average costing of production

Until now, we have assumed that there has been no opening WIP. In reality, this is unlikely to be the case.

- Work remaining in process (WIP) and transfers out of a process (fully-completed units) can be valued on different bases: weighted average method and the FIFO method.
- These methods are similar to the valuation methods studied when we looked at materials in an earlier chapter.

- In the weighted average method opening inventory values are added to current costs to provide an overall average cost per unit.
- No distinction is made between units in process at the start of a period and those added during the period.

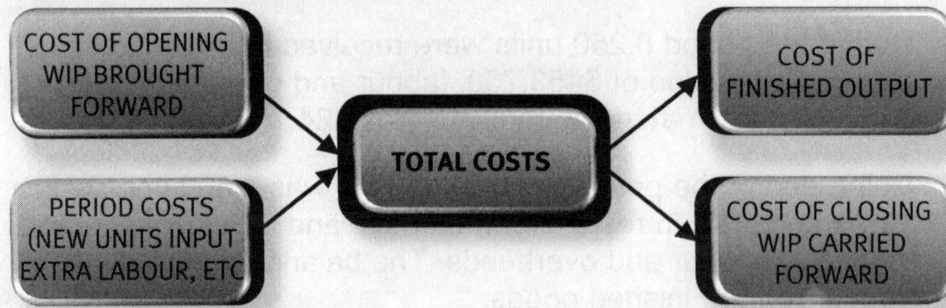

e.g

Illustration 12 – Weighted average costing of production

BR Ltd makes a product requiring several successive processes. Details of the first process for August are as follows:

Opening WIP:	400 units
Degree of completion:	
Materials (valued at $19,880)	100 %
Conversion (valued at $3,775)	25 %
Units transferred to Process 2	1,700 units
Closing WIP	300 units
Degree of completion:	
Materials	100 %
Conversion	50 %
Costs incurred in the period:	
Material	$100,000
Conversion	$86,000

There were no process losses.

Required:

Prepare the process account for August using the weighted average method.

Solution

Process 1 Account

	Units	$		Units	$
Opening WIP	400	23,655	Transferred to Process 2	1,700	184,394
Materials	1,600	100,000	Closing WIP	300	25,261
Conversion		86,000			
	2,000	209,655		2,000	209,655

Statement of EUs					
	Output	Materials		Conversion	
		%	EUs	%	EUs
Transferred to Process 2	1,700	100%	1,700	100%	1,700
Closing WIP	300	100%	300	50%	150
Total units	2,000		2,000		1,850
Costs: Opening WIP			19,880		3,775
Period			100,000		86,000
Total cost			119,880		89,775
Cost per EU			$59.94		$48.527

Valuation of transfers to Process 2:

Materials	= (1,700 x $59.94)	=	$101,898
Conversion	= (1,700 x $48.527)	=	$82,496
Total		=	$184,394

Valuation of Closing WIP:

Materials	= (300 x $59.94)	=	$17,982
Conversion	= (150 x $48.527)	=	$7,279
Total		=	$25,261

Test your understanding 6

A business makes one product that passes through a single process. The business uses weighted average costing. The details of the process for the last period are as follows:

Materials	$98,000
Labour	$60,000
Production overheads	$39,000
Units added to the process	1,000

There were 200 units of opening WIP which are valued as follows:

Materials	$22,000
Labour	$6,960
Production overheads	$3,000

There were 300 units of closing WIP fully complete as to materials but only 60% complete for labour and 50% complete for overheads.

Calculate the following:

(a) The value of the completed output for the period.
(b) The value of the closing WIP.

7 FIFO costing of production

In the weighted average method opening inventory values are added to current costs to provide an overall average cost per unit. With FIFO, opening WIP units are distinguished from those units added in the period.

- With FIFO it is assumed that the opening WIP units are completed first.
- This means that the process costs in the period must be allocated between:
  - opening WIP units
  - units started and completed in the period (fully-worked units)
  - closing WIP units.
- This also means that if opening WIP units are 75% complete with respect to materials and 40% complete with repect to labour, only 25% 'more work' will need to be carried out with respect to materials and 60% with respect to labour.

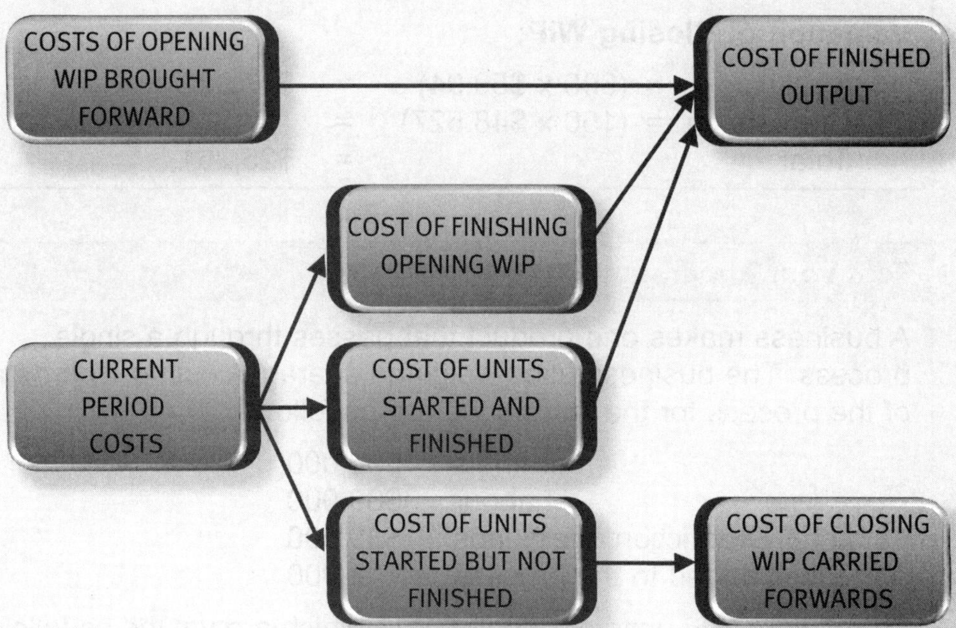

- This is a very important point to remember when calculating the EUs of materials and conversion costs and is demonstrated in the following illustration.

e.g

Illustration 13 – FIFO costing of production

BR Ltd makes a product requiring several successive processes. Details of the first process for August are as follows:

Opening WIP:	400 units
Degree of completion:	
Materials (valued at $19,880)	100%
Conversion (valued at $3,775)	25%
Units transferred to Process 2	1,700 units
Closing WIP	300 units
Degree of completion:	
Materials	100%
Conversion	50%
Costs incurred in the period:	
Material	$100,000
Conversion	$86,000

There were no process losses.

Required:

Prepare the process account for August using the FIFO method.

Solution

Process 1 Account

	Units	$		Units	$
Opening WIP	400	23,655	Transferred to Process 2	1,700	183,534
Materials	1,600	100,000	Closing WIP	300	26,121
Conversion		86,000			
	2,000	209,655		2,000	209,655

Statement of EUs

	Output	Materials		Conversion	
		%	EUs	%	EUs
Opening WIP completed	400	0	0	75	300
Fully-worked in process	1,300	100	1,300	100	1,300
Closing WIP	300	100	300	50	150
Total	2,000		1,600		1,750
Costs			$100,000		$86,000
Cost per EU			$62.50		$49.143

Value of units passed to Process 2:

Opening WIP value from last period = $19,880 + $3,775 = $23,655
Opening WIP completed this period:
Conversion only = 300 x $49.143 = $14,743

Fully-worked current period

Materials	= 1,300 x $62.50	=	$81,250
Conversion	= 1,300 x $49.143	=	$63,886
Total		=	$145,136
Total value of units transferred to next process		=	$183,534

Expandable text

Additional notes for solution to Illustration 13

Materials

Units transferred to Process 2	1,700
Closing WIP	300
Opening WIP	(400)
Material units added in period	1,600

Of the 1,600 units added in the process, 1,300 (units added less closing WIP) were started and finished in the period.

Opening WIP

Note that the opening WIP is 100% complete with respect to materials and therefore no further work or costs are involved in completing the opening WIP units.

Similarly, the opening WIP is 25% complete with respect to conversion costs and therefore 75% of the conversion work/costs are still outstanding.

Costs to complete opening WIP and fully-worked units

Each unit started and finished in the period costs $(62.50 + 49.143) = $111.643

1,300 units were fully-worked in the process = 1,300 x $111.643 = $145,136

Costs to complete 400 units of opening WIP = 300 units (conversion EUs) x $49.143 = $14,743

Costs to complete units transferred to Process 2

Cost of completing 1,700 units (1,300 fully-worked plus 400 opening WIP) = $145,136 + $ 14,743 = $159,879

Total cost of units transferred to Process 2 = cost of completing 1,700 units plus costs already incurred in opening WIP, i.e. $(19,880 + 3,775) = $23,655

Therefore, cost of 1,700 units transferred to Process 2 = $159,879 + $23,655 = $183,534

Value of closing WIP

Value of closing WIP = 300 EUs x $62.50 = $18,750 (materials) plus 150 x $49.143 = $7,371.45 = $26,121.45

Test your understanding 7

AXL Ltd operates a process costing system. Details of Process 1 are as follows.

All materials used are added at the beginning of the process. Labour costs and production overhead costs are incurred evenly as the product goes through the process. Production overheads are absorbed at a rate of 100% of labour costs.

The following details are relevant to production in the period:

	Units	Materials	Labour and production overheads
Opening inventory	200	100% complete	75% complete
Closing inventory	100	100% complete	50% complete

Opening inventory

Costs associated with these opening units are $1,800 for materials. In addition $4,000 had been accumulated for labour and overhead costs.

Period costs

Costs incurred during the period were:

Materials	$19,000
Labour costs	$19,000

During the period, 2,000 units were passed to Process 2. There were no losses.

The company uses a FIFO method for valuing process costs.

Calculate the total value of the units transferred to Process 2.

8 Losses made part way through production

In the examples we have looked at so far, the losses have occurred at the end of the process. It is possible that losses (or gains) could be identified part way through a process. In such a case, EUs must be used to assess the extent to which costs were incurred at the time at which the loss was identified.

e.g

Illustration 14 – Losses made part way through production

BLT manufactures chemicals and has a normal loss of 15% of material input. Information for February is as follows:

Material input 200 kg costing $5 per kg
Labour and overheads $4,100
Transfers to finished goods 160 kg
Losses are identified when the process is 40% complete
No opening or closing WIP.

Required:

Prepare the process account for February.

Solution

1 Normal loss is 15% of input, i.e. 15% x 200 kg = 30 kg
Actual loss is 40 kg. Thus abnormal loss is 10 kg.

2 Calculate the expected number of EUs of output (where expected output is actual finished units plus the abnormal loss).

EUs of output

	Total	EUs Materials	EUs Conversion
Finished units	160	160	160
Abnormal loss	10	10	4
Total EUs	170	170	164

3 Process costs:

	$
Materials: 200 x $5	1,000
Labour and overhead	4,100
	5,100

4 Calculate the cost per EU (used to value finished units and abnormal losses).

Materials $\frac{\$1,000}{170} = \$5.88$

Conversion $\frac{\$4,100}{164} = \$25$

Total cost of completed unit = $(5.88 + 25) = $30.88

5 Write up the process account and normal and abnormal loss accounts.

Process account

	Kg	$		Kg	$
Materials	200	1,000	Normal loss	30	-
Labour and overheads		4,100	Finished goods (W1)	160	4,941
			Abnormal loss (W2)	10	159
	200	5,100		200	5,100

Workings

(W1) 160 x $30.88 = $4,941
(W2) Abnormal loss (10 x $5.88) + (4 x $25) = $159

Normal loss account

	Kg	$		Kg	$
Process account	30	-			

Abnormal loss account

	Kg	$		Kg	$
Process account	10	159	Income statement		159
	10	159			159

Normal and abnormal losses (or gains) must be recorded and valued. Remember that abnormal losses (or gains) do not affect the cost per EUs calculation.

9 Joint and by-products

9.1 Introduction

The nature of process costing is such that processes often produce more than one product. These additional products may be described as either joint products or by-products. Essentially joint products are both main products whereas by-products are incidental to the main products.

9.2 Joint products

Joint products are two or more products separated in the course of processing, each having a sufficiently high saleable value to merit recognition as a main product.

- Joint products include products produced as a result of the oil-refining process, for example, petrol and paraffin.
- Petrol and paraffin have similar sales values and are therefore equally important (joint) products.

9.3 By-products

By-products are outputs of some value produced incidentally in manufacturing something else (main products).

- By-products, such as sawdust and bark, are secondary products from the timber industry (where timber is the main or principal product from the process).
- Sawdust and bark have a relatively low sales value compared to the timber which is produced and are therefore classified as by-products.

10 Treatment of joint costs

10.1 Accounting treatment of joint products

The distinction between joint and by-products is important because the accounting treatment of joint products and by-products differs.

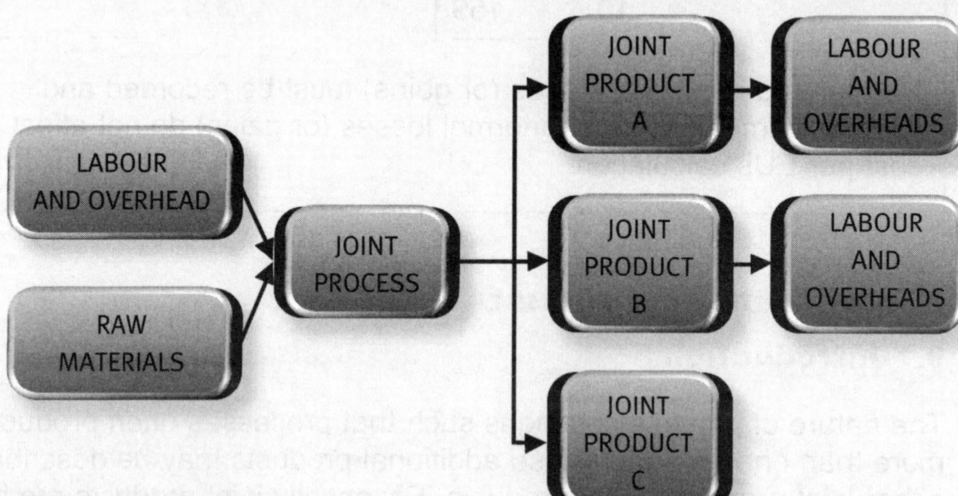

- Joint process costs occur before the split-off point. They are sometimes called pre-separation costs or common costs.
- The joint costs need to be apportioned between the joint products at the split-off point to obtain the cost of each of the products in order to value closing inventory and cost of sales.

- The basis of apportionment of joint costs to products is usually one of the following:
  - sales value of production (also known as market value)
  - production units
  - net realisable value.

e.g

Illustration 15 – Treatment of joint costs

The following information is relevant for a production process for Period 1:

	$
Direct material cost	10,000
Direct labour cost	5,000
Overheads	3,000
Total cost	18,000

The process produces joint products A and B, which are then sold at the prices given below. The output figure represents all of the output from the process.

	Product A	**Product B**
Units of output	2,000	8,000
Price per unit	$5	$2.50

Required:

Calculate the cost of sales, and gross profit for products A and B assuming:

(i) joint costs are apportioned by market value

(ii) joint costs are apportioned by production units.

Solution

(a) Market value basis

	Product A	**Product B**	**Total**
Sales value	$10,000	$20,000	$30,000
Joint costs apportioned (see working)	$6,000	$12,000	$18,000
Gross profit	$4,000	$8,000	$12,000

Working

Total joint costs = $(10,000 + 5,000 + 3,000) = $18,000

Joint costs apportioned to Product A = $\frac{10,000}{30,000}$ x $18,000 = $6,000

Joint costs apportioned to Product B = $\frac{20,000}{30,000}$ x $18,000 = $12,000

(b) Production units basis

	Product A	Product B	Total
Sales value	$10,000	$20,000	$30,000
Apportioned joint costs (see working)	$3,600	$14,400	$18,000
Gross profit	$6,400	$5,600	$12,000

Working

Total output units = 2,000 + 8,000 = 10,000

Joint costs allocated to Product A = $\frac{2,000}{10,000}$ x $18,000 = $3,600

Joint costs allocated to Product B = $\frac{8,000}{10,000}$ x $18,000 = $14,400

10.2 Accounting treatment of by-products

As by-products have an insignificant value the accounting treatment is different.

- The costs incurred in the process are shared between the joint products alone. The by-products do not pick up a share of the costs, like normal loss.
- The sales value of the by-product at the split-off point is treated as a reduction in costs instead of an income, again just the same as normal loss.
- If the by-product has no known value at the split-off point but does have a value after further processing, the net income of the by-product is used to reduce the costs of the process.

Net income (or net realisable value) =
Final sales value – Further processing costs.

e.g

Illustration 16 – Treatment of joint costs

Process M produces two joint products (A and B) and one by-product (C). Joint costs are apportioned on the basis of sales units.

The following information is relevant.

	Product A	Product B	Total
Sales units	2,000	8,000	10,000
Apportioned joint cost	$3,600	$14,400	$18,000

It is now possible to sell by-product C after further processing for $0.50 per unit. The futher processing costs are $0.20 per unit. 2,000 units of by-product C are produced.

Required:

How are the joint costs of $18,000 apportioned when by-product C is produced?

Solution

With the production of by-product C, joint costs are reduced by the net income from the process.

Net income from process = $(0.5 – 0.2) x 2,000 = $600

Joint costs are now $17,400 ($18,000 – $600)

	Product A	**Product B**	**Total**
Sales units	2,000	8,000	10,000
Apportioned joint costs	$3,480	$13,920	$17,400

Total output units = 2,000 + 8,000 = 10,000

Joint costs allocated to Product A = $\frac{2,000}{10,000}$ x $17,400 = $3,400

Joint costs allocated to Product B = $\frac{8,000}{10,000}$ x $17,400 = $13,920

Test your understanding 8

A company operates a manufacturing process which produces joint products A and B, and by-product C.

Manufacturing costs for a period total $272,926, incurred in the manufacture of:

Product A	16,000 kgs (selling price $6.10 per kg)
Product B	53,200 kgs (selling price $7.50 per kg)
Product C	2,770 kgs (selling price $1.20 per kg)

Product B requires further processing after separation from the other two products. This costs a total of $201,930.

Product C also requires further processing to make it saleable, and this costs $0.40 per kg.

Calculate the total profit earned by Products A and B in the period, using the net realisable values (net income) to apportion joint costs.

11 Process accounts for joint and by-products

You may be required to deal with joint and by-products when preparing process accounts. Joint products should be treated as 'normal' output from a process. The treatment of by-products in process accounts is slightly more complicated.

- There is no information value in calculating a cost for a by-product or measuring its profitability. The accounting treatment of a by-product in process costing is similar to the treatment of normal loss.
- The by-product income could be treated as additional income in the income statement. However, it is more usual to deduct the by-product income from the cost of the process that produces it.
- The by-product income is therefore credited to the process account and debited to a by-product account.
- To calculate the EUs in a period, by-products (like normal loss) are zero EUs.
- When by-products are produced, the cost per EU of direct materials is calculated as follows:

$$\frac{\text{Material costs incurred} - \text{Scrap value of normal loss} - \text{Sales value of by-product}}{\text{EUs for materials}}$$

- We can now consolidate what we have learned in this chapter by looking at how joint and by-products are recorded in a process account.

e.g

Illustration 17 – Process accounts for joint and by-products

The output from a process consists of two joint products, JP1 and JP2, and a by-product BP. The following data relates to November:

Materials input (18,500 units): cost	$134,000
Conversion costs	$89,500
Normal loss (1,000 units): scrap value	$500
Abnormal loss: (500 units)	$7,000
Output:	
By-product BP (2,000 units): sales value	$6,000
Joint-product JP1: 10,000 units	
Joint-product JP2: 5,000 units	

Required:

Prepare the process account for November, assuming that the common costs are apportioned to joint products on the basis of output units.

Solution

	Units	$	$
Direct materials	18,500		134,000
Conversion costs	–		89,500
	18,500		223,500
Scrap value of normal loss	1,000	500	
By-product sales income	2,000	6,000	
Abnormal loss	500	7,000	
	3,500		13,500
Cost of finished output	15,000		210,000

If common costs are apportioned on a units basis, the process account would be:

Process account

	Units	$		Units	$
Direct materials	18,500	134,000	Normal loss	1,000	500
Conversion costs		89,500	Abnormal loss	500	7,000
			By-product BP	2,000	6,000
			Joint product JP1	10,000	140,000
			Joint product JP2	5,000	70,000
	18,500	223,500		18,500	223,500

Working

	JP1	JP2	Total
Units produced	10,000	5,000	15,000
Cost per unit ($210,000/15,000)	$14	$14	
Apportionment of common costs	$140,000	$70,000	$210,000

Test your understanding 9

The following information relates to a company that produces two joint products, X and Y and one by-product, Z, in a process.

Data for December

Materials input (43,750 units): cost	$266,500
Conversion costs	$105,000
Abnormal loss: (3,750 units)	$37,500
Joint products output:	
Joint-product X: 18,000 units	$180,000
Joint-product Y: 15,000 units	$150,000

Normal loss is 1,000 units. Units lost have a scrap value of $1 per unit.

6,000 units of by-product Z are produced. Each unit is sold for $0.50 per unit.

Prepare the process account for December.

Chapter summary

Joint and by-products

- Joint products are two or more products separated in processing, each having sufficiently high saleable value
- By-products are outputs of some value produced at the same time as joint products

Job costing

Form of specific order costing used when customer orders a specific job to be done. Each job is priced separately and is unique.

DIFFERENT TYPES OF PRODUCTION

Batch costing

Form of specific order costing which is very similar to job costing. Each batch is a separately identifiable cost unit which is given a batch number.

Simple process costing

Costing method used when mass production of many identical products takes place, e.g, manufacture of bars of chocolate or cans of soup.

All products manufactured are indistinguishable from each other and so an average cost per unit is calculated for each process.

Process costing with gains and losses

- Normal loss = expected loss. Value is $0 unless it has a scrap value.
- Abnormal loss is extra unexpected loss.
- Abnormal gain occurs when actual loss is less than expected.
- Abnormal loss and gain are valued at same value as good output.

Process costing with opening WIP

Weighted average method does not distinguish between opening WIP units and units added in process. FIFO method distinguishes between opening WIP, units started and finished in process ('fully- worked' units) and closing WIP.

Process costing with WIP and EUs

Not fair to allocate full unit cost to a part-processed unit. Idea behind the concept of EUs is that a part-processed unit can be expressed as a proportion of a fully- completed unit.

Process costs are allocated to units in a process on the basis of EUs.

Test your understanding answers

Test your understanding 1

Job costing is customer-driven with customers ordering a specific job to be done. It is also possible for production to be completed within a single accounting period and therefore the correct answer is C.

Test your understanding 2

	$
Direct materials 50 kg x $4	200
Direct labour 30 hours x $9	270
Variable production overhead 30 x $6	180
Fixed overheads $80,000/20,000 x 30	120
Other overheads	40
Total cost (75%)	810
Profit $810.00 x 25/75	270
Job cost (100%)	1,080

Note: a net profit of 25% on sales means that total cost represents 75% of the job cost and the profit represents 25% of the job cost. The profit can therefore be calculated as 25/75ths of the total cost. Similarly, if a net profit of 30% on sales (or a 30% margin) were applicable, the total cost would represent 70% of the job cost and the profit would represent 30% of the job cost and could be calculated as 30/70ths of the total cost.

Test your understanding 3

Average cost per unit = $\frac{\text{Costs of production}}{\text{Expected or normal output}}$

Costs of production = $(24,000 + 5,000 + 4,000 + 3,000) = $36,000

Expected or normal output = 1,000 units

Average cost per unit in Process 1= $\frac{\$36,000}{1,000}$ = $36 per unit

Process 2 Account

	Units	$		Units	$
Transfer from Process 1	1,000	24,000			
Additional raw materials		5,000			
Direct labour		4,000			
Departmental overheads		3,000	Transfer to Process 3	1,000	36,000
	1,000	36,000		1,000	36,000

Note that the units completed in Process 1 form the opening WIP in Process 2 and that the units completed in Process 2 form the opening WIP in Process 3.

Test your understanding 4

Process 2 Account

	Kg	$		Kg	$
Transfer from Process 1	500	750	Normal loss	25	25
Additional raw materials	300	300	Finished goods	755	2,265
Direct labour		800	Abnormal loss	20	60
Departmental overheads		500			
	800	2,350		800	2,350

Normal loss = 5% of transfer from Process 1 = 500 kg x 0.05 = 25 kg

Scrap value of normal loss = 25 kg x $1 = $25

Cost per unit = ($2,350 – $25) / (800 kg – 25 kg) = $3

Abnormal gains and losses account

	$		$
Process 1	60.00	Scrap (20 $1)	20.00
		Income statement	40.00
	60.00		60.00

Scrap account

	$		$
Process 1 (normal loss)	25.00	Cash (45 $1)	45.00
Abnormal gain and loss	20.00		
	45.00		45.00

Test your understanding 5

Statement of EUs					
	Output	Materials		Conversion	
		%	EUs	%	EUs
Fully-worked	6,650	100	6,650	100	6,650
Closing WIP	1,600	100	1,600	60	960
Total units			8,250		
Costs:			$453,750 $24,750		$350,060
Total cost			$478,500		$350,060
Cost per EU			$58		$46

The value of finished goods is (W1) $ 691,600

The value of WIP is (W2) $ 136,960

Workings

(W1)
Value of finished goods:
Materials: 6,650 x $58 = $385,700
Conversion: 6,650 x $46 = $305,900
Total = $691,600

(W2)
Value of closing WIP:

Materials: 1,600 x $58	=	$92,800
Conversion: 960 x $46	=	$44,160
Total	=	$136,960

Test your understanding 6

(a)

	%	Materials EU	%	Labour EU	%	Overheads EU
Output	100	900	100	900	100	900
Closing WIP	100	300	60	180	50	150
Total EUs		1,200		1,080		1,050
		$		$		$
Costs – period		98,000		60,000		39,000
Opening WIP		22,000		6,960		3,000
Total costs		120,000		66,960		42,000
Cost per unit (Total costs/total EUs)		$100		$62		$40

Value of completed output = 900 x $(100 + 62 + 40) = $181,800

(b)

		$
Materials	300 x $100	30,000
Labour	180 x $62	11,160
Overheads	150 x $40	6,000
Value of closing WIP		47,160

Test your understanding 7

Statement of EUs					
	Output	Materials		Conversion	
		%	EUs	%	EUs
Opening WIP completed	200	0	0	25	50
Fully-worked in process	1,800	100	1,800	100	1,800
Closing WIP	100	100	100	50	50
Total	2,100		1,900		1,900
Costs			$19,000		$19,000 + $19,000*= $38,000
Cost per EU			$10		$20

* Overheads are absorbed at 100% of labour cost.

Labour cost = $19,000, ∴ overheads = $19,000.

Value of units passed to Process 2:

Opening WIP value from last period	= $1,800 + $4,000	= $5,800
Opening WIP completed this period:		
Conversion only	= 50 x $20	= $1,000
Fully-worked current period		
Materials	= 1,800 x $10	= $18,000
Conversion	= 1,800 x $20	= $36,000
Total		= $54,000
Total value of units transferred to Process 2		**= $60,800**

Test your understanding 8

Net revenue from product C = $(1.2 – 0.4) = $0.80

Costs to apportion = Joint process costs – net revenue from product C
= $272,926 – (2,770 x $0.80)
= $270,710

	A	B	Total
	$	$	$
Revenue	97,600	399,000	496,600
Further processing costs	–	(201,930)	(201,930)

Net realisable values	97,600	197,070	294,670
Joint costs	(89,664)	(181,046)	(270,710)
Total profits	7,936	16,024	23,960

Total net realisable values = $(97,600 + 197,070) = $294,670

Joint costs apportioned to Product A $= \frac{97,600}{294,670} \times \$270,710 = \$89,664$

Joint costs apportioned to Product B $= \frac{197,070}{294,670} \times \$270,710 = \$181,046$

Test your understanding 9

Process account

	Units	$		Units	$
Direct materials	43,750	266,500	Normal loss (W1)	1,000	1,000
Conversion costs		105,000	Abnormal loss	3,750	37,500
			By-product Z (W2)	6,000	3,000
			Joint product X	18,000	180,000
			Joint product Y	15,000	150,000
	43,750	371,500		43,750	371,500

Workings:

(W1)
Scrap value of normal loss units = 1,000 x $1 = $1,000

(W2)
By-product Z value = 6,000 x $0.50 = $3,000

chapter

12

Service and operation costing

Chapter learning objectives

Upon completion of this chapter you will be able to:

- give examples of situations where the use of service/operation costing is appropriate
- illustrate, using simple numerical examples, suitable unit cost measures that may be used in different service/operation situations
- carry out service cost analysis in simple service industry situations using data supplied.

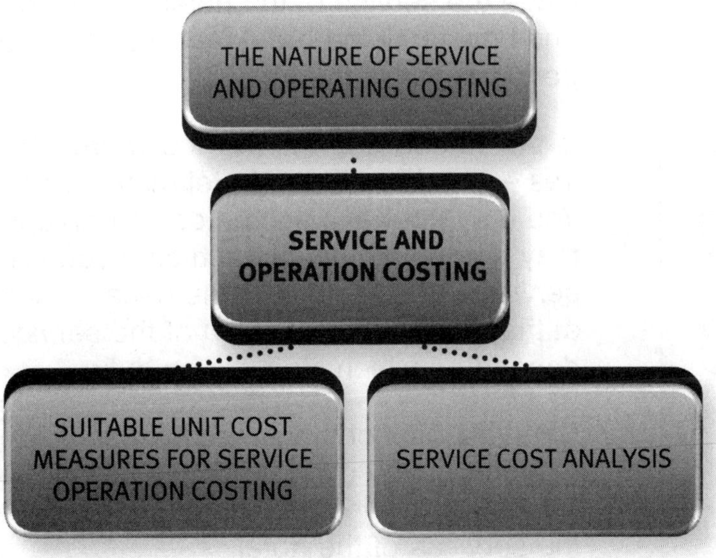

1 The nature of service and operation costing

1.1 Service costing

Service costing is used when an organisation or department provides a service. There are four main differences between the 'output' of service industries and the products of manufacturing industries.

- **Intangibility** – output is in the form of 'performance' rather than tangible ('touchable') goods.
- **Heterogeneity** – the nature and standard of the service will be variable due to the high human input.
- **Simultaneous production and consumption** – the service that you require cannot be inspected in advance of receiving it.
- **Perishability** – the services that you require cannot be stored.

e.g

Illustration 1 – The nature of service and operation costing

Examples of service industries include the following:

- hotel
- college
- hairdressers
- restaurant.

We can ask the following questions about, e.g. the hotel industry.

1 Is output in the form of performance?
Yes – the hotel provides a bed and possibly breakfast. You will judge the service of the hotel on how comfortable the bed was and how tasty the breakfast was. You cannot really 'touch' the performance of the hotel.

2 Is the standard of the service variable?
Yes – your stay at the hotel may vary each time you stay there. You may not have such a comfortable bed and your breakfast may not be very tasty each time you visit. The standard of service is therefore variable because lots of different staff work at the hotel – the standard of the service you receive may depend on which staff are on duty.

3 Can you inspect the services in advance of receiving them?
In general, you cannot sleep in a hotel bed or eat breakfast at the hotel until you have booked in and made a contract to buy the services of the hotel.

4 Can the hotel services be stored?
No! You cannot take your bed away with you, nor can you keep your breakfast – it must be eaten during the morning of your stay.

Test your understanding 1

List as many service industries that you can think of.

2 Suitable unit cost measures for service/operation costing

2.1 Unit cost measures for service costing

One of the main difficulties in service costing is the establishment of a suitable cost unit. In some situations it may be necessary to calculate a composite cost unit.

- A composite cost unit is more appropriate if a service is a function of two variables.
- Examples of composite cost units are as follows:
  - tonne-miles for haulage companies
  - patient-days for hospitals
  - passenger-miles for public transport companies
  - guest-days for hotel services.
- Alternatively, service organisations may use several different cost units to measure the different kinds of service that they are providing.
- The following cost units might be used by a hotel:

Service	**Cost unit**
Restaurant	Meals served
Function facilities	Hours

2.2 Cost per service unit

The total cost of providing a service will include labour, materials, expenses and overheads (the same as the costs associated with the products produced in manufacturing industry).

	$
Direct materials	X
Direct labour	X
Direct expenses	X
Overheads absorbed	X
TOTAL COST	XX

- In service costing, it is not uncommon for labour to be the only direct cost involved in providing a service and for overheads to make up most of the remaining total costs.
- In service costing it is sometimes necessary to classify costs as being fixed, variable or semi-variable. If costs are semi-variable, it is necessary to separate them into their fixed and variable constituents using the high/low method.
- The cost per service unit is calculated by establishing the total costs involved in providing the service and dividing this by the number of service units used in providing the service.
- The calculation of a cost per service unit is as follows.

$$\textbf{Cost per service unit} = \frac{\textbf{Total costs for providing the service}}{\textbf{Number of service units used to provide the service}}$$

e.g

Illustration 2 – Suitable unit cost measures for service/operation costing

The canteen of a company records the following income and expenditure for a month.

	$	$
Income		59,010
Food	17,000	
Drink	6,000	
Bottled water	750	
Fuel costs (gas for cooking)	800	
Maintenance of machinery	850	
Repairs	250	
Wages	15,500	
Depreciation	1,000	

During the month the canteen served 56,200 meals.

Required:

Calculate the average cost per meal served and the average income per meal served.

Solution

Total canteen expenditure in month = $42,150

Total meals served in the month = 56,200

Average cost per meal served $= \frac{\$42,150}{56,200} = \$0.75$ per meal

Average income per meal $= \frac{\$59,010}{56,200} = \$1.05$ per meal

Test your understanding 2

Which of the following are characteristics of service costing?

(i) High levels of direct labour costs as a proportion of total cost.
(ii) Use of composite cost units.
(iii) Use of equivalent units.

A (i) only
B (i) and (ii) only
C (ii) only
D (ii) and (iii) only

3 Service cost analysis

If organisations in the same service industry use the same service cost units then comparisons between the companies can be made easily, as the following example of a service cost statement shows.

e.g

Illustration 3 – Service cost analysis

The following figures were taken from the annual accounts of two electricity supply boards working on uniform costing methods.

Meter reading, billing and collection costs:

	Board A	**Board B**
	$000	$000
Salaries and wages of:		
Meter readers	150	240
Billing and collection staff	300	480
Transport and travelling	30	40
Collection agency charges	–	20
Bad debts	10	10
General charges	100	200
Miscellaneous	10	10
	600	1,000
Units sold (millions)	2,880	9,600
Number of consumers (thousands)	800	1,600
Sales of electricity (millions)	$18	$50
Size of area (square miles)	4,000	4,000

Comparative costs for Boards A and B may be collected as follows and are useful in showing how well (or otherwise) individual services are performing.

Electricity Boards A and B
Comparative costs – year ending 31.12X5

	Board A $000	% of total	**Board B** $000	% of total
Salaries and wages:				
Meter reading	150	25.0	240	24.0
Billing and collection	300	50.0	480	48.0
Transport/travelling	30	5.0	40	4.0
Collection agency	-	-	20	2.0
Bad debts	10	1.7	10	1.0
General charges	100	16.6	200	20.0
Miscellaneous	10	1.7	10	1.0
	600	100.0	1,000	100.0

The information contained in the following table is much more useful for comparison purposes than the meter reading and billing costs information given above.

	$	$
Cost per:		
Million units sold	208	104
Thousand consumers	750	625
$m of sales	33,333	20,000
Square mile area	150	250

Test your understanding 3

Happy Returns Ltd operates a haulage business with three vehicles. The following estimated cost and performance data is available:

Petrol	$0.50 per kilometre on average
Repairs	$0.30 per kilometre
Depreciation	$1.00 per kilometre, plus $50 per week per vehicle
Drivers' wages	$300.00 per week per vehicle
Supervision and general expenses	$550 per week
Loading costs	$6.00 per tonne

During week number 26 it is expected that all three vehicles will be used, 280 tonnes will be loaded and a total of 3,950 kilometres travelled (including return journeys when empty) as shown in the following table:

Journey	Tonnes carried (one way)	Kilometres (one way)
1	34	180
2	28	265
3	40	390
4	32	115
5	26	220
6	40	480
7	29	90
8	26	100
9	25	135
	280	1,975

Calculate the average cost per tonne-kilometre in week 26.

Chapter summary

The nature of service and operation costing

- Intangibility
- Heterogeneity
- Simultaneous production and consumption
- Perishability

Examples of service industries:

- Hotels
- Airlines
- Public transport
- College/university
- Accountancy/audit firms
- Utility companies
- Distribution/haulage companies

Service and operation costing

Used when an organisation or department provides a service.

Suitable unit cost measures for service operation coasting

Composite cost unit used if service is function of two variables, for example:

- Patient-day
- Passenger-mile
- Guest-day
- Tonne-mile (or km)

Service cost analysis

If organisations in the same industry use the same service cost units then comparisons between companies can be made easily

Test your understanding answers

Test your understanding 1

Here are a few. You may have thought of others. Don't forget to ask questions 1-4 above if you are unsure whether it is appropriate to classify an industry as being a service industry:

- hotel
- airline, train and bus companies
- hairdressers
- taxi company
- college/university
- firm of accountants/auditors
- distribution company
- utility company (gas/electricity/telephone)
- banks
- insurance companies
- hospitals.

Test your understanding 2

B

Direct labour costs may be a high proportion on the total cost of providing a service and composite cost units are characteristic features of service costing. (i) and (ii) are therefore applicable and the correct answer is B.

Test your understanding 3

Total costs in Week 26		$
	$/km	
Petrol	0.50	
Repairs	0.30	
Depreciation	1.00	
	1.80 x 3,950	7,110
	$/week	
Depreciation ($50 x 3)	150	
Wages ($300 x 3)	900	
Supervision and general expenses	550	

	1,600
Loading costs ($6 x 280)	1,680
	10,390
Tonne-km in week 26 (see working)	66,325

(Costs averaged over the outward journeys, not the return, as these are necessary, but carry no tonnes.)

$$\text{Average cost per tonne-kilometre} = \frac{\text{Total cost}}{\text{Total tonne-kilometres}} = \frac{\$10,390}{66,325} = \$0.157$$

Working

Journey	Tonnes carried (one way)	Kilometres (one way)	Tonne-kilometres
1	34	180	6,120
2	28	265	7,420
3	40	390	15,600
4	32	115	3,680
5	26	220	5,720
6	40	480	19,200
7	29	90	2,610
8	26	100	2,600
9	25	135	3,375
	280	1,975	66,325

chapter

13

Budgeting

Chapter learning objectives

Upon completion of this chapter you will be able to:

- explain why organisations use budgeting, planning, control, communication, co-ordination, authorisation, motivation, evaluation
- explain the stages in the budget process, including the administrative procedures
- explain, giving examples, the term 'principal budget factor' (or 'limiting factor')
- from data supplied, prepare budgets for sales
- from data supplied, or derived, about the sales budget, prepare budgets for production
- from data supplied, or derived, about the production budget, prepare budgets for material usage
- from data supplied, or derived, about the materials usage budget, prepare budgets for material purchases
- from data supplied, or derived, about the production budget, prepare budgets for labour
- from data supplied, or derived, about the production budget, prepare budgets for overheads
- explain, and prepare from information provided: fixed, flexible, flexed budgets.

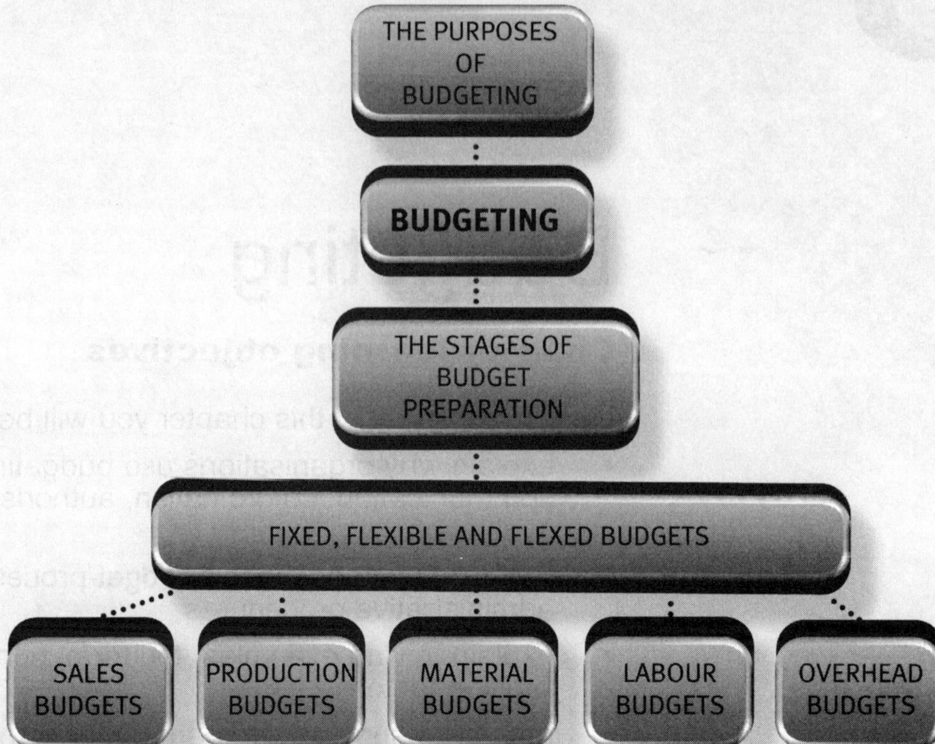

1 The purposes of budgeting

1.1 Budget theory

A budget is a quantitative expression of a plan of action prepared in advance of the period to which it relates.

Budgets set out the costs and revenues that are expected to be incurred or earned in future periods.

- For example, if you are planning to take a holiday, you will probably have a budgeted amount that you can spend. This budget will determine where you go and for how long.
- Most organisations prepare budgets for the business as a whole. The following budgets may also be prepared by organisations:
  - Departmental budgets.
  - Functional budgets (for sales, production, expenditure and so on).
  - Income statements (in order to determine the expected future profits).
  - Cash budgets (in order to determine future cash flows).

1.2 Purposes of budgeting

The main aims of budgeting are as follows:

- **Planning for the future** – in line with the objectives of the organisation.
- **Controlling costs** – by comparing the plan of the budget with the actual results and investigating significant differences between the two.
- **Co-ordination** of the different activities of the business by ensuring that managers are working towards the same common goal (as stated in the budget).
- **Communication** – budgets communicate the targets of the organisation to individual managers.
- **Motivation** – budgets can motivate managers by encouraging them to beat targets or budgets set at the beginning of the budget period. Bonuses are often based on 'beating budgets'. Budgets, if badly set, can also demotivate employees.
- **Evaluation** – the performance of managers is often judged by looking at how well the manager has performed 'against budget'.
- **Authorisation** – budgets act as a form of authorisation of expenditure.

2 The stages in budget preparation

2.1 How are budgets prepared?

Before any budgets can be prepared, the long-term objectives of an organisation must be defined so that the budgets prepared are working towards the goals of the business.

Once this has been done, the budget committee can be formed, the budget manual can be produced and the limiting factor can be identified.

- **Budget committee is formed** – a typical budget committee is made up of the chief executive, budget officer (management accountant) and departmental or functional heads (sales manager, purchasing manager, production manager and so on). The budget committee is responsible for communicating policy guidelines to the people who prepare the budgets and for setting and approving budgets.
- **Budget manual is produced** – an organisation's budget manual sets out instructions relating to the preparation and use of budgets. It also gives details of the responsibilities of those involved in the budgeting process, including an organisation chart and a list of budget holders.
- **Limiting factor is identified** – in budgeting, the limiting factor is known as the principal budget factor. Generally there will be one factor that will limit the activity of an organisation in a given period. It is usually sales that limit an organisation's performance, but it could be anything else, for example, the availability of special labour skills.

If sales is the principal budget factor, then the sales budget must be produced first.

- **Final steps in the budget process** – once the budget relating to the limiting factor has been produced then the managers responsible for the other budgets can produce them. The entire budget preparation process may take several weeks or months to complete. The final stages are as follows.

  1 Initial budgets are prepared. Budget managers may sometimes try to build in an element of budget slack – this is a deliberate over-estimation of costs or under-estimation of revenues which can make it easier for managers to achieve their targets.

  2 Initial budgets are reviewed and integrated into the complete budget system.

  3 After any necessary adjustments are made to initial budgets, they are accepted and the master budget is prepared (budgeted income statement, balance sheet and cash flow). This master budget is then shown to top management for final approval.

  4 Budgets are reviewed regularly. Comparisons between budgets and actual results are carried out and any differences arising are known as variances.

2.2 Budget preparation

The preparation of budgets involves the following seven steps and is illustrated as follows.

e.g

Illustration 1 – The stages in budget preparation

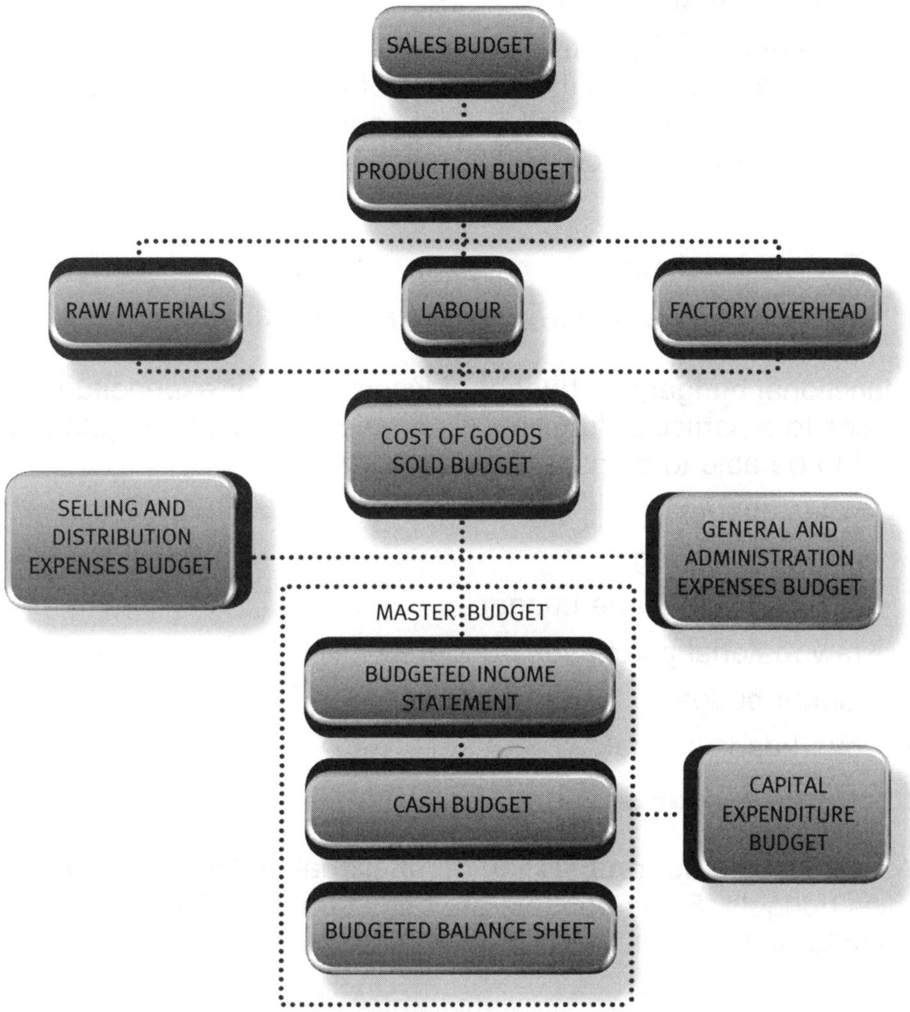

- The diagram shown above is based on sales being the principal budget factor.This is why the sales budget is shown in Step 1.
- Remember that if labour were the principal budget factor, then the labour budget would be produced first and this would determine the production budget.
- Once the production budget has been determined then the remaining functional budgets can be prepared.

2.3 Continuous budgets

- **Continuous budget** – this type of budget is prepared a year (or budget period) ahead and is updated regularly by adding a further accounting period (month, quarter) when the first accounting period has expired. If the budget period is a year, then it will always reflect the budget for a year in advance. Continuous budgets are also known as rolling budgets.

Test your understanding 1

A principal budget factor is:

A the highest value item of cost
B a factor that limits the activities of an undertaking
C a factor common to all budget centres
D a factor controllable by the manager of the budget centre.

3 Sales budgets

3.1 Budget preparation – functional budgets

A functional budget is a budget of income and/or expenditure which applies to a particular function. The main functional budgets that you need to be able to prepare are as follows:

- sales budget
- production budget
- raw material usage budget
- raw material purchases budget
- labour budget
- overheads budget.

3.2 Sales budgets

We shall begin our preparation of functional budgets by looking at sales budgets. Sales budgets are fairly straightforward to prepare as the following illustration will demonstrate.

Illustration 2 – Sales budgets

A company makes two products – PS and TG. Sales for next year are budgeted to be 5,000 units of PS and 1,000 units of TG. Planned selling prices are $95 and $130 per unit respectively.

Required:

Prepare the sales budget for the next year.

Solution

	Total	PS	TG
Sales units	6,000	5,000	1,000
Sales value	$605,000	$475,000	$130,000

Workings

Sales – PS = 5,000 x $95 = $475,000
Sales – TG = 1,000 x $130 = $130,000

Test your understanding 2

A company makes two products – A and B. The products are sold in the ratio 1:1. Planned selling prices are $100 and $200 per unit respectively. The company needs to earn $900,000 revenue in the coming year.Required:

Prepare the sales budget for the coming year.

4 Production budgets

Budgeted production levels can be calculated as follows:

Budgeted production = Forecast sales + Closing inventory of finished goods – Opening inventory of finished goods

Illustration 3 – Production budgets

A company makes two products, PS and TG. Forecast sales for the coming year are 5,000 and 1,000 units repectively.

The company has the following opening and required closing inventory levels.

	PS units	TG units
Opening inventory	100	50
Required closing inventory	1,100	50

Required:

Prepare the production budget for the coming year.

Solution

Production budget

	PS units	TG units
Sales budget	5,000	1,000
+ Closing inventory	1,100	50
– Opening inventory	(100)	(50)
Budgeted production in units	6,000	1,000

Test your understanding 3

Newton Ltd manufactures three products. The expected sales for each product are shown below.

	Product 1	Product 2	Product 3
Sales in units	3,000	4,500	3,000

Opening inventory is expected to be:

Product 1	500 units
Product 2	700 units
Product 3	500 units

Management have stated their desire to reduce inventory levels, and closing inventory is budgeted as:

Product 1	200 units
Product 2	300 units
Product 3	300 units

Required:

Complete the following.

(a) The number of units of product 1 to be produced is [ ]

(b) The number of units of product 2 to be produced is [ ]

(c) The number of units of product 3 to be produced is [ ]

5 Material budgets

There are two types of material budget that you need to be able to calculate, the usage budget and the purchases budget.

- The **material usage budget** is simply the budgeted production for each product multiplied by the quantity (e.g. kg) required to produce one unit of the product.
- The **material purchases budget** is made up of the following elements.

Material purchases budget = Material usage budget + Closing inventory – Opening inventory

e.g

Illustration 4 – Material budgets

A company produces Products PS and TG and has budgeted to produce 6,000 units of Product PS and 1,000 units of Product TG in the coming year.

The data about the materials required to produce Products PS and TG is given as follows.

Finished products:

	PS per unit	TG per unit
Kg of raw material X	12	12
Kg of raw material Y	6	8

Direct materials:

	Raw material X kg	Raw material Y kg
Desired closing inventory	6,000	1,000
Opening inventory	5,000	5,000

Standard rates and prices:

Raw material X	$0.72 per kg
Raw material Y	$1.56 per kg

Required:

Prepare the following:

(a) The material usage budget.

(b) The material purchase budget.

Solution

Material budgets

	Material X kg	Material Y kg
For production of PS (W1)	72,000	36,000
For production of TG (W2)	12,000	8,000
Material usage budget	84,000	44,000
+ Closing inventory	6,000	1,000
– Opening inventory	5,000	5,000
Material purchases budget (units)	85,000	40,000
	$	$
Material purchases budget ($)		
X $0.72 per kg x 85,000	61,200	
Y $1.56 per kg x 40,000		62,400

Workings

(W1) Budgeted production of Product PS = 6,000 units
Therefore: 6,000 x 12 kg per unit = 72,000 kg of Material X required.
Therefore: 6,000 x 6 kg per unit = 36,000 kg of Material Y required.

(W2) Budgeted production of Product TG = 1,000 units
Therefore: 1,000 x 12 kg per unit = 12,000 kg of Material X required.
Therefore: 1,000 x 8 kg per unit = 8,000 kg of Material Y required.

Test your understanding 4

Newton Ltd manufactures three products. The expected production levels for each product are shown below.

	Product 1	Product 2	Product 3
Budgeted production in units	2,700	4,100	2,800

Three types of material are used in varying amounts in the manufacture of the three products. Material requirements are shown below:

	Product 1	Product 2	Product 3
Material M1	2 kg	3 kg	4 kg
Material M2	3 kg	3 kg	4 kg
Material M3	6 kg	2 kg	4 kg

The opening inventory of material is expected to be:

Material M1	4,300 kg
Material M2	3,700 kg
Material M3	4,400 kg

Management are keen to reduce inventory levels for materials, and closing inventory levels are to be much lower. Expected levels are shown below:

Material M1	2,200 kg
Material M2	1,300 kg
Material M3	2,000 kg

Material prices are expected to be 10% higher than this year and current prices are \$1.10/kg for material M1, \$3.00/kg for material M2 and \$2.50/kg for material M3.

Required:

Complete the following.

(a) (i) The quantity of material M1 to be used is [ ] kg

(ii) The quantity of material M2 to be used is [ ] kg

(iii) The quantity of material M3 to be used is [ ] kg

(b) (i) The quantity of material M1 to be purchased is [ ] kg

These purchases have a value of $ [ ]

(ii) The quantity of material M2 to be purchased is [ ] kg

These purchases have a value of $ [ ]

(iii) The quantity of material M3 to be purchased is [ ] kg

These purchases have a value of $ [ ]

6 Labour budgets

Labour budgets are simply the number of hours multiplied by the labour rate per hour as the following illustration shows.

e.g

Illustration 5 – Labour budgets

A company produces Products PS and TG and has budgeted to produce 6,000 units of Product PS and 1,000 units of Product TG in the coming year.

The data about the labour hours required to produce Products PS and TG is given as follows.

Finished products:

	PS per unit	TG per unit
Direct labour hours	8	12

Standard rate for direct labour = $5.20 per hour

Required:

Prepare the labour budget for the coming year.

Solution

		Hours		$
For Product PS	6,000 x 8 hrs	48,000		
For Product TG	1,000 x 12 hrs	12,000		
		60,000	@ $5.20	312,000

Test your understanding 5

Newton Ltd manufactures three products. The expected production levels for each product are shown below.

	Product 1	Product 2	Product 3
Budgeted production in units	2,700	4,100	2,800

Two types of labour are used in producing the three products. Standard times per unit and expected wage rates for the forthcoming year are shown below:

	Product 1	Product 2	Product 3
Hours per unit			
Skilled labour	3	1	3
Semi-skilled labour	4	4	2

Skilled labour is to be paid at the rate of $9/hour and semi-skilled labour at the rate of $6/hour.

Required:

Complete the following.

(a) The number of hours of skilled labour required is ______

The cost of this labour is $ ______

(b) The number of hours of semi-skilled labour required is ______

The cost of this labour is $ ______

Test your understanding 6

A contract cleaning firm estimates that it will take 2,520 actual cleaning hours to clean an office block. Unavoidable interruptions and lost time are estimated to take 10% of the workers' time. If the wage rate is $8.50 per hour, the budgeted labour cost will be:

A $19,278
B $21,420
C $23,562
D $23,800

7 Overhead budgets

The following illustration demonstrates the calculation of overhead budgets.

e.g

Illustration 6 – Overhead budgets

A company produces Products PS and TG and has budgeted to produce 6,000 units of Product PS and 1,000 units of Product TG in the coming year.

The following data about the machine hours required to produce Products PS and TG and the standard production overheads per machine hour is relevant to the coming year.

	PS per unit	TG per unit
Machine hours	8	12

Production overheads per machine hour

Variable	$1.54 per machine hour
Fixed	$0.54 per machine hour

Required:

Calculate the overhead budget for the coming year.

Solution

Overhead budget

		$
Variable costs	60,000 hours x $1.54	92,400
Fixed costs	60,000 hours x $0.54	32,400
		124,800

Workings

Machine hours – Product PS = 6,000 units x 8 hours = 48,000 machine hours

Machine hours – Product TG = 1,000 units x 12 hours = 12,000 machine hours

Total machine hours = 48,000 + 12,000 = 60,000

Test your understanding 7

Newton Ltd manufactures three products. The expected production levels for each product are shown below.

	Product 1	Product 2	Product 3
Budgeted production in units	2,700	4,100	2,800

Two types of labour are used in producing the three products. Standard times per unit and expected wage rates for the forthcoming year are shown below:

	Product 1	Product 2	Product 3
Hours per unit			
Skilled labour	3	1	3
Semi-skilled labour	4	4	2

Production overheads per labour hour are as follows:

Variable $3.50 per labour hour
Fixed $5.50 per labour hour

Required:

Calculate the overhead budget.

8 Fixed, flexible and flexed budgets

8.1 Budgetary control cycle

At the beginning of this chapter we listed the main purposes of budgeting, one of which was 'controlling costs – by comparing the plan of the budget with the actual results and investigating any significant differences between the two' – this is known as **budgetary control**.

The budgetary control cycle can be illustrated as follows.

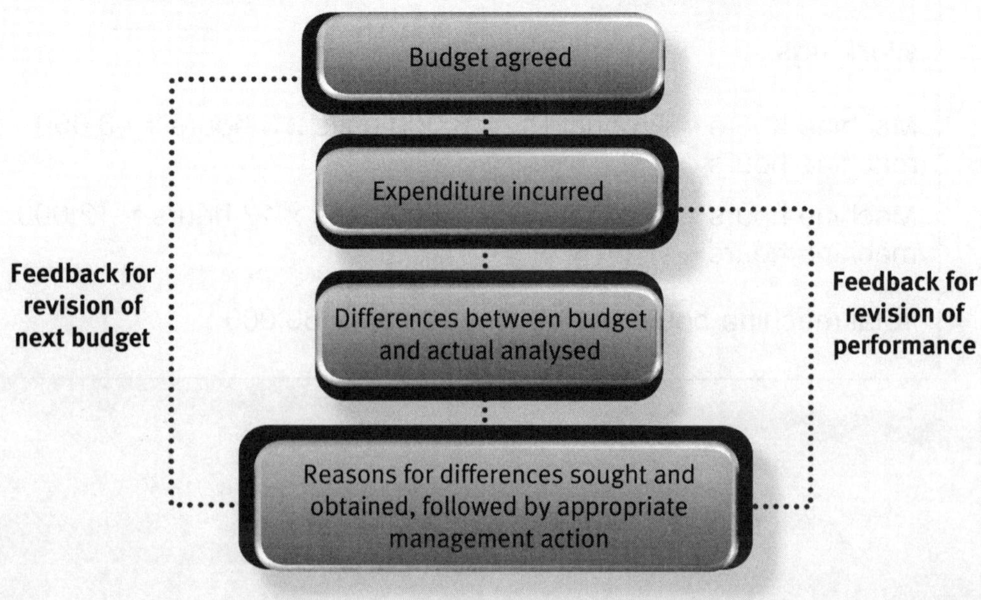

8.2 Fixed budgets

The simplest form of budget report compares the original budget against actual results and is known as a fixed budget.

- Any differences arising between the original budget and actual results are known as variances. Variances may be either adverse or favourable.
- Adverse variances (Adv) or (A) decrease profits.
- Favourable variances (Fav) or (F) increase profits.
- An example of a budget report is shown below.

Budget	Actual		
Sales units	1,000	1,200	
Production units	1,300	1,250	
	$	$	$
			Variance
Sales revenue	10,000	11,500	1,500 Fav
- labour costs	2,600	2,125	475 Fav
- materials costs	1,300	1,040	260 Fav
- overheads	1,950	2,200	250 Adv
	5,850	5,365	485 Fav
Cost of sales			
Profit	4,150	6,135	1,985 Fav

- The fixed budget shown above is not particularly useful because we are not really comparing like with like. For example, the budgeted sales were 1,000 units but the actual sales volume was 1,200 units.
- The overall sales variance is favourable, but from the report shown we don't know how much of this variance is due to the fact that actual sales were 200 units higher than budgeted sales (or whether there was an increase in the sales price).
- Similarly, actual production volume was 50 units less than the budgeted production volume, so we are not really making a very useful comparison. It is more useful to compare actual results with a budget that reflects the actual activity level. Such a budget is known as a **flexed budget**.

8.3 Flexed budgets

A **flexed** budget is a budget which recognises different cost behaviour patterns and is designed to change as the volume of activity changes.

- When preparing flexed budgets it will be necessary to identify the cost behaviour of the different items in the original budget.
- In some cases you may have to use the high/low method in order to determine the fixed and variable elements of semi-variable costs.

e.g

Illustration 7 – Fixed, flexible and flexed budgets

Wye Ltd manufactures one product and when operating at 100% capacity can produce 5,000 units per period, but for the last few periods has been operating below capacity.

Below is **the flexible** budget prepared at the start of last period, for three levels of activity at below capacity:

Level of activity	70%	80%	90%
	$	$	$
Direct materials	7,000	8,000	9,000
Direct labour	28,000	32,000	36,000
Production overheads	34,000	36,000	38,000
Administration, selling and distribution overheads	15,000	15,000	15,000
Total cost	84,000	91,000	98,000

In the event, the last period turned out to be even worse than expected, with production of only 2,500 units. The following costs were incurred:

	$
Direct materials	4,500
Direct labour	22,000
Production overheads	28,000
Administration, selling and distribution overheads	16,500
Total cost	71,000

Required:

Use the information given above to prepare the following.

(a) A flexed budget for 2,500 units.

(b) A budgetary control statement.

Solution

(a) Flexed budget for 2,500 units

	$
Direct materials (W1) (2,500 x $2)	5,000
Direct labour (W2) (2,500 x $8)	20,000
Production overheads (W3)	30,000
Administration, selling and distribution overheads (W4)	15,000
Total cost	70,000

Workings

1 Material is a variable cost – \$2 per unit

$$\text{Variable material cost} = \frac{\$7{,}000}{70\% \times 5{,}000} = \$2 \text{ per unit}$$

2 Labour is a variable cost – \$8 per unit.

$$\text{Variable labour cost} = \frac{\$28{,}000}{70\% \times 5{,}000} = \$8 \text{ per unit}$$

3 Production overheads are semi-variable. Using the high/low method, the variable cost is \$4 per unit, the fixed cost is \$20,000. The cost for 2,500 units therefore = \$20,000 + (2,500 x \$4) = \$30,000.

70% activity = 70% x 5,000 = 3,500
90% activity = 90% x 5,000 = 4,500

$$\text{Variable cost per unit} = \frac{\$(38{,}000 - 34{,}000)}{4{,}500 - 3{,}500} = \$4 \text{ per unit}$$

Total fixed cost by substituting at high activity level:

Total cost	=		\$38,000
Total variable cost	=	4,500 x \$4	\$18,000
Fixed cost	=		\$20,000

4 Other overheads are fixed.

(b)

	Budget for 2,500 units	Actual	Variance

	Fixed budget	Flexed budget	Actual results	Expenditure Variances
Production (units)	20,000	17,600	17,600	
	\$	\$	\$	\$
Indirect labour	20,000	17,600	19,540	(1,940) (A)
Consumables	800	704	1,000	(296) (A)
Other variable	4,200	3,696	3,660	36 (F)
	25,000	22,000	24,200	(2,200) (A)
Depreciation	10,000	10,000	10,000	-
Other fixed	5,000	5,000	5,400	(400) (A)
	40,000	37,000	39,600	(2,600) (A)

Remove

This data may be displace. Not need for the quiz please see next pg to answer part (b). Mony

	$	$	$
Direct materials	5,000	4,500	500 (F)
Direct labour	20,000	22,000	2,000 (A)
Production overheads	30,000	28,000	2,000 (F)
Administration, selling and distribution overheads	15,000	16,500	1,500 (A)
Total cost	70,000	71,000	1,000 (A)

8.4 Flexed budgets and budget variances

As we have already said, the comparison of actual results against a flexed budget is much more useful than a comparison against an original fixed budget.

- However, we cannot just ignore the original budget altogether as it forms part of the operational plan and management will want to see how the actual results compare with budgeted profits.
- The overall differences between the original budget and actual results are known as total budget variances.
- Total budget variances can be analysed into volume and expenditure variances. Consider the budget report shown in the following illustration.

e.g

Illustration 8 – Fixed, flexible and flexed budgets

	Fixed budget	Flexed budget	Actual results	Expenditure Variances
Production (units)	20,000	17,600	17,600	
	$	$	$	$
Indirect labour	20,000	17,600	19,540	(1,940) (A)
Consumables	800	704	1,000	(296) (A)
Other variable	4,200	3,696	3,660	36 (F)
	25,000	22,000	24,200	(2,200) (A)
Depreciation	10,000	10,000	10,000	-
Other fixed	5,000	5,000	5,400	(400) (A)
	40,000	37,000	39,600	(2,600) (A)

- The total variance is the difference between fixed budget and actual results.
- The volume variance reflects the difference in costs which are due to the actual activity level being different to budgeted activity level. The volume variance is the difference between the fixed and flexible budget.

- The expenditure variance reflects the difference in costs due to actual expenditure differing from fixed budget figures. The expenditure variance is the difference between flexed budget and actual results.
- We can analyse these expenditure variances further in order to establish reasons why the variances have occurred. We will be looking at expenditure variances further in the next chapter.

Test your understanding 8

The following details have been extracted from the cost card of Product X which is manufactured by the XYZ chemical company. The company uses an absorption costing system.

	$
Direct labour	7.60
Variable overhead	3.90
Direct materials	8.40
Fixed overhead	5.10
	25.00

The fixed overhead charged to each unit of the product is based on a monthly production of 2,000 units.

During October 20X3, the actual production amounted to 2,150 units, and costs incurred were as follows.

	$
Direct materials	18,100
Direct labour	14,980
Variable overhead	8,160
Fixed overhead	9,950

Calculate the following total expenditure variances stating whether they are adverse or favourable.

(i) Direct materials.
(ii) Direct labour.
(iii) Variable overhead.
(iv) Fixed overhead.

Chapter summary

The purposes of budgeting

- Planning
- Control
- Co-ordination
- Authorisation
- Communication
- Motivation
- Evaluation

BUDGETING

The stages of budget preparation

1. Budget committee formed
2. Budget manual produced
3. Limiting factor identified and its corresponding budget prepared
4. Initial functional budgets prepared
5. Initial budgets reviewed and integrated into complete budget system
6. Top management give final approval
7. Budgets reviewed regulary and variances arising are investigated

Fixed, flexible and flexed budgets

- Original budget = fixed
- Flexed budget recognises different cost behaviour patterns and is designed to change volume of activity changes

SALES BUDGETS | **PRODUCTION BUDGETS** | **MATERIAL BUDGETS** | **LABOUR BUDGETS** | **OVERHEAD BUDGETS**

Note that if sales is the limiting factor (principal budget factor) then sales demand is what limits the activities of an organisation and so the sales budget must be prepared first.
Once the sales budget has been prepared, the production budget can be prepared, followed by the material, labour and overhead budgets.

Test your understanding answers

Test your understanding 1

B The scale of operations may be limited by various factors, e.g. sales, labour, material, cash or machinery.

The limiting factor must be identified at the first stage of the budgeting process, since it will determine all the other budgets. In this context the limiting factor is referred to as the principal budget factor.

Test your understanding 2

Sales budget

	Total	A	B
Sales units (see working)	6,000	3,000	3,000
Selling price per unit		$100	$200
Sales value	$900,000	$300,000	$600,000

Working

Total sales revenue = $900,000

$300 revenue is earned every time a mix of one unit of Product A and one unit of Product B is sold ($100 + $200).

Number of 'mixes' to be sold to earn $900,000 = $\frac{\$900,000}{\$300}$ = 3,000 'mixes'

3,000 'mixes' = 3,000 units of Product A and 3,000 units of Product B.

Test your understanding 3

(a) The number of units of product 1 to be produced is [ ]

(b) The number of units of product 2 to be produced is [ ]

(c) The number of units of product 3 to be produced is [ ]

Workings:

	Product 1	**Product 2**	**Product 3**
Sales forecast	3,000	4,500	3,000
+ Closing inventory	200	300	300
- Opening inventory	500	700	500
Production budget	2,700	4,100	2,800

Test your understanding 4

(a) (i) The quantity of material M1 to be used is 28,900 kg

(ii) The quantity of material M2 to be used is 31,600 kg

(iii) The quantity of material M3 to be used is 35,600 kg

(b) (i) The quantity of material M1 to be purchased is 26,800 kg

These purchases have a value of $ 32,428

(ii) The quantity of material M2 to be purchased is 29,200 kg

These purchases have a value of $ 96,360

(iii) The quantity of material M3 to be purchased is 33,200 kg

These purchases have a value of $ 91,300

Working

	Material M1	**Material M2**	**Material M3**
Product 1 usage	5,400	8,100	16,200
Product 2 usage	12,300	12,300	8,200
Product 3 usage	11,200	11,200	11,200
Materials usage budget	28,900	31,600	35,600

	Material M1	**Material M2**	**Material M3**
Material usage	28,900	31,600	35,600
+ Closing inventory	2,200	1,300	2,000
- Opening inventory	4,300	3,700	4,400
Material purchases budget (units)	26,800	29,200	33,200
Material price per kg	$1.21	$3.30	$2.75
Material purchases budget (value)	$32,428	$96,360	$91,300

Note: Material prices are as follows:

M1 : $1.10 x 1.1 = $1.21
M2 : $3.00 x 1.1 = $3.30
M3 : $2.50 x 1.1 = $2.75

Material usages are as follows:

Product 1 – Material M1 usage = 2 x 2,700 = 5,400
Product 2 – Material M1 usage = 3 x 4,100 = 12,300
Product 3 – Material M1 usage = 4 x 2,800 = 11,200

KAPLAN PUBLISHING 292

Product 1 – Material M2 usage = 3 x 2,700 = 8,100
Product 2 – Material M2 usage = 3 x 4,100 = 12,300
Product 3 – Material M2 usage = 4 x 2,800 = 11,200

Product 1 – Material M3 usage = 6 x 2,700 = 16,200
Product 2 – Material M3 usage = 2 x 4,100 = 8,200
Product 3 – Material M3 usage = 4 x 2,800 = 11,200

Test your understanding 5

(a) The number of hours of skilled labour required is **20,600**

The cost of this labour is $ **185,400**

(b) The number of hours of semi-skilled labour required is **32,800**

The cost of this labour is $ **196,800**

Workings:

	Skilled	Semi-skilled
Product 1 hours	8,100	10,800
Product 2 hours	4,100	16,400
Product 3 hours	8,400	5,600
Labour budget (hours)	20,600	32,800
Labour rate per hour	$9	$6
Labour budget ($)	185,400	196,800

Product 1 – skilled hours = 3 x 2,700 = 8,100
Product 2 – skilled hours = 1 x 4,100 = 4,100
Product 3 – skilled hours = 3 x 2,800 = 8,400

Product 1 – semi-skilled hours = 4 x 2,700 = 10,800
Product 2 – semi-skilled hours = 4 x 4,100 = 16,400
Product 3 – semi-skilled hours = 2 x 2,800 = 5,600

Test your understanding 6

The correct answer is D.

The budgeted labour cost is $23,800

Actual expected total time = $\frac{2,520}{0.9}$ = 2,800 hours

Budgeted labour cost = 2,800 x $8.50 = $23,800

Test your understanding 7

Number of hours of skilled labour = 20,600 (see working)
Number of hours of semi-skilled labour = 32,800 (see working)

Total hours worked = 20,600 + 32,800 = 53,400

		$
Variable costs	53,400 hours x $3.50	186,900
Fixed costs	53,400 hours x $5.50	293,700
		480,600

Working

Product 1 – skilled hours = 3 x 2,700 = 8,100
Product 2 – skilled hours = 1 x 4,100 = 4,100
Product 3 – skilled hours = 3 x 2,800 = 8,400

Total skilled hours = 8,100 + 4,100 + 8,400 = 20,600

Product 1 – semi-skilled hours = 4 x 2,700 = 10,800
Product 2 – semi-skilled hours = 4 x 4,100 = 16,400
Product 3 – semi-skilled hours = 2 x 2,800 = 5,600

Total semi-skilled hours = 10,800 + 16,400 + 5,600 = 32,800

Test your understanding 8

	Budget for 2,150 units	Actual	Variance	
	$	$	$	
(i) Direct materials (W1)	18,060	18,100	40	(A)
(ii) Direct labour (W2)	16,340	14,980	1,360	(F)
(iii) Variable overhead (W3)	8,385	8,160	225	(F)
(iv) Fixed overhead (W4)	10,965	9,950	1,015	(F)

Workings

Direct materials = 2,150 x $8.40 = $18,060
Direct labour = 2,150 x $7.60 = $16,340
Variable overhead = 2,150 x $3.90 = $ 8,385
Fixed overhead = 2,150 x $5.10 = $10,965

chapter

14

Standard costing

Chapter learning objectives

Upon completion of this chapter you will be able to:

- explain, for a manufacturing business, the purpose and principles of standard costing: targets, feedback/variances, ease of accounting
- establish, from information supplied, the standard cost per unit under marginal costing
- establish, from information supplied, the standard cost per unit under absorption costing
- calculate, from information supplied, the sales price and volume variances
- for given or calculated sales variances, interpret and explain possible causes, including possible interrelationships between them
- calculate, from information supplied, the materials total, price and usage variances
- for given or calculated materials variances, interpret and explain possible causes, including possible interrelationships between them
- calculate, from information supplied, the labour total, price and efficiency variances
- for given or calculated labour variances, interpret and explain possible causes, including possible interrelationships between them
- calculate, from information supplied, the variable overhead total, expenditure and efficiency variances
- for given or calculated variable overhead variances, interpret and explain possibe causes, including possible interrelationships between them
- calculate, from information supplied, fixed overhead total and expenditure variances

- calculate, from information supplied, where appropriate, fixed overhead volume, capacity and efficiency variances
- for given or calculated fixed overhead variances, interpret and explain possible causes, including possible interrelationships between them
- using given variances and standard figures, calculate actual figures
- using given variances and actual figures, calculate standard figures
- using given or derived variances, produce an operating statement to reconcile budgeted profit with actual profit under standard absorption costing
- using given or derived variances, produce an operating statement to reconcile budgeted profit or contribution with actual profit or contribution under standard marginal costing.

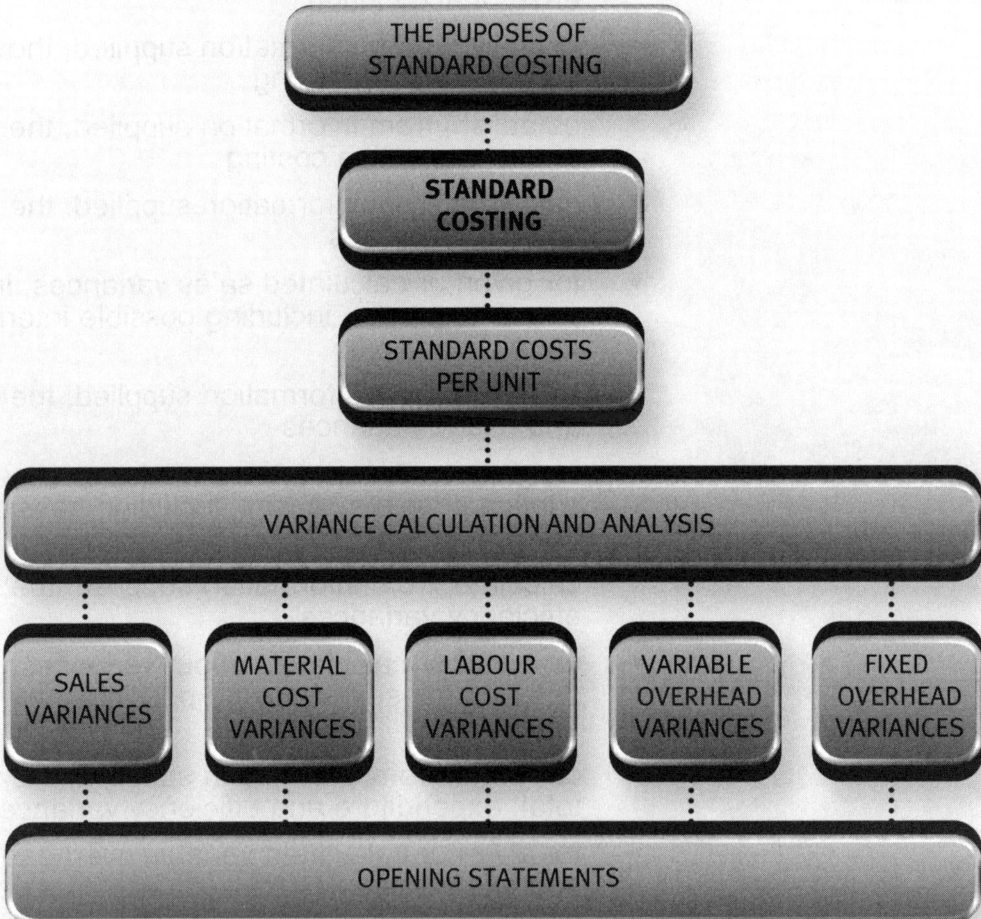

1 The purposes of standard costing

1.1 Introduction to standard costing

A **standard cost** is the planned unit cost of a product or service.

In order to prepare budgets we need to know what an individual unit of a product or service is expected to cost.

- Standard costs represent 'target' costs and they are therefore useful for planning, control and motivation.
- As well as being the basis for preparing budgets, standard costs are also essential for calculating and analysing variances.
- Variances provide 'feedback' to management indicating how well, or otherwise, the company is doing.
- Standard costs also provide an easier method of accounting since it enables simplified records to be kept.
- A standard cost may be computed on either a marginal cost basis, including only variable costs, or under absorption costing.

1.2 Types of cost standards

There are four main types of cost standards.

- **Basic standards.**
- **Ideal standards.**
- **Attainable standards.**
- **Current standards.**

Expandable text

- **Basic standards** – these are long-term standards which remain unchanged over a period of years. Their sole use is to show trends over time for items such as material prices, labour rates, and labour efficiency. They are also used to show the effect of using different methods over time. Basic standards are the least used and the least useful type of standard.
- **Ideal standards** – these standards are based upon perfect operating conditions. Perfect operating conditions include: no wastage; no scrap; no breakdowns; no stoppages; no idle time. In their search for perfect quality, Japanese companies use ideal standards for pinpointing areas where close examination may result in large cost savings. Ideal standards may have an adverse motivational impact because they are unlikely to be achieved.
- **Attainable standards** – these standards are the most frequently encountered type of standard. They are based upon efficient (but not perfect) operating conditions. These standards include allowances for the following: normal or expected

material losses; fatigue; machine breakdowns. Attainable standards must be based on a high performance level so that with a certain amount of hard work they are achievable (unlike ideal standards).

- **Current standards** – these standards are based on current levels of efficiency in terms of allowances for breakdowns, wastage, losses and so on. The main disadvantage of using current standards is that they do not provide any incentive to improve on the current level of performance.

2 Standard costs per unit

2.1 Standard cost cards

Once estimated, standard costs are usually collected on a standard cost card.

e.g

Illustration 1 – Standard costs per unit

K Ltd manufactures Product 20K. Information relating to this product is given below.

Budgeted output for the year:	900 units
Standard details for one unit:	
Direct materials:	40 square metres at $5.30 per square metre
Direct wages:	Bonding department 24 hours at $5.00 per hour Finishing department 15 hours at $4.80 per hour

Budgeted costs and hours per annum are as follows:

	$	Hours
Variable overhead		
Bonding department	45,000	30,000
Finishing department	25,000	25,000

Fixed overhead apportioned to this product:

Production	$36,000
Selling, distribution and administration	$27,000

Note: Variable overheads are recovered (absorbed) using hours, fixed overheads are recovered on a unit basis.

Required:

Prepare a standard cost card in order to establish the standard cost of one unit of Product 20K and enter the following subtotals on the card:

1 prime cost
2 marginal cost
3 total absorption cost
4 total standard cost.

Solution

Standard cost card – Product 20K	$
Direct materials (40 x $5.30)	212
Direct labour:	
Bonding (24 hours at $5.00)	120
Finishing (15 hours at $4.80)	72
1 **Prime cost**	404
Variable overhead:	
Bonding ($45,000/30,000 x 24 hours)	36
Finishing ($25,000/25,000 x 15 hours)	15
2 **Marginal cost**	455
Production overheads ($36,000/900)	40
3 **Total absorption cost**	495
Non-production overheads ($27,000/900)	30
4 **Total standard cost**	525

Test your understanding 1

The following statement shows budgeted and actual costs for the month of October for Department X.

Month ended 31 October	Original budget $	Actual result $
Sales	600,000	550,000
Direct materials	150,000	130,000
Direct labour	200,000	189,000
Production overhead		
Variable with direct labour	50,000	46,000
Fixed	25,000	29,000
Total costs	425,000	394,000
Profit	175,000	156,000
Direct labour hours	50,000	47,500
Sales and production units	5,000	4,500

Note: There is no opening and closing inventory.

(a) Calculate the standard cost per unit under absorption costing.

(b) Calculate standard cost per unit under marginal costing.

3 Sales variances

3.1 Introduction

There are two causes of sales variances: a difference in the selling price, and a difference in the sales volume, giving:

- sales price variance
- sales volume variance.

3.2 Sales volume variance

The sales volume variance calculates the effect on profit of the actual sales volume being different from that budgeted. The effect on profit will differ depending upon whether a marginal or absorption costing system is being used.

- Under absorption costing any difference in units is valued at the standard profit per unit.

- Under marginal costing any difference in units is valued at the standard contribution per unit.
- In neither case is the standard selling price used. This is because when volumes change, so do production costs and the purpose of calculating the variance is to find the effect on profit.

3.3 Sales price variance

The sales price variance shows the effect on profit of selling at a different price from that expected.

e.g

Illustration 2 – Sales variances

The following data relates to 20X8.

Actual sales:	1,000 units @ $650 each
Budgeted output and sales for the year:	900 units
Standard selling price:	$700 per unit
Budgeted contribution per unit:	$245
Budgeted profit per unit:	$205

Required:

Calculate the sales volume variance (under absorption and marginal costing) and the sales price variance.

Solution

Sales volume variance (absorption costing)

Budgeted sales	900 units
Actual sales	1,000 units

100 units extra sold x Budgeted profit x $205
= $20,500 (F) (more sold so higher profit)

Sales volume variance (marginal costing)

Budgeted sales	900	units
Actual sales	1,000	units
	100	units extra sold
x Budgeted contribution	x $245	
	= $24,500	(F) (more sold so higher profit).

Sales price variance

Budgeted selling price	$700	
Actual selling price	$650	
	$50	
x Quantity sold	x 1,000	
	= $50,000	(A) (lower price charged so lower profit).

Test your understanding 2

Radek Ltd has budgeted sales of 400 units at $2.50 each. The variable costs are expected to be $1.80 per unit, and there are no fixed costs.

The actual sales were 500 units at $2 each and costs were as expected.

Calculate the sales price and sales volume variances (using marginal costing).

Test your understanding 3

W Ltd budgeted sales of 6,500 units but actually sold only 6,000 units. Its standard cost card is as follows:

	$
Direct material	25
Direct wages	8
Variable overhead	4
Fixed overhead	18
Total standard cost	55
Standard gross profit	5
Standard selling price	60

The actual selling price for the period was $61.

Calculate the sales price and sales volume variances for the period (using absorption costing).

3.4 Possible causes of sales variances

Causes of sales variances include the following:

- unplanned price increases (sales price variance)
- unplanned price reduction, for example, when trying to attract additional business (sales price variance)
- unexpected fall in demand due to recession (sales volume variance)
- additional demand attracted by reduced price (sales volume variance)
- failure to satisfy demand due to production difficulties (sales volume variance).

4 Materials cost variances

4.1 Introduction

There are three different materials variances that you need to know about:

- materials total variance
- materials price variance
- materials usage variance.

4.2 Materials total variance

The materials total variance is the difference between:

(a) the standard material cost of the actual production (flexed budget) and

(b) the actual cost of direct material.

- It can be analysed into two sub-variances: a materials price variance and a materials usage variance.
- A materials price variance analyses whether the company paid more or less than expected for materials.
- The purpose of the materials usage variance is to quantify the effect on profit of using a different quantity of raw material from that expected for the actual production achieved.

e.g

Illustration 3 – Material cost variances

The following information relates to the production of Product X.

Extract from the standard cost card of Product X

	$
Direct materials	
(40 square metres x $5.30 per square metre)	212

Actual results for direct materials in the period: 1,000 units were produced and 39,000 square metres of material costing $210,600 in total were used.

Required:

Calculate the materials total, price and usage variances for Product X in the period.

Solution

(i) Actual quantity x Actual price		$210,600	
(i) – (ii)	**Price variance**		$3,900 (A)
(ii) Actual quantity x Standard price			
39,000 x $5.30		$206,700	
(iii) – (ii)	**Usage variance**		$5,300 (F)
(iii) Standard quantity x Standard price (For actual production)			
1,000 x 40 x $5.30		$212,000	
(iii) – (i)	**Total variance**		$1,400 (F)

Proof: The materials total variance is the sum of the price and usage variances, i.e. $5,300 (F) + $3,900 (A) = $1,400 (F).

Test your understanding 4

James Marshall Ltd makes a single product with the following budgeted material costs per unit:

2 kg of material A at $10/kg

Actual details:

Output 1,000 units
Material purchased and used 2,200 kg
Material cost $20,900

Calculate materials price and usage variances.

4.3 Possible causes of materials variances

Materials price variances may be caused by:

- supplies from different sources
- unexpected general price increases
- changes in quantity discounts
- substitution of one grade of material for another
- materials price standards are usually set at a mid-year price so one would expect a favourable price variance early in a period and an adverse variance later on in a budget period.

Materials usage variances may be caused by:

- a higher or lower incidence of scrap
- an alteration to product design
- substitution of one grade of material for another. A lower grade of material may be more difficult to work with, so there may be a higher wastage rate and, in turn, an adverse usage variance may arise.

5 Labour cost variances

5.1 Introduction

There are three different labour variances that you need to know about:

- labour total variance
- labour price variance
- labour efficiency variance.

5.2 Labour total variance

The labour total variance is the difference between:

(a) the standard direct labour cost of the actual production (flexed budget); and

(b) the actual cost of direct labour.

- A labour price variance analyses whether the company paid more or less than expected for labour.
- A labour efficiency variance analyses whether the company used more or less labour than expected.

e.g

Illustration 4 – Labour cost variances

The following information relates to the production of Product X.

Extract from the standard cost card of Product X

	$
Direct labour:	
Bonding (24 hrs @ $5 per hour)	120
Finishing (15 hrs @ $4.80 per hour)	72

Actual results for wages:

Production	1,000 units produced
Bonding	23,900 hours costing $131,450 in total
Finishing	15,500 hours costing $69,750 in total

Required:

Calculate the labour total, price and efficiency variances in each department for Product X in the period.

Solution

Labour variances in Bonding department

Actual quantity x actual price		$131,450	
	Price variance		$11,950 (A)
Actual quantity x standard price			
23,900 x $5.00 hours		$119,500	
	Efficiency variance		$500 (F)
Standard quantity x standard price			
(For actual production)			
1,000 x 24 hours x $5.00		$120,000	

The labour total variance in the Bonding department is the sum of the price and efficiency variances, i.e.

$11,950 (A) + $500 (F) = $11,450 (A)

Proof: The labour total variance in the Bonding department is the difference between:

(a) the standard direct labour cost of the actual production (flexed budget) $120,000 and

(b) the actual cost of direct labour $131,450.

Difference = $(131,450 – 120,000) = $11,450 (A) which is what was calculated above.

Labour variances in Finishing department

Actual quantity x Actual price		$69,750	
	Price variance		$4,650 (F)
Actual quantity x Standard price			
15,500 hours x $4.80		$74,400	
	Efficiency variance		$2,400 (A)
Standard quantity x Standard price			
(For actual production)			
1,000 x 15 hours x $4.80		$72,000	

The labour total variance in the Finishing department is the sum of the price and efficiency variances, i.e.

$4,650 (F) + $2,400 (A) = $2,250 (F)

Proof: The labour total variance in the Finishing department is the difference between:

(a) the standard direct labour cost of the actual production (flexed budget) $72,000 and

(b) the actual cost of direct labour $69,750.

Difference = $(72,000 – 69,750) = $2,250 (F) which is what was calculated above.

Test your understanding 5

Roseberry Ltd makes a single product and has the following budgeted information:

Budgeted production	1,000 units
Budgeted labour hours	3,000 hours
Budgeted labour cost	$15,000

Actual results:

Output	1,100 units
Hours paid for	3,400 hours
Labour cost	$17,680

Calculate labour total, price and efficiency variances.

5.3 Possible causes of labour variances

Labour price variances may be caused by:

- an unexpected national wage award
- overtime or bonus payments which are different from planned/budgeted
- substitution of one grade of labour for another higher or lower grade.

Labour efficiency variances may be caused by:

- changes in working conditions or working methods, for example, better supervision
- consequences of the learning effect
- introduction of incentive schemes or staff training
- substitution of one grade of labour for another higher or lower grade.

6 Variable overhead variances

6.1 Introduction

Variable overhead variances are very similar to those for materials and labour because, like these direct costs, the variable overhead cost also changes when activity levels change.

The most common examination question assumes that variable overhead costs vary with labour hours worked. This results in the calculation of the following variable overhead variances:

- variable overhead total variance
- variable overhead expenditure variance
- variable overhead efficiency variance.

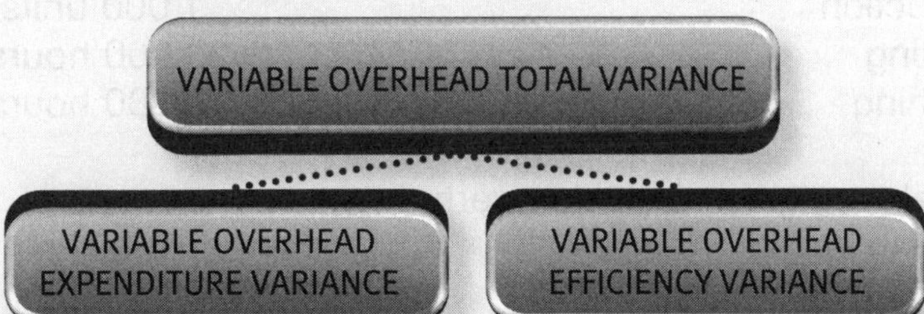

6.2 Variable overhead total variance

It is normally assumed that variable overheads vary with direct labour hours of input and the variable overhead total variance will therefore be due to one of the following:

- the variable overhead cost per hour was different to that expected (an expenditure variance)
- working more or fewer hours than expected for the actual production (an efficiency variance)

Expandable text

- if variable overhead cost changes, not as a result of a change in direct labour hours, but as a result of a change in the production volume it is not possible to calculate the sub-variances: expenditure and efficiency
- in such situations, only the variable overhead total variance can be calculated using the standard variable overhead cost per unit.

Illustration 5 – Variable overhead variances

The following information relates to the production of Product X.

Extract from the standard cost card of Product X

	$
Direct labour:	
Bonding (24 hrs @ $5 per hour)	120
Finishing (15 hrs @ $4.80 per hour)	72
Variable overhead:	
Bonding (24 hrs @ $1.50 per hour)	36
Finishing (15 hrs @ $1 per hour)	15

Actual results for production and labour hours worked:

Production	1,000 units produced
Bonding	23,900 hours
Finishing	15,500 hours

Actual results for variable overheads:

Bonding	Total cost $38,240
Finishing	Total cost $14,900

Required:

Calculate the variable overhead total, expenditure and efficiency variances in each department for Product X for the period.

Solution

Variable overhead variances in Bonding department

Actual quantity x Actual price		$38,240	
	Expenditure variance		$2,390 (A)
Actual quantity x Standard price			
23,900 hours x $1.50		$35,850	
	Efficiency variance		$150 (F)
Standard quantity x Standard price (for actual production)			
1000 x 24 hours x $1.50		$36,000	
	Total variance		$2,240 (A)

The variable overhead total variance in the Bonding department is the sum of the expenditure and efficiency variances, i.e.

$2,390 (A) + $150 (F) = $2,240 (A)

Proof: The variable overhead total variance in the Bonding department is the difference between:

(a) the standard variable overhead of the actual production (flexed budget) $36,000 and

(b) the actual cost of the variable overhead $38,240.

Difference = $(36,000 – 38,240) = $2,240 (A) which is what was calculated above.

Variable overhead variances in Finishing department

Actual quantity x Actual price		$14,900	
	Expenditure variance		$600 (F)
Actual quantity x Standard price			
15,500 hours x $1.00		$15,500	

	Efficiency variance		$500 (A)
Standard quantity x Standard price (for actual production)			
1000 x 15 hours x $1		$15,000	
	Total variance		$100 (F)

The variable overhead total variance in the Finishing department is the sum of the expenditure and efficiency variances, i.e.

$600 (F) + $500 (A) = $100 (F)

Proof: The variable overhead total variance in the Finishing department is the difference between:

(a) the standard variable overhead of the actual production (flexed budget) $15,000 and

(b) the actual cost of the variable overhead $14,900.

Difference = $(15,000 – 14,900) = $100 (F) which is what was calculated above.

Test your understanding 6

The budgeted output for Carr Ltd for May was 1,000 units of product A. Each unit requires two direct labour hours. Variable overheads are budgeted at $3/labour hour.

Actual results:

Output	900	units
Labour hours worked	1,980	hours
Variable overheads	$5,544	

Calculate variable overhead total, expenditure and efficiency variances.

6.3 Possible causes of variable overhead variances

Variable overhead expenditure variances may be caused by:

- incorrect budgets being set at the beginning of a period.
- overheads consisting of a number of items, such as: indirect

materials, indirect labour, maintenance costs, power, etc. Consequently, any meaningful interpretation of the expenditure variance must focus on individual cost items.

Variable overhead efficiency variances may be caused by:

- changes in working methods and condition, for example, better supervision
- consequences of the learning effect
- introduction of incentive schemes or staff training
- substitution of one grade of labour for another higher or lower grade.

Note that the possible causes of variable overhead efficiency variances are the same as those for the labour efficiency variance.

7 Fixed overhead variances

7.1 Introduction

Fixed overhead variances show the effect on profit of differences between actual and expected fixed overheads.

- By definition, actual and expected fixed overheads do not change when there is a change in the level of activity, consequently many of the variances calculated are based upon budgets.
- However, the effect on profit depends upon whether a marginal or absorption costing system is being used.

7.2 Fixed overhead variances in a marginal costing system

As you know, marginal costing does not relate fixed overheads to cost units. There is no under- or over-absorption and the fixed overhead incurred is the amount shown in the income statement (as a period cost).

- Since fixed overhead costs are fixed, they are not expected to change when there is a change in the level of activity.
- Fixed overhead variances in a marginal costing system are as follows:
  - fixed overhead total variance
  - fixed overhead expenditure variance
    - note that the fixed overhead total variance equals the fixed overhead expenditure variance in a marginal costing system.

7.3 Fixed overhead variances in an absorption costing system

- In absorption costing, fixed overheads are related to cost units by using absorption rates. This means that the calculation of fixed overhead variances in an absorption costing system is slightly more complex than in a marginal costing system.
- The fixed overhead variances in an absorption costing system are as follows:
  - fixed overhead total variance
  - fixed overhead expenditure variance
  - fixed overhead volume variance.

- The fixed overhead total variance is equivalent to the under- or over-absorption of overhead in a period.
- The fixed overhead volume variance can be further subdivided into a capacity and efficiency variance.
- We shall look at each of these variances in detail as we progress through this section of the chapter.

7.4 Fixed overhead total variance

Note the differences between this variance under the different costing methods.

- The fixed overhead total variance measures the difference between the budgeted fixed overhead and the actual fixed overhead in a marginal costing system. Under marginal costing, this variance is equal to the fixed overhead expenditure variance.
- In an absorption costing system, the fixed overhead total variance measures the effect on profit of there being a difference between the actual cost incurred and the amount absorbed by the use of the absorption rate based on budgeted costs and activity. Under absorption costing, this variance can be further subdivided into an expenditure and volume variance.

7.5 Fixed overhead expenditure variance

The fixed overhead expenditure variance shows the effect on profit of the actual fixed overhead expenditure differing from the budgeted value. It is calculated in exactly the same way for both marginal and absorption costing.

	$
Actual expenditure	X
Less: Budgeted expenditure	X
Fixed overhead expenditure variance	X

7.6 Fixed overhead volume variance

The fixed overhead volume variance is a measure of the amount of under- or over-absorption of overheads that arises because the actual production volume is different from the budgeted production volume.

- Production volumes can be measured in units or standard hours produced.
- Standard hours produced = actual units produced x standard hours per unit.
- There is no volume variance in a marginal costing system.

	$
Budgeted expenditure	X
Less: Actual units x Fixed overhead absorption rate per unit (FOAR)	X
Fixed overhead volume variance	X

Alternatively:

	$
Budgeted expenditure	X
Less: Standard hours for actual production x FOAR per standard hour	X
Fixed overhead volume variance	X

e.g

Illustration 6 – Fixed overhead variances

The following information is available for a company for Period 4.

Budget

Fixed production overheads	$22,960
Unit	6,560

Actual

Fixed production overheads	$24,200
Unit	6,460

Required:

Calculate the following:

(a) FOAR per unit
(b) fixed overhead expenditure variance for marginal costing
(c) fixed overhead expenditure variance for absorption costing
(d) fixed overhead volume variance for marginal costing
(e) fixed overhead volume variance for absorption costing
(f) fixed overhead total variance for marginal costing
(g) fixed overhead total variance for absorption costing.

Solution

(a) FOAR = $22,960/6,560 = $3.50 per unit

(b) Fixed overhead expenditure variance for marginal costing.

Actual expenditure	$24,200
Less Budgeted expenditure	$22,960
Fixed overhead expenditure variance	$ 1,240 (A)

(c) The fixed overhead expenditure variance for absorption costing is calculated in exactly the same way as that for marginal costing.

(d) There is no fixed overhead volume variance for marginal costing. This is because under maraginal costing, fixed overheads are not expected to change when there is a change in volume of activity.

(e) Fixed overhead volume variance for absorption costing.

Budgeted expenditure	$22,960
Less Actual units x FOAR per unit*	$22,610
Fixed overhead volume variance	$350 (A)

* (6,460 x $3.50 = $22,610)

The variance is adverse because fewer units were produced than expected.

(f) The fixed overhead total variance for marginal costing is the same as the expenditure variance for marginal costing, i.e. $1,240 (A).

(g) The fixed overhead total variance for absorption costing is the total of the expenditure and volume variances for absorption costing, i.e. $1,240 (A) + $350 (A) = $1,590 (A).

Proof: the fixed overhead total variance in an absorption costing system is the same as any under/over-absorption of overhead.

Actual overhead	$24,200
Absorbed overhead (6,460 x $3.50)	$22,610
Fixed overhead total variance (under-absorption)	$1,590 (A)

The variance is adverse because overheads are under-absorbed.

7.7 Fixed overhead capacity and efficiency variances

In absorption costing systems, the fixed overhead volume variance can be subdivided into capacity and efficiency variances.

- The capacity variance measures whether the workforce worked more or fewer hours than budgeted for the period:

	$
Budgeted expenditure	X
Less Actual hours x FOAR per hour	X
Fixed overhead volume capacity variance	X

- The efficiency variance measures whether the workforce took more or less time than expected in producing their output for the period:

	$
Standard hours for actual production x FOAR per hour	X
Less Actual hours x FOAR per hour	X
Fixed overhead volume efficiency variance	X

- Together, these two sub-variances explain why the level of activity was different from that budgeted, i.e. they combine to give the fixed overhead volume variance.

e.g

Illustration 7 – Fixed overhead variances

The following information is available for a company for Period 4.

Budget

Fixed production overheads	$22,960
Units	6,560

The standard time to produce each unit is 2 hours

Actual

Fixed production overheads	$24,200
Units	6,460
Labour hours	12,600 hrs

Required:

Calculate the following:

(a) FOAR per hour
(b) fixed overhead capacity variance
(c) fixed overhead efficiency variance
(d) fixed overhead volume variance.

Solution

(a) FOAR = $22,960/13,120 = $1.75 per hour

Budgeted hours = 6,560 units x 2 hours = 13,120 hours

(b) Budgeted expenditure	$22,960	
Capacity variance		$910 (A)
(c) Actual hours x FOAR = 12,600 x $1.75	$22,050	
Efficiency variance		$560 (F)
Standard hours x FOAR = 6,460 x 2 x $1.75	$22,610	

(d) The fixed overhead volume variance is the sum of the capacity and efficiency variances, i.e.

$910 (A) + $560 (F) = 350 (A). This can be proved as follows.

Budgeted expenditure	$22,960
Less: standard hours x FOAR per hour (6,460 x 2 hours x $1.75)	$22,610
	$350 (A)

You will also note that this is the same value that was calculated for the fixed overhead volume variance in **Illustration 6** above.

Test your understanding 7

Gatting Ltd produces a single product. Fixed overheads are budgeted at $12,000 and budgeted output is 1,000 units.

Actual results:

Output	1,100 units
Overheads incurred	$13,000

Calculate the following:

(a) under/over-absorption
(b) fixed overhead expenditure variance
(c) fixed overhead volume variance
(d) fixed overhead total variance.

7.8 Possible causes of fixed overhead variances

Fixed overhead expenditure variances may be caused by:

- changes in prices relating to fixed overhead expenditure, for example, increase in factory rent
- seasonal differences, e.g. heat and light costs in winter. When the annual budget is divided into four equal quarters, no allowances are given for seasonal factors and the fact that heat and light costs in winter are generally much higher than in the summer months. (Of course, over the year, the seasonal effect is cancelled out.)

Fixed overhead volume variances may be caused by:

- changes in the production volume due to changes in demand or alterations to stockholding policies
- changes in the productivitiy of labour or machinery
- lost production through strikes.

7.9 Possible interrelationships between variances

The cause of a particular variance may affect another variance in a corresponding or opposite way. This is known as interrelationships between variances. Here are some examples:

- if supplies of a specified material are not available, this may lead to a favourable price variance (use of cheaper material), an adverse usage variance (more wastage caused by cheaper material), an adverse fixed overhead volume variance (production delayed while material was unavailable) and an adverse sales volume variance (inability to meet demand due to production difficulties)
- a new improved machine becomes available which causes an adverse fixed overhead expenditure variance (because this machine is more expensive and depreciation is higher) offset by favourable wages efficiency and fixed overhead volume variances (higher productivity)
- workers trying to improve productivity (favourable labour efficiency variance) might become careless and waste more material (adverse materials usage variance)
- in each of these cases, if one variance has given rise to the other, there is an argument in favour of combining the two variances and ascribing them to the common cause. In view of these possible interrelationships, care has to be taken when implementing a bonus scheme. If the chief buyer is rewarded for producing a favourable price variance, this may cause trouble later as shoddy materials give rise to adverse usage variances.

8 Operating statements – total absorption costing

Variances are often summarised in an operating statement (or reconciliation statement).

e.g

Illustration 8 – Operating statements – total absorption costing

Absorption costing operating statement

			$
Budgeted profit			
Sales volume variance **(using profit per unit)**			____
Standard profit on actual sales			
Sales price variance			____
Cost variances:			
	F $	**A** $	
Material price			
Material usage			
Labour rate			
Labour efficiency			
Variable overhead rate			
Variable overhead efficiency			
Fixed overhead volume – Production			
Fixed overhead expenditure – Production			
Fixed overhead expenditure – Non-production	____	____	
Total			____
Actual profit			____

(Note the underlines in bold highlight the differences from the marginal costing version.)

Test your understanding 8

Chapel Ltd manufactures a chemical protective called Rustnot. The following standard costs apply for the production of 100 cylinders:

		$
Materials	500 kgs @ $0.80 per kg	400
Labour	20 hours @ $1.50 per hour	30
Fixed overheads	20 hours @ $1.00 per hour	20
		450

Chapel Ltd uses absorption costing.

The monthly production/sales budget is 10,000 cylinders.
Selling price = $6 per cylinder.

For the month of November the following actual production and sales information is available:

Produced/sold		10,600 cylinders
Sales value		$63,000
Material purchased and used	53,200 kgs	$42,500
Labour	2,040 hours	$3,100
Fixed overheads		$2,200

The following variances were calculated for November:

Sales volume variance	$900 (F)
Sales price variance	$600 (A)
Materials price variance	$60 (F)
Materials usage variance	$160 (A)
Labour rate variance	$40 (A)
Labour efficiency variance	$120 (F)
Fixed overhead expenditure variance	$200 (A)
Fixed overhead volume variance	$120 (F)

Prepare an operating statement for November using the variances given above.

If you wish to gain further practice in calculating variances, use the information given in the question to calculate the variances. The Expandable Text after the solution shows how the individual entries in the operating statement were calculated.

Expandable text

Workings

(W1) **Budgeted profit**

	$
10,000 cylinders @ $1.50	15,000

(W2) Actual profit

		$	$
Sales			63,000
Less:	Materials	42,500	
	Labour	3,100	
	Fixed overheads	2,200	
			47,800
			15,200

Variances

(W3) **Sales price and volume**

The budgeted selling price is $6 per cylinder. Actual sales were 10,600 cylinders for $63,000. If the actual cylinders sold had been sold at the budgeted selling price of $6 then sales would have been:

10,600 x $6 = $63,600.

Thus the difference in selling price resulted in a lower sales value by $600. This is an adverse selling price variance.

The budgeted volume was 10,000 cylinders costing $4.50 each. At the budgeted selling price of $6 each this is a budgeted profit of $1.50 per cylinder.

Actual sales volume was 10,600 cylinders, 600 more than budget. These extra 600 cylinders will increase profit by:

600 x $1.50 = $900.

This is a favourable sales volume variance.

(W4) **Materials price and usage**

The standard price of the raw material is $0.80 per kg. If the actual quantity of 53,200 kg had been bought at the standard price this would have been:

53,200 kg x $0.80/kg = $42,560.

The actual cost was $42,500. This is a saving caused by price – it is a favourable price variance of $60.

Each 100 cylinders should use 500 kgs of material. Therefore the 10,600 cylinders produced should use:

10,600 x 500 kg/100 = 53,000 kgs.

The actual usage was 53,200 kgs. These additional 200 kgs of material have a value (using standard prices) of:

200 kgs x $0.80 = $160.

This is an adverse materials usage variance.

(W5) **Labour**

The standard labour rate is $1.50 per hour. The actual labour hours was 2,040 hours, so if they had been paid at the standard rate per hour, the wage cost would have been:

2,040 x $1.50 = $3,060.

The actual wage cost was $3,100. This extra $40 is the adverse wage rate variance.

Each 100 cylinders should take 20 hours to produce. The actual production was 10,600 cylinders so these should have taken:

10,600 x 20/100 = 2,120 hours.

Actual hours were 2,040 hours, a saving of 80 hours. These hours (valued at the standard rate) are worth:

80 x $1.50 = $120.

This is a favourable labour efficiency.

(W6) **Fixed overheads**

The standard fixed overhead cost is $20 per 100 cylinders. Monthly production is budgeted at 10,000 cylinders. Therefore the budgeted fixed overhead cost is:

10,000 x $20/100 = $2,000.

The actual cost was $2,200. The extra cost of $200 is an adverse fixed overhead expenditure variance.

But the actual production was 10,600 cylinders, 600 more than budgeted. This extra volume of 600 units (valued at the standard absorption rate of $20/100 units) is:

600 x $20/100 = $120.

This is a favourable fixed overhead volume variance.

9 Operating statements – marginal costing

The main differences between absorption and marginal costing operating statements are as follows:

- The marginal costing operating statement has a sales volume variance that is calculated using the standard contribution per unit (rather than a standard profit per unit as in absorption costing).
- There is no fixed overhead volume variance.

e.g

Illustration 9 – Operating statement – marginal costing

Marginal costing operating statement

			$
Budgeted profit			
Sales volume variance (using contribution per unit)			____
Standard profit on actual sales			
Sales price variance			____

Cost variances:			
	F	A	
	$	$	
Material price			
Material usage			
Labour rate			
Labour efficiency			
Variable overhead rate			
Variable overhead efficiency			
Fixed overhead expenditure – Production			
Fixed overhead expenditure – Non-production	____	____	
Total			____
Actual profit			____

Note

The sales volume variance is calculated using the standard contribution per unit.

There is no fixed overhead volume variance (and therefore capacity and efficiency variances) in a marginal costing operating statement.

Test your understanding 9

Place an 'X' in the relevant column to show which variances are found in marginal costing (MC) and which are found in absorption costing (AC) operating statements.

Variance	MC	AC
Sales volume profit variance		
Sales volume contribution variance		
Material cost variances		
Labour cost variances		
Variable overhead variances		
Fixed overhead expenditure variance		
Fixed overhead volume variance		
Fixed overhead capacity variance		
Fixed overhead efficiency variance		
Fixed overhead total variance		

10 Working backwards

One way that the examiner can easily test your understanding of variances is to ask you to calculate the following instead of straightforward variance calculations:

- actual figures from variances and standards
- standards from variances and actual figures.

Illustration 10 – Working backwards

ABC Ltd uses standard costing. It purchases a small component for which the following data are available:

Actual purchase quantity	6,800 units
Standard allowance for actual production	5,440 units
Standard price	$0.85/unit
Material price variance (Adverse)	($544)

Required:

Calculate the actual price per unit of material.

		$
Actual quantity x Actual price = 6,800 x AP	=	?
Actual quantity x Standard price = 6,800 x $0.85	=	5,780
Material price variance (given)	=	544 (A)

Because the material price variance is adverse, this means that the actual cost of the materials was $544 more than standard, i.e.

Actual quantity (6,800) x Actual price = $(5,780 + 544) = $6,324

Actual price per unit = $\frac{\$6,324}{\text{Actual quantity}} = \frac{\$6,324}{\$6,324} = \$0.93$

Test your understanding 10

A business has budgeted to produce and sell 10,000 units of its single product. The standard cost per unit is as follows:

Direct materials	$15
Direct labour	$12
Variable overhead	$10
Fixed production overhead	$8

During the period the following variances occurred:

fixed overhead expenditure variance	$ 4,000 adverse
fixed overhead volume variance	$12,000 favourable

Calculate the following.

(a) Actual fixed overheads in the period.
(b) Actual production volume in the period.

Illustration 11 – Working backwards

In a period, 11,280 kilograms of material were used at a total standard cost of $46,248. The material usage variance was $492 adverse.

Required:

Calculate the standard allowed weight of material for the period.

Solution

$$\text{Standard price} = \frac{\$46,248}{11,280} = \$4.1 \text{ per kg}$$

$$\begin{array}{l}\text{Material usage}\\ \text{variance in kg}\end{array} = \frac{\text{Usage variance in \$}}{\text{Standard price per kg}} = \frac{\$492\text{ (A)}}{\$4.1} = 120 \text{ kg}$$

If the usage variance is adverse, then this means that the actual quantity was greater than the standard quantity, i.e.

Standard quantity allowed = Actual quantity – material usage variance in kg

= 11,280 – 120 = 11,160 kg

This can be proved as follows:

	$
Actual quantity x Standard price = (11,280 x $4.1) =	46,248
Standard quantity x Standard price = (11,160 x $4.1) =	45,756
Material usage variance =	492 (A)

Test your understanding 11

In a period 6,500 units were made and there was an adverse labour efficiency variance of $26,000. Workers were paid $8 per hour, total wages were $182,000 and there was a nil rate variance.

Calculate how many standard labour hours there were per unit.

Chapter summary

The puposes of standard costing

- Provide 'targets'
- Useful for planning, control and decision making
- Essential for calculating and analysing variances
- Variances provide 'feedback' to management
- Easier method of accounting
- Standards may be on marginal or absorption costing basis

STANDARD COSTING

Standard costs per unit

- Collected on standard cost card
- Allow variances to be calculated
- In marginal costing includes variable costs only
- In absorption costing includes a fixed cost per unit also

Variance calculation and analysis

You need to know how to calculate and interpret the following variances

- **SALES VARIANCES**
- **MATERIAL COST VARIANCES**
- **LABOUR COST VARIANCES**
- **VARIABLE OVERHEAD VARIANCES**
- **FIXED OVERHEAD VARIANCES**

Opening statements

- Variances summarised in operating statement
- Reconcile budgeted profit (or contribution) with actual profit
- Marginal costing operating statements do not have fixed overhead volume variances (and therefore capacity and efficiency variances)
- Marginal costing operating statements calculate a sales volume variance using standard contribution per unit
- Absorption costing operating statements calculate a sales volume variance using standard profit per unit

Test your understanding answers

Test your understanding 1

(a) Standard cost per unit under absorption costing

	$
Direct materials	150,000
Direct labour	200,000
Production overhead	
Variable	50,000
Fixed	25,000
Total production cost	425,000

Budgeted production units = 5,000
Standard cost per unit (absorption costing) = $425,000/5,000 units = $85

(b) Standard cost per unit under marginal costing

	$
Direct materials	150,000
Direct labour	200,000
Variable overhead costs	50,000
Total variable cost	400,000

Budgeted production units = 5,000
Standard cost per unit (marginal costing) = $400,000/5,000 units = $80

Test your understanding 2

Price variance = ($2.50 – $2.00) x 500	=	$250 (A)
Volume variance = (500 – 400) x $0.70*	=	$70 (F)
		$180 (A)

*Standard contribution per unit = $(2.50 – 1.80) = $0.70

Test your understanding 3

Price variance = ($60 – $61) x 6,000	=	$6,000 (F)
Volume variance = (6,500 – 6,000) x $5*	=	$2,500 (A)
		$3,500 (F)

* Standard gross profit per unit

Test your understanding 4

Material variances	$	$
Actual quantity x Actual price =	20,900	
Price variance		1,100 (F)
Actual quantity x Standard price		
= 2,200 x $10 =	22,000	
Usage variance		2,000 (A)
Standard quantity x Standard price		
= 1,000 x 2 x $10 =	20,000	
Total variance		900 (A)

Test your understanding 5

Labour variances	$	$
Actual hours x Actual rate =	17,680	
Price variance		680 (A)
Actual hours x Standard rate		
= 3,400 hours x $5 ($15,000/3,000 = $5 per hour) =	17,000	
Efficiency variance		500 (A)
Standard hours x Standard rate		
= 1,100 x 3 hours x $5 =	16,500	
Total variance		1,180 (A)

Test your understanding 6

Variable overhead variances	$	$
Actual hours x Actual rate =	5,544	
Expenditure variance		396 (F)
Actual hours x Standard rate		
= 1,980 hours x $3 =	5,940	
Efficiency variance		540(A)
Standard hours x Standard rate		
= 900 x 2 hours x $3 =	5,400	
Total variance		144 (A)

Variable overhead variances:	$	$
Actual hours x Actual rate =	5,544	
Expenditure variance		396 (F)
Actual hours x Standard rate		
= 1,980 hours x $3 =	5,940	
Efficiency variance		540(A)
Standard hours x Standard rate		
= 900 x 2 hours x $3 =	5,400	
Total variance		144 (A)

The variable overhead total variance is the sum of the expenditure and efficiency variances, i.e.

$396 (F) + $540 (A) = $144 (A).

Proof: The variable overhead total variance in the Finishing department is the difference between:

(a) the standard variable overhead of the actual production (flexed budget) $5,400 and

(b) the actual cost of the variable overhead $5,544.

Difference = $(5,400 – 5,544) = $144 (A) which is what was calculated above.

Test your understanding 7

(a) FOAR per unit = $12,000/1,000 = $12 per unit

Under/over-absorption		
Overheads absorbed = 1,100 x $12	$13,200	
Overheads incurred	$13,000	
Over-absorption	$200	

(b) Fixed overhead expenditure variance

Actual expenditure	$13,000	
Budgeted expenditure	$12,000	
Expenditure variance	$1,000	(A)

(c) Fixed overhead volume variance

Budgeted expenditure	12,000	
Actual units x FOAR (1,100 x $12)	13,200	
Volume variance	$1,200	(F)

(d) Fixed overhead total variance

The fixed overhead total variance is the sum of the expenditure and volume variances.

Fixed overhead expenditure variance	$1,000	(A)
Fixed overhead volume variance	$1,200	(F)
Fixed overhead total variance	$200	(F)

Proof: the fixed overhead total variance is the same as the over-absorbed overhead ($200) as calculated in part (a) above.

Test your understanding 8

Chapel Ltd – Operating statement for November

Budgeted profit (W1)			15,000
Sales volume variance (W3)			900
Sales price variance (W3)			(600)
			15,300
Cost variances:			
	F	**A**	
Materials price (W4)	60		
Materials usage (W4)		160	
Labour rate (W5)		40	
Labour efficiency (W5)	120		
Fixed overhead expenditure (W6)		200	
Fixed overhead volume (W6)	120		
Total	300	400	(100)
Actual profit (W2)			15,200

Test your understanding 9

Variance	**MC**	**AC**
Sales volume profit variance		**X**
Sales volume contribution variance	**X**	
Material cost variances	**X**	**X**
Labour cost variances	**X**	**X**
Variable overhead variances	**X**	**X**
Fixed overhead expenditure variance	**X**	**X**
Fixed overhead volume variance		**X**
Fixed overhead capacity variance		**X**
Fixed overhead efficiency variance		**X**
Fixed overhead total variance	**X**	**X**

Test your understanding 10

(a) The actual fixed overheads are calculated as follows.

Actual fixed overheads	?	
Budgeted fixed overheads ($8 x 10,000)	$80,000	
Fixed overhead expenditure variance	$4,000	(A)

Because the fixed overhead expenditure variance is adverse, this means that the actual fixed overheads were $4,000 more than budgeted.

Actual fixed overheads = Budgeted fixed overheads + Fixed overhead expenditure variance

= $80,000 + $4,000 = $84,000

(b) The actual production volume is calculated as follows.

$$\text{The fixed overhead volume variance (in units)} = \frac{\text{Fixed overhead volume variance in \$}}{\text{Standard fixed overhead rate per unit}}$$

$$= \frac{\$12{,}000}{\$8} = 1{,}500 \text{ units (F)}$$

Because the variance is favourable, this means that 1,500 more units were produced than budgeted, i.e. 10,000 + 1,500 = 11,500 units.

This can also be proved as follows.

Budgeted expenditure	$80,000	
Actual units x standard fixed overhead rate per unit ? x $8	?	
Fixed overhead volume variance	$12,000	(F)

Actual units x standard fixed overhead rate per unit = $80,000 + $12,000 = $92,000

$$\text{Actual units} = \frac{\$92{,}000}{\$8} = 11{,}500 \text{ units}$$

Test your understanding 11

	$	$
Actual hours x Actual rate	182,000	
Rate variance		Nil
Actual hours x Standard rate		
= ? x $8 = 4	182,000	
Efficiency variance		26,000 (A)
Standard hours x Standard rate		
= 6,500 x Standard hours x $8 =	156,000	

∴ Standard labour hours per unit = $\frac{\$156{,}000}{}$ x $8 = 3

Appendix: spreadsheets

Chapter learning objectives

Upon completion of this chapter you will be able to:

- explain the role, features and uses of a spreadsheet package.

This section has been included as an appendix as many students will already have detailed knowledge of such software through practical experience. However, spreadsheets are examinable and should be expected to come up every time in the exam.

1 Spreadsheets

1.1 Introduction

For those unfamiliar with spreadsheet packages, this appendix will provide the basic introduction needed to feel confident to 'get into' Microsoft Excel and carry out simple information analysis tasks.

- This package has been chosen because it is the most popular and therefore the most likely to be used in your college or work environment.
- The editions and programs that you are using may not be the same as those used in this appendix. In that case, the screens you produce will not be identical to those shown here.
- However, all spreadsheet packages will have the basic features described in this appendix and access to a different package will not cause too many problems.
- If you are at all unsure, you should read the manual that accompanies your chosen spreadsheet.

1.2 What is a spreadsheet?

A spreadsheet is a computer package that is used to manipulate data. The word spreadsheet has its origins in the large sheets of paper used by accountants, over which they spread their figures and calculations in neat rows and columns.

- A spreadsheet could be defined as a table of rows and columns that intersect to form cells.
- Each row is identified by a number.
- Each column is identified by a letter (or letters).
- Each cell has a unique identifier formed by a letter (or letters) and a number.
- Numbers, text or formulae may be entered into these cells.
- A formula normally involves a mathematical calculation on the content of other cells, the result being inserted in the cell containing the formula. These are not visible when you are entering data but reside in the background.
- Because most business worksheets are quite large, extending beyond the edge of the computer screen, the screen is in effect a 'window' into the worksheet.
- Some or all of a spreadsheet can be printed out directly or saved on disk for insertion into reports or other documents using a word processing package.

2 Accessing a spreadsheet

2.1 Excel

The instructions that follow are for the Excel for Windows (or similar) package.

If you do not have access to Excel it will be assumed that you can use a similar package and you should refer to your manual for the basic mouse clicks.

In order to explain the role, features and uses of a spreadsheet package, the following instructions should be read and attempted in full if you are unfamiliar with the use of spreadsheets. If you are confident with using spreadsheets check through the notes for any areas you may not have covered previously.

2.2 Basic spreadsheet terms

Make sure you learn the following basic spreadsheet terms if you don't know them already.

- **Worksheet:** a worksheet or spreadsheet is the basis of all the work you do. It could be considered to be the electronic equivalent of an accountant's ledger.
- **Workbook:** is a collection of worksheets. The workbook is simply a folder that binds together your worksheets. When you open a new workbook, it automatically contains 16 worksheets.
- **Cells:** the worksheet is divided into columns and rows. The intersection of a column and a row is known as a 'cell'. To refer to a particular cell, use its column and row location. This is called a 'cell address', for example A1, B22, etc.
- **Columns:** each column is referenced by one or two letters in the column heading. The whole worksheet consists of 256 columns, labelled A through IV.
- **Rows:** each row is referenced by the row number shown in the row heading to the left of a row. There are 65,536 rows in Excel.
- **Sheet tabs:** these are between the worksheet and the status bar and are used to move between worksheets in your workbook.
- **Window:** you can only see part of the worksheet at any time; you could consider the screen to be a window onto the worksheet. You have the facility to move this window, so that you can view any part of the spreadsheet.
- **Cell pointer:** look at the cell that is highlighted; this highlighted area is known as the cell pointer. It indicates the cell in which you are currently working. The current cell location is also displayed on the edit line above the spreadsheet.

A good way of testing your understanding of spreadsheets in an examination is to ask you to select the correct definition of one of the basic spreadsheet terms from a list of possible options.

2.3 Running a spreadsheet program

The way to gain access to a spreadsheet package depends upon the type of computer system in use.

- A **menu** may be available to allow access to the chosen software by entering a single number or letter or by use of a cursor or mouse.

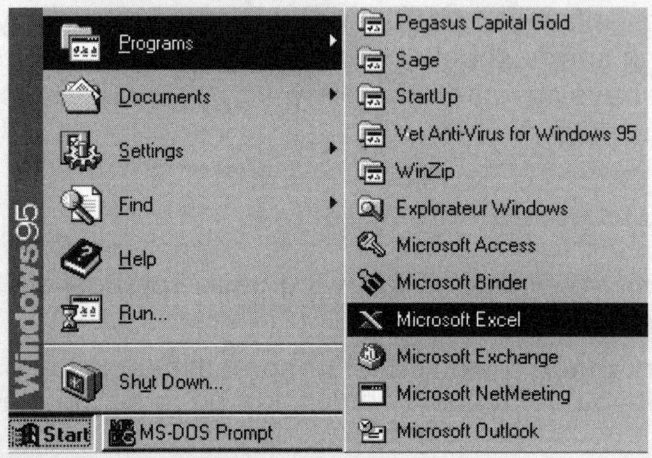

- If you are working in a **Windows** environment, you will access the spreadsheet package using the mouse.
- Click on the Start button in the bottom left hand corner of the Window.
- Keep the mouse button depressed and highlight the 'Programs' and then the package that you want to use. Click on the icon.
- The opening screen in Microsoft Excel might look like this.

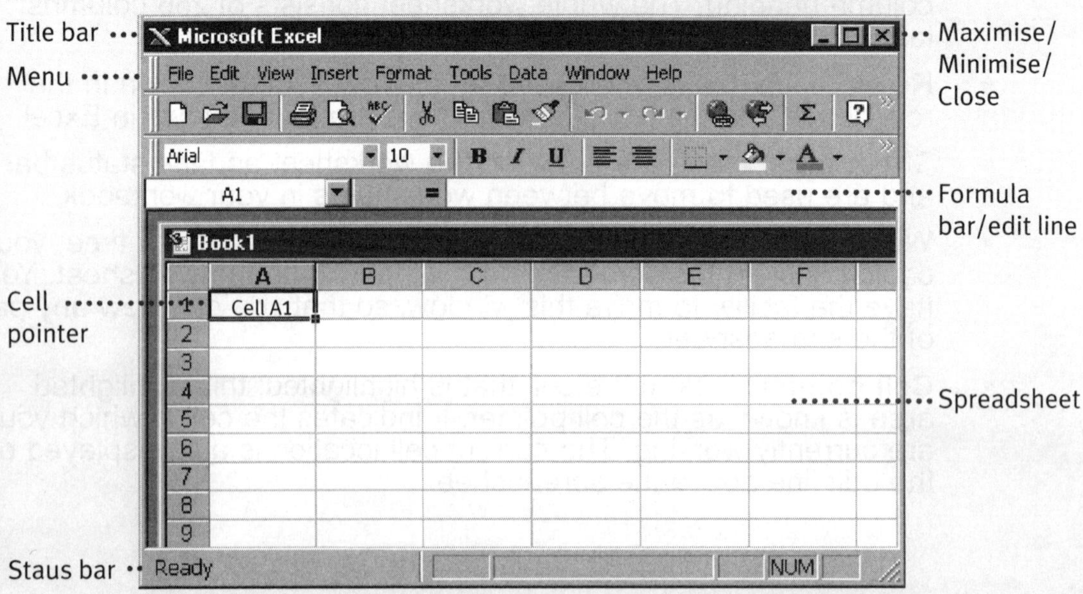

(Yours might look a little different if you have a different version of Excel).

- On the screen you will see the **title bar**, the **menu bar, the function tool bar** and in the top right corner the buttons to **minimise**, **maximise**/restore and close the worksheet. As with most Windows programs you can change the size and move the Excel Window.
- If your screen does not have a formula bar, a formatting bar or a toolbar you can show these by accessing **View** and then **Toolbars** from the menu at the top of the screen. You can then select (or deselect) what you want to show on the screen. A tick signifies that it is switched on.
- The toolbars are below the menu bar. Clicking on any of these buttons provides a shortcut to selecting options from the menu bar. If you pause the pointer over a button a label will appear and, in the **status bar**, Excel will tell you what that button does.
- The **formula bar** is between the spreadsheet and the toolbar. This provides you with information about the contents of the active cell. The co-ordinates of the active cell are displayed on the left-hand side of the formula bar.
- The **status bar** is at the bottom of the screen. It gives you information about your spreadsheet, such as when you are opening or saving a file and whether you have CAPS LOCK, NUM LOCK or SCROLL LOCK on.
- **Scroll bars** are used to move your spreadsheet both up and down and left to right. The vertical scroll bar (on the right hand side of the spreadsheet) is used to move up and down. The horizontal scroll bar (below the spreadsheet and above the status bar) is used to move left and right.

2.4 Creating a new file

When you first open Excel, a blank spreadsheet appears on the screen and you can start typing straight away. At this point you can work on an established spreadsheet or start on a new one by creating a file.

- From the file menu choose the NEW option, and a new Excel workbook will appear on the screen. Once you have created a document, you must save it if you wish to use it in the future.

2.5 Saving a file

To save a file, carry out the following instructions:

- From the **FILE** menu choose the **SAVE AS** option.
- A dialogue box will appear.
- If necessary, use the DRIVE drop down menu to select the relevant drive; if you are saving to floppy disk, it is generally the 'a:' or 'b:' drive.
- In the **FILE NAME** text box type in the name you wish to use (up to 8 characters). All spreadsheet packages automatically add a three-digit extension to your filename. In Lotus it will begin with wk and in Excel it will begin with xl.

- Click on the **OK** button.
- When you have saved a file once, you do not need to choose the **SAVE AS** option again, but simply choose **SAVE** from the **FILE** menu or click on the icon on the tool bar (picture of a floppy disk).

2.6 Closing a file/Quitting

When you have finished working on a spreadsheet and you have saved it, you will need to close it down.

- You can do this by either pressing the button at the top right hand side of the worksheet with a cross on it or by choosing the CLOSE or EXIT option from the FILE menu.
- If you only want to exit Excel briefly and prefer not to close down the whole package you can switch to another application or back to the Windows Program Manager by pressing <Alt><Tab> repeatedly. This allows you to step through all the opened packages in rotation.
- If you have changed the file, Excel will ask if you wish to save the changes you made before closing. Click on the appropriate button.

3 Moving around the spreadsheet

3.1 Cell pointer

As you know, a whole worksheet consists of many columns and rows. On opening a spreadsheet, you can only see a small part of it – generally columns A to H and rows 1 to 16.

- The screen is like a window onto the worksheet and you have the facility to move this window so that you can view any part of the worksheet.
- The cell pointer highlights the cell you are currently in.
- By moving the cell pointer you are able to enter information into any cell of the worksheet. There are a number of ways of moving the cell pointer, but the easiest way is to use the mouse.
- You can move around the spreadsheet by positioning the **mouse pointer** over the appropriate cell and clicking to select that cell.
- If the cell address you want is outside the range shown in the current window, it is possible to move down or across the spreadsheet by clicking on the scroll bars to the side or below the Window.
- Alternatively, you can use the arrow keys on the keyboard.

3.2 Moving directly to a cell: the GOTO command

Sometimes you may want to move to a specific address in the spreadsheet that is too far from your present position to warrant using the arrow keys to get there. On the top of the keyboard you can see a row of keys labelled F1 through to F12; these are known as 'function keys'.

- When the function keys are pressed, a special function is invoked. For example, the F5 key is the GOTO key in both Excel and Lotus 123.
- If you wish to go to cell D19, press F5 and a dialogue box will appear. You are prompted to enter an address or range. Enter D19 and the cell pointer will go directly to cell D19.

3.3 The help facility

Excel has a comprehensive help facility, which provides both **general** help and **context sensitive** help.

- To invoke the help command press the 'Help' button on the menu bar, the ? box on the toolbar or the shortcut key F1.
- To obtain information on any particular subject shown, move the mouse pointer over the required topic and click, or you may be prompted to type in a question.
- Context sensitive help is available either when a help button is displayed in a dialogue box or when an error message is flashed onto the screen.
- Asking for help at this stage by either clicking on the help button, ? box or by pressing F1 will result in the help window appearing at the topic relevant to the problem encountered.

4 Entering data

4.1 Putting data onto a worksheet

Entering data on a worksheet is very easy. You simply type your entry at the keyboard, press return and whatever you typed will be placed in the current cell, i.e. where the cell pointer is.

- As you type, each character will be displayed on the edit line at the top of the screen. The entry is not put onto the worksheet until you press the return key.
- When you have finished entering data you can either press the <Enter> key on the keyboard or click on the Enter Box (a green tick) on the formula bar.
- If you change your mind about entering the data then either press the <Esc> key on the keyboard or click on the Cancel Box (a red cross) on the formula bar.
- If you have made a mistake, you can press the 'backspace key' (the key above the ENTER key) to delete what you have done one character at a time. If you have already pressed the ENTER key, you can delete it by highlighting the cell or cells and pressing the Delete key.

- There are three types of data that can be entered into your worksheet – text, numbers and formulae.

4.2 Entering text

Text is entered by simply typing into a cell. Typing any letter at the beginning of a cell entry causes it to be accepted as a 'label', rather than a 'value'.

- If the text you enter is longer than the width of the cell then the text will 'run over' into the next cell. But if the next cell also contains data/information then you will only see part of the text you entered, i.e. the label will be truncated.
- There will be times when you want a spreadsheet to treat a number or a formula as text. To do this you must type an apostrophe in front of the number or formula you are entering, e.g. '01707 320903 or '=A4+D5.

4.3 Entering numbers

Numbers can be entered on a spreadsheet by simply typing into a cell.

- If the space in the cell is insufficient, the number will be shown in an exponential form on the spreadsheet, but the number will still be retained in full in the formula bar.
- If you want to see the contents of cells in full, the columns can be widened to accommodate the number (or text).
- It is not necessary to put the commas in manually when entering large numbers (1,000 or more), because it is easy to format the data to display commas and decimal places to make the data easier to understand. For example:
  - if you wish to enter 123,456, enter 123456 into a cell and press Enter
  - move the cursor back onto that cell, click on 'Format' in the menu bar, then 'Cells'

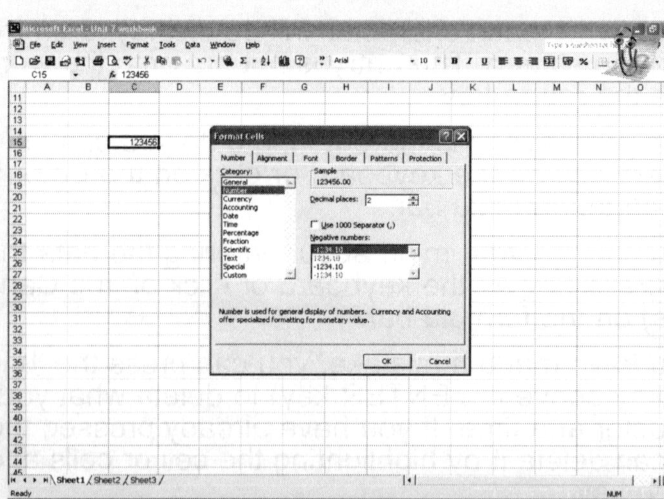

- choose the 'Number' tab and then 'Number' from the category list
- now reduce the decimal places to '0' by clicking on the down arrow and tick the 'Use 1000 separator' box
- press OK. Your number should now be shown as 123,456
- you can also use the 'Currency' option from the category list to put $s in front.

4.4 Entering formulae

The arithmetic operations and method of writing the basic formulae are very similar in all packages The **BODMAS (Brackets, Of, Division, Multiplication, Addition, Subtraction)** rule must be used to evaluate an arithmetic problem:

- use brackets to clarify the correct order of operations and evaluate expressions within the brackets first
- calculate 'of' expressions (e.g. 20% of the total)
- perform division and multiplication before addition and subtraction
- work from left to right if the expression contains only addition and subtraction.

4.5 Steps involved in entering formulae

To enter a formula:

- select the cell where you want to enter the formula
- press the equal sign (=) on the keyboard (or click on the sign in the formula bar, if one is shown)
- key in the formula directly from the keyboard or use the mouse to select the cells you want in the formula. There are no spaces in a formula
- press the <Enter> key
- when you have entered a formula, the resulting value appears in that cell. The formula is only visible in the formula bar
- typical formulae:

= (A6+C10)-E25	Adds A6 with C10 and subtracts E25
= (H19*A7)/3	Multiplies H19 with A7 and divides the total by 3
= SUM(L12:L14)	A quick way of adding L12 + L13 + L14

- an even quicker way to add a row or column of numbers is to click the button in the toolbar for Lotus 1-2-3. The equivalent button in MS Excel is the Greek symbol Σ sigma.

4.6 Statistical functions

The basic commands for statistical functions that operate on lists of values are also very similar throughout the range of spreadsheet packages. Examples of these are:

- SUM The sum of the values in list
- AVG The average of the values in list
- A formula always starts with an equal sign (=) in Excel. If you start it with an equal sign (=) in Lotus 123, it automatically converts it to a plus (+) sign.
- Formulae consist of numbers, cell co-ordinates (e.g. A2, F7), operators and functions. Operators perform actions on numbers and co-ordinates. Examples of operators are plus, minus, divide and multiply. Functions perform more advanced actions on numbers and co-ordinates.

4.7 Adding basic formulae

Excel allows you to build up mathematical formulae to perform many useful functions, e.g. add up data, find average values, produce variances, add or subtract VAT, etc. Some basic formulae are commonly used in financial spreadsheets.

- **Multiply** – type an = in the formula bar and click on first cell, then type a * (to multiply) and click on second cell.
- **Add** – type "=" in the formula bar (or click on the = sign), click on the first cell, then type "+" and click on second cell.

4.8 Copying

Shown below are the Cut, Copy and Paste buttons toolbar at the top of the screen on both Excel (left) and Lotus.

- **Cut** then **paste** is used to **move** cells from one area of the spreadsheet to another.
- **Copy** then **paste** is used to **copy** cells from one area to another.
- Copying and pasting or cutting and pasting operations always have two parts:
  - define the range you want to copy or cut **from**; then
  - define the range that you want to copy or move to.
- You can copy formulae to different cells by the same method. Note that the cell references change automatically when formulae are copied – this is known as relative copying.
- If you do not wish for cell references to be changed automatically when copying formulae to different cells you can insert $ signs before the column reference, or the row reference or both. This is known as absolute copying.

5 Improving the appearance of a spreadsheet

5.1 Formatting numbers

To make monetary data 100% clearer it should be formatted into monetary amounts. For columns with a '$' at the top:

- highlight the column of figures to be formatted
- click on 'Format' on the menu bar, then choose 'Cells'
- on the category list choose 'Currency'. It will probably automatically assign a '$' and 2 decimal places. Click OK.

5.2 Formatting text

Making a spreadsheet look good is more than just a cosmetic exercise. Proper formatting, underlining and emboldening can make the spreadsheet easier to follow, draw attention to important figures and reduce the chance of errors.

- For example, to change the font to Times New Roman throughout a spreadsheet: click on the first cell with an entry in it and drag the mouse to the last cell with an entry in it. The area covered should be shaded. Go to the Format menu and select Cells. Select the Font tab and then the chosen style.
- For example, to put titles in bold: click and drag the cursor over them, then click on the **B** button (**B**old) on the tool bar. Alternatively, all entries in a row or column can be selected by clicking on the letter at the head of the column or the number at the very left of the row.
- For example, to change the width of a column: place the mouse pointer in the column heading at the intersection and a two headed arrow should appear. Drag this to the right until the column is wide enough. Adjust the width of the other columns to accommodate the entries comfortably.
- For example, to align column headings use the align buttons on the formatting toolbar (to the right of the underline U).
- For example, to underline totals by highlighting the cells containing the totals: click on 'Format' on the menu bar, then click on 'Cells' then 'Border' tab, and a window similar to the following will appear.

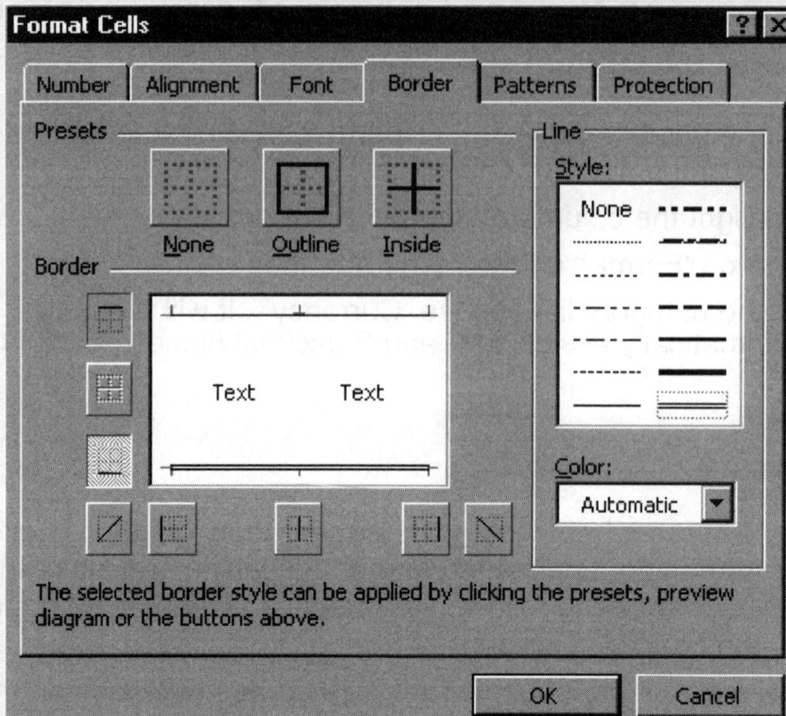

- The box on the left shows the edges of the cell or selection of cells, which will have a border.
- The box on the right shows the types of lines that are available.
- Click on the top line on the left-hand list and then on the single, non-bold line (probably already selected) in the right hand options.
- The top of the 'totals' cells should now have a single underlining.
- Now click on the bottom line and then on the double under-lining style. Click on OK.

6 Uses of spreadsheets

6.1 Introduction

Much of the data of a company is likely to be held on a number of spreadsheets. They are a convenient way of setting up all sorts of charts, records and tables, including:

- budgeting and forecasting
- reporting performance
- variance analysis
- CVP analysis
- inventory valuation.

Spreadsheets can be used for anything with a rows and columns format.

6.2 'What if?' analysis

- The power of spreadsheets is that the data held in any one cell can be made dependent on that held in other cells.
- This means that changing a value in one cell can set off a chain reaction of changes through other related cells.
- This allows 'what-if?' analysis to be quickly and easily carried out, e.g. 'what if sales are 10% lower than expected?'

6.3 Budgeting and forecasting

Preparing budgets and forecasts are classic applications of spreadsheets, as they allow estimates to be changed without having to recalculate everything manually, e.g. here is an extract from a cash flow forecast.

	A	B	C	D	E
1	**Revised cashflow forecast for 05/06**				
2	**£000**	**Jul-05**	**Aug-05**	**Sep-05**	**Oct-05**
3					
4	**Sales receipts**	**1867**	**1828**	**1893**	**1939**
5					
6	**Payments**				
7	Purchases	1691	1644	1701	1798
8	Overheads	57	57	57	57
9	Capex	50	50	50	25
10	Bank loan	12	12	12	12
11	VAT	160			171
12	CT				
13	Bank o/d interest	2	2	2	1
14		**1972**	**1765**	**1822**	**2064**
15					
16	Net cash in/out flow	**-105**	**63**	**71**	**-125**
17					
18	Bal b/f *	-134	-239	-176	-105
19	Bal c/f	-239	-176	-105	-230
20					

Apart from the formatting to make the forecast easy to read, the key formulae are as follows:

- Total payments: e.g. B14: = SUM(B7:B13)
- Net cashflow: e.g. B16: = +B4-B14
- Bal c/f: e.g. B19: = +B18+B16

6.4 Reporting performance

Performance appraisal usually involves calculating ratios, possibly involving comparatives between companies and from one year to the next.

- A neat way of doing this is to input the raw data, such as financial statements on one sheet and calculate the ratios on another.
- For example, here is an extract from the five years results for a company called Parkland, input on a sheet titled "historic data":

	A	Formula Bar		D	E	
1						
2					Rutwater	
3	£'000		2005	2004	2003	2
4						
5	Revenue		319,361	316,197	309,119	30
6	Cost of sales		-81,428	-84,627	-83,039	-8
7	Gross profit		237,933	231,570	226,080	22
8						

- Here are some ratios that have been set up on a separate sheet (titled "current and historic ratios") in the same workbook:

	A	B	C	D	E
1					
2	**Historic ratio analysis**				**Rutwater**
3			**2005**	**2004**	**2003**
4					
5	RoC		11.7%	12.5%	12.5%
6	Margin		27.8%	27.8%	26.8%
7	Asset turnover		£0.42	£0.45	£0.47
8	Gross margin		74.5%	73.2%	73.1%
9	EBITDA margin		49.2%	48.1%	47.2%
10					

- Don't worry about the detail of the ratios – you will encounter them at some stage in your studies.
- Taking just one as an example, gross margin – this is calculated as gross profit divided by revenue. The answer has been formatted to show as a percentage to one decimal place and the formula for cell C8 is as follows: ='Historic data'!C7/'Historic data'!C5
- The 'historic data'! part indicates which worksheet the information came from. While this looks complex, setting up the formula was simply a matter of clicking on the correct cells in the first place:
  - On the sheet "current and historic ratios" click on cell C8 and press "="
  - Switch to sheet "historic data" and click on cell C7
  - Type "/"
  - Click on cell C5 while still on sheet "historic data"
  - Press enter and you will automatically return to the "current and historic ratios" sheet.

6.5 Variance analysis

Variance analysis involves management comparing actual results with budget and then investigating the differences. A relatively simple statement could be along the lines of the following:

Variance Report

Project Name: ____________________

Employee Name: ____________________

ID#	Task Name	Planned Effort (Baseline)	Actual Effort (or Estimated Completion)	Variance / Slippage	Comments
				0.0	
				0.0	
				0.0	
				0.0	
				0.0	
				0.0	

7 Advantages and disadvantages of spreadsheets

7.1 Introduction

Many users use spreadsheets to store data, even though the data could be better managed in a database.

- This confusion stems from the basic similarity that the key function of both spreadsheets and databases is to store and manipulate data.
- However, there are some distinct advantages and disadvantages to both spreadsheets and databases that define their usefulness as a data management tool.
- To store large amounts of raw data, it is best to use a database. This is especially true in circumstances where two or more users share the information.

7.2 Advantages of spreadsheets

Spreadsheets are designed to analyse data and sort list items, not for long-term storage of raw data. A spreadsheet should be used for 'crunching' numbers and storage of single list items. Advantages of spreadsheets include the following.

- Spreadsheet programs are relatively easy to use.
- Little training is required to get started with using spreadsheets.
- Most data managers are familiar with spreadsheets.
- They also include graphing functions that allow for quick reporting and analysis of data. There is more on the graphics function of spreadsheets at the end of this section.

7.3 Disadvantages of spreadsheets

Disadvantages of spreadsheets include the following.

- Data must be re-copied over and over again to maintain it in separate data files.
- Spreadsheets are not able to identify data errors efficiently.
- Spreadsheets lack detailed sorting and querying abilities.
- There can be sharing violations among users wishing to view or change data at the same time.
- Spreadsheets are restricted to a finite number of records, and can require a large amount of hard-drive space for data storage.

7.4 Graphics

As we have already said, one of the major advantages of using a spreadsheet package is the ease with which graphs and charts can be generated.

- For example, suppose we want to present the following information about customer invoices graphically:

DC Carers Ltd	$58.68
F Browns Ltd	$32.31
J Cables Ltd	$134.68
J Hoggs Ltd	$271.43
L Quick Ltd	$1,098.63

- The easiest way to do this is to use the chart wizard, with the icon:

- With the two columns in the spreadsheet selected, you can click on the Chart Wizard and select the type of chart or graph that you prefer and experiment with changing the data labels and percentages. An example is shown below.

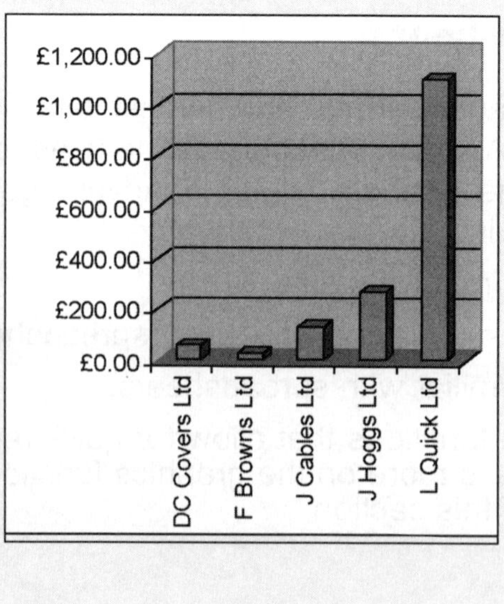

Test your understanding 1

Which of the following is not an advantage of spreadsheet software over manual approaches?

A Security

B Speed

C Accuracy

D Legibility

Test your understanding 2

Angelina wants to calculate the expected value of the following cash flows using a spreadsheet

	A	B	C
1	Cash flow	Probability	CF × probability
2	250	0.3	
3	350	0.2	
4	450	0.4	
5	600	0.1	
6	Total	1	

What should the formulae be in

A Cell C3

B Cell C6?

Test your understanding 3

The following spreadsheet has been set up to look at the relationship between 20 sets of data relating to production volume (x) and costs (y).

		A	B	C	D	E
1		x	y	xy	x^2	y^2
25	Totals					

What formula is required to calculate the variable cost per unit?

Test your understanding answers

Test your understanding 1

A A computer-based approach exposes the firm to threats from viruses, hackers and general system failure.

Test your understanding 2

A =C1*C2

B =SUM(C2:C5)

Test your understanding 3

The variable cost per unit is the gradient ("b") of the linear regression line, given in this case by

$$b = \frac{n\Sigma xy - (\Sigma x)(\Sigma y)}{n\Sigma x^2 - (\Sigma x)^2} = (20*C25\text{-}A25*B25)/(20*D25\text{-}A25\hat{}2)$$

Questions

MULTIPLE CHOICE QUESTIONS

Chapter 1: The nature and purpose of management accounting

Q 1 Data is information that has been processed in such a way as to make it meaningful for use by management in making decisions.

Is this statement TRUE or FALSE?

(1 mark)

Q 2 Which of the following is not a fundamental attribute of good information?

A Complete

B Concise

C Cost effective

(1 mark)

Q 3 Which of the following steps does not form part of the planning process?

A Set objectives for achievement

B Identify ways in which objectives can be achieved

C Take corrective action to improve chances of achieving objectives

(1 mark)

Q 4 Which of the following is the appropriate name for planning which considers how the functional heads within a business unit will coordinate employees on a day-to-day basis?

A Strategic planning

B Tactical planning

C Operational planning

(1 mark)

Q 5 The manager of a division is responsible for costs and revenues as well as capital invested.

Which is the appropriate classification for the division?

A Revenue centre

B Investment centre

C Profit centre

(1 mark)

Q 6 **The following assertions relate to management accounting:**

i) The purpose of management accounting is to provide accounting information to the managers of the business and other internal users.

ii) Management accounts are only concerned with the cost of goods, services and operations.

Which of the following statements are true?

A Assertion i) and ii) are both correct

B Only assertion i) is correct

C Only assertion ii) is correct

(1 mark)

Chapter 2: Types of Cost and Cost Behaviour

Q 7 **Which of the following costs should not be included in the stock valuation of a manufacturing business?**

A Depreciation on the plant and machinery

B Salary of salesman

C Factory supervisor's salary

D Electricity for factory

(2 marks)

Q 8 **A shop carries out repairs on customers' electrical items, eg televisions, video recorders, etc.**

Which of the following is an example of an indirect variable cost?

A Business rates for repair shop

B Salary of repair shop supervisor

C Repair person paid per hour worked

D Electricity for recharging repair tools

(2 marks)

Q 9 **The following diagram represents a cost behaviour pattern.**

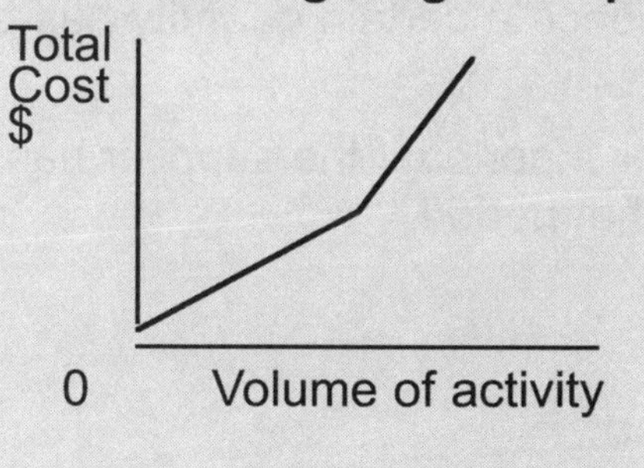

Which of the following statements is consistent with the above diagram?

A Annual factory costs when the electricity supplier sets a tariff based on a fixed charge plus a constant unit cost for consumption but subject to a maximum annual charge.

B Weekly total labour cost when workers are paid an hourly wage during normal working hours and a higher hourly rate if they are required to work outside those hours.

C Total direct material cost for a period if the supplier charges a lower unit cost on all units once a certain quantity has been purchased in that period.

D Total direct material cost for a period if the supplier has agreed to a maximum charge for that period.

(2 marks)

Q **10** **The following diagram represents a cost behaviour pattern.**

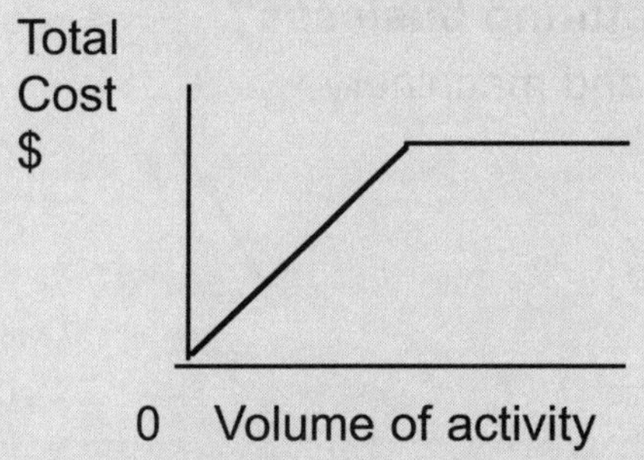

Which of the following statements is consistent with the above diagram?

A Annual factory costs when the electricity supplier sets a tariff based on a fixed charge plus a constant unit cost for consumption but subject to a maximum annual charge

B Weekly total labour cost when workers are paid an hourly wage during normal working hours and a higher hourly rate if they are required to work outside those hours

C Total direct material cost for a period if the supplier charges a lower unit cost on all units once a certain quantity has been purchased in that period

D Total direct material cost for a period if the supplier has agreed to a maximum charge for that period

(2 marks)

11 The telephone costs of a business are likely to be classified as a stepped fixed cost.

Is this statement TRUE or FALSE?

A True

B False

(1 mark)

12 A company has a performance related pay scheme in operation.

What is the most appropriate cost classification for the salaries of the managers?

A Fixed cost

B Stepped fixed cost

C Semi-variable cost

(1 mark)

13 Which of the following statements is correct?

A Only direct production costs should be included in stock valuation

B All indirect costs should be treated as non-production costs.

C The sum of direct costs is known as prime cost.

D Indirect costs per unit are always larger than direct costs per unit.

(2 marks)

14 The costs and output of a business for the last quarter of the year were as follows:

	Output (units)	**Cost ($)**
Oct	1800	8850
Nov	2000	8750
Dec	800	3950

Using the high low method which of the following represents the estimated cost in January of producing 1500 units if the monthly fixed costs are expected to increase by $100 at the start of next year?

A 6750

B 6850

C 7380

D 7480

(2 marks)

Q

15 A business has experienced the following labour costs:

Output (units)	Cost ($)
7000	86,000
12000	141,000
9000	97,500

Fixed costs increase by $15000 for output in excess of 10,000 units.

Using the high low method what is the estimated cost of producing 14000 units ?

A 142000

B 157,000

C 163,000

D 178,000

(2 marks)

Chapter 3: Business mathematics

Q

16 Expected values are of most use as a prediction tool when considering the result of a one-off outcome.

Is this statement TRUE or FALSE?

A True

B False

(1 mark)

Q

17 A company has estimated that sales next year may be $200,000 (probablility 0.6), $300,000 (probablility 0.3) or $400,000.

What is the expected value of sales to be used in next year's forecast?

A 250,000

B 305,000

C 450,000

(1 mark)

Q 18 Regression analysis has been used to find the line of best fit for two variables, x and y and the correlation coefficient has then been calculated to assess the reliability of the line as a forecasting tool.

What is the value of the correlation coefficient for the line that will provide the most reliable forecast?

A -0.9

B 0

C +0.2

(1 mark)

Q 19 Regression analysis has been used to calculate the line of best fit from a series of data. Using this line to predict a value which lies between the two extreme values observed historically is known as extrapolation.

Is this statement TRUE or FALSE?

A True

B False

(1 mark)

Q 20 Regression analysis has produced the following results from the batch production costs for each of the past 5 months.

$\Sigma x=540$, $\Sigma y=755$, $\Sigma x^2 = 61{,}000$, $\Sigma xy = 83{,}920$

Which of the following is the appropriate value for b in the regression line to 2 decimal places?

A -1.40

B 0.01

C 0.89

D 1.40

(2 marks)

Q **21 A company is preparing its budgets for next year. The following regression equation has been found to be a reliable estimate of XYZ's deseasonalised sales in units:**

y =10x + 150

Where y = total sales units and x refers to the accountancy period.

What is the expected figure for actual sales in accounting period 19 (which is Q1)?

A 255

B 315

C 340

(1 mark)

Chapter 4: Ordering and accounting for inventory

Q **22 Which of the following could be used to document the transfer of materials from one production department to another?**

A Materials requisition note

B Materials returned note

C Materials transfer note

(1 mark)

Q **23 The following represent the materials transactions for a company for a year:**

	$'000
Materials purchases	240
Issued to production	215
Materials written off	12
Returned to stores	6
Returned to suppliers	2

The material stock at 31 December 20X1 was $42,000.

What was the opening balance on the materials inventory account at 1 January 20X1?

A $1,000

B $25,000

C $33,000

D $59,000

(2 marks)

24 Continuous stocktaking is the process of checking the balance of every item of inventory on the same date, usually at the end of an accounting period.

Is this statement TRUE or FALSE?

A True

B False

(1 mark)

25 Wasted inventory that is expected to arise due to the breaking up of bulk material receipts into smaller quantities must be written off against profits in the period incurred.

Is this statement TRUE or FALSE?

A True

B False

(1 mark)

Chapter 5: Order quantities and reorder levels

26 The objective of holding buffer inventory is to take advantage of quantity discounts.

Is this statement TRUE or FALSE ?

A True

B False

(1 mark)

27 Which of the following is not a stockholding cost:

A The opportunity cost of capital tied up

B The cost of insurance

C Shipping and handling costs

D Stock obsolescence

(2 marks)

28 A manufacturer uses 100,000 components costing $1each at a constant rate throughout the year. The cost of making a single order for more components is $10 and the holding costs for each component are 0.5% of the average inventory value.

What is the EOQ?

A 1,411

B 14,142

C 20,000

(1 mark)

Q

29 A retailer has a steady demand for rugby balls at 50 a month. Each ball costs $6 from the supplier. The costs involved in placing an order are $10 and the stockholding costs are 20% of the stockholding value per annum.

How many orders will be placed per annum?

A 1.73

B 6

C 8.48

D 100

(2 marks)

Q

30 Annual demand for raw material is 1,000,000 units. Each unit costs 15 cents. Procurement costs for each order are $20 and lead time has been estimated as 2 days. There are 250 working days per annum, the carrying cost of inventory is 10 cents per unit and the cost of a stockout is 20 cents per unit. What is the optimal reorder level?

A 125

B 8,000

C 20,000

(1 mark)

Q

31 A company buys each item of inventory at a purchase price of $30. The cost of capital is 9% p.a. The company pays rent of $10,000 p.a. for the warehouse. Each item takes up 1.5 square metres in the warehouse which could be sublet at $10 per square metre per annum. Admin costs associated with each order are $0.50 per unit. In addition the company pays $15,000 p.a. salary to the storeman.

What is the correct value of h in the EOQ formula?

A $27.70

B $28.20

C $32.70

D $33.20

(2 marks)

Chapter 6: Accounting for labour

Q

32 Which of the following should be classified as direct labour?

A The site foreman of a building company

B Workers assembling components on a production line

C The storeman handling parts requisitions in a factory.

(1 mark)

33 Task-related activity time records are more commonly used to record time spent working in manufacturing industries rather than service industries.

Is this statement TRUE or FALSE?

A True

B False

(1 mark)

34 A company employs 100 direct workers in the factory, who are paid a basic rate of $5 per hour for a 35 hour week. In addition to working their normal hours last month, each worker was asked to work an additional 5 hours overtime per week to meet general production requirements. All overtime hours are paid at time and a half. As a result of some faulty material, 150 hours of direct labour time were registered as idle.

What is the indirect labour cost for last month, assuming a 4 week period?

A $750

B $2,000

C $5,750

D $15,750

(2 marks)

35 An employee receives a bonus according to the Rowan scheme. The employee's basic rate of pay is $6 per hour. The allowed time for the job was 1 hour and the employee completed it in 40 minutes.

What is the total payment for the job (to the nearest cent) ?

A $1.33

B $ 4.00

C $ 5.00

D $ 5.33

(2 marks)

36 At 31 March 20x1 an organisation had 5,400 employees. During the previous year 750 had left the organisation, although the management had decided that only 600 needed replacing and had recruited accordingly.

What was the labour turnover rate for the year to 31 March 20X1 (to 2 decimal places) ?

A 10.96%

B 11.11%

C 11.27%

D 13.89%

(2 marks)

37 The data below relates to last month's production of product Z:

Standard time allowed per unit = 20 minutes

Budgeted hours available = 210 hours

Actual output = 600 units in 220 hours

Which of the following is the correct labour capacity and efficiency ratio?

	Labour capacity	Labour efficiency
A	95.24%	90.91%
B	95.24%	104.76%
C	104.76%	90.91%
D	104.76%	95.24%

(2 marks)

Chapter 7: Accounting for overheads

38 A company manufactures two products, E and F, in a factory divided into two production cost centres, Primary and Finishing. In order to determine a budgeted fixed overhead cost per unit of product, the following budgeted data are relevant.

	Primary	Finishing
Allocated and apportioned fixed costs	$84,000	$93,000
Direct labour - minutes per unit		
E	36	25
F	30	40

Budgeted production is 9,000 units of E and 6,000 units of F. Fixed overheads are to be absorbed on a direct labour hour basis.

What is the budgeted fixed overhead cost of a unit of product E?

A $10

B $11

C $12

D $13

(2 marks)

Q **39** Billecarte Ltd manufactures two products, Zonk and Tink, in a factory divided into two production cost centres, Machining and Assembly. In order to find a fixed overhead cost per unit, the following budgeted data are relevant.

	Machining	**Assembly**
Direct and allocated fixed costs	$120,000	$72,000
Labour hours per unit		
Zonk	0.50 hours	0.20 hours
Tink	1.00 hours	0.25 hours

Budgeted production is 4,000 units of each product (8,000 units in all) and fixed overheads are to be absorbed by reference to labour hours.

What should be the budgeted fixed overhead cost of a unit of Zonk?

A $28

B $24

C $20

D $18

(2 marks)

Q **40 A manufacturing company has three production departments and needs to apportion budgeted fixed overheads between them.**

Budgeted costs for the year are as follows:

	$
Rent & Rates	36,000
Supervisors salary	84,000
Machine depreciation	132,000
	252,000

The following additional information is available:

	Dept X	Dept Y	Dept Z
Number of employees	10	8	17
Area (sq m)	1,050	5,250	5,700
Value of plant and machinery	200	275	525

What is the total budgeted monthly fixed cost for department Y, to the nearest $?

A $71,250

B $65,400

C $5,938

D $5,450

(2 marks)

Q

41 Products alpha and beta are made in a factory that has two production cost centres: assembly and finishing. Budgeted production is 8,000 alpha and 10,000 beta. Fixed overheads are absorbed on a labour hour basis.

The following budgeted information is available:

	Production	Finishing
Allocated and apportioned fixed costs	$ 55,000	$ 63,000
Direct labour hours per unit		
Product alpha	1.5 hrs	2 hrs
Product beta	1 hr	0.5 hrs

What is the budgeted fixed cost per unit for product beta?

A $3.46

B $4.00

C $9.75

D $10.425

(2 marks)

Q 42 Here are three statements on the determination of overhead absorption rates:

(1) Costs can be allocated where it is possible to identify the department that caused them.

(2) Costs need to be apportioned where they are shared by more than one department.

(3) Service centre costs should not be included in unit overhead costs.

Which of these statements are correct?

A (1) and (2) only

B (1) and (3) only

C (2) and (3) only

D (1), (2) and (3)

(2 marks)

Q 43 The following statements refer to overhead absorption:

(1) Factory rent and rates are typically allocated to departments rather than apportioned.

(2) A single product firm does not need to apportion overhead to find a cost per unit.

(3) If departmental overhead recovery rates are similar it makes little difference if overheads are applied on a departmental or business wide basis.

Which of these statements are correct?

A (1) and (2) only

B (1) and (3) only

C (2) and (3) only

D (1), (2) and (3)

(2 marks)

Q 44 A manufacturing company has the following budgeted and actual results for the year:

Budgeted fixed overhead expenditure	$504,000
Budgeted activity	42,000 machine hours
Actual fixed overhead expenditure	$515,000
Actual activity	45,000 machine hours

What is the result of using the pre-determined fixed overhead rate for the year?

A $11,000 under-absorbed

B $25,000 under-absorbed

C $25,000 over-absorbed

D $36,000 overabsorbed

(2 marks)

Q

45 A manufacturing organisation has two production departments (Machining and finishing) and two service departments (Quality controL and Maintenance). After primary apportionment the overheads for the factory are as follows:

What is the total overhead to be apportioned to the Finishing department?

	Total	Machining	Finishing	QC	Maintenance
Overheads	$633,000	$220,000	$160,000	$140,000	$113,000
Work done by QC		45%	35%	-	20%
Work done by Maint'ce		30%	40%	30%	-

A $124,750

B $284,750

C $285,821

D $348,250

(2 marks)

Chapter 8: Marginal and absorption costing

Q

46 Annual fixed costs are expected to be $120,000. The company's product sells for $20 per unit with variable costs of $12 per unit.

What is the break-even point?

A 5,000 units

B 10,000 units

C 15,000 units

D 20,000 units

(2 marks)

Q **47 A company manufactures and sells a single product with a variable cost per unit of $36. It has a contribution to sales ratio of 25%. The company has weekly fixed costs of $18,000.**

What is the weekly break-even point (in units)?

A 1,500

B 1,600

C 1,800

D 2,000

(2 marks)

Q **48 The management accountant of a company has calculated his firm's break-even point from the following data:**

	$
Selling price per unit	20
Variable costs per unit	8
Fixed overheads for next year	79,104

It is expected that next year the firm will produce and sell 7500 units.

What is the margin of safety?

A 12.1%

B 13.8%

C 47.3%

D 89.6%

(2 marks)

Q **49 An organisation manufactures and sells a single product and has produced the following budget for the coming year:-**

	$000	$000
Sales revenue (20,000 units)		5,000
Manufacturing costs		
Variable	1,400	
Fixed	1,600	
Selling costs		
Fixed	1,200	
Variable	400	
Cost of sales		(4,600)
Profit		400

If negligible inventories are held, what is the break-even point (in units)?

A 8,890

B 10,000

C 15,556

D 17,500

(2 marks)

Q

50 A company manufactures two products, Alpha and Beta. For every one alpha, it must sell two beta.

Product information, based on producing the maximum number of each product, is as follows:

	Alpha $ per unit	**Beta $ per unit**
Sales price	58	36
Variable overhead	28	20
Fixed overhead	13	9
Profit per unit	17	7
Maximum demand	30,000 units	60,000 units

What is the break even point in units ?

	Alpha	Beta
A	5,000	10,000
B	10,000	20,000
C	15,000	30,000
D	30,000	60,000

(2 marks)

Q

51 The following statements relate to costing and overheads:

i) Products create a demand for support activities in service cost centres in direct proportion to the volume of each product manufactured

ii) Where overheads form a large proportion of total costs, then the arbitrary nature of apportionment is more of an issue

iii) When closing inventory levels are lower than opening inventory levels, marginal costing gives a lower profit than absorption costing

iv) Only fixed and variable production costs should be included in unit costs for inventory valuation purposes under absorption costing

Which TWO of the statements are correct?

A Statements i) and iii)

B Statements i) and iv)

C Statements ii) and iii)

D Statements ii) and iv)

(2 marks)

Q 52 The number of units of finished goods inventory at the end of a period is greater than at the beginning.

What would the effect be of using the marginal costing method of inventory valuation?

A less operating profit than the absorption costing method

B the same operating profit as the absorption costing method

C more operating profit than the absorption costing method

D more or less operating profit than the absorption costing method depending on the ratio of fixed to variable costs

(2 marks)

Q 53 Accounting standards support the use of the marginal costing approach to inventory valuation when preparing the published accounts of a company, as it achieves a better matching of sales and expenses for the period.

Is this statement TRUE or FALSE?

A True

B False

(2 marks)

Q 54 A business has just completed its first year of trading. The following information has been collected from the accounting records.

	$
Variable cost per unit	
Manufacturing	6.00
Selling and administration	0.20
Fixed costs	
Manufacturing	90,000
Selling and administration	22,500

Production was 75,000 units and sales were 70,000 units. The selling price was $8 per unit throughout the year.

What is the difference in annual net income using marginal costing for inventory valuation, rather than absorption costing?

A $8,500

B $7,500

C $6,000

D $2,500

(2 marks)

Chapter 9: Relevant Costing

Q

55 **Which of the following costs is relevant for decision making?**

A Common costs

B Avoidable fixed overheads

C Committed costs

(1 mark)

Q

56 **A company is evaluating a project that requires three types of material (A, B and C). All material is required at the commencement of the project. Data relating to the material requirements are as follows.**

Material type	Quantity needed for the project	Quantity currently in inventory	Original purchase price of inventory	Current purchase price	Current resale price
	tonnes	tonnes	$/tonne	$/tonne	$/tonne
A	200	300	19	22	20
B	700	200	26	36	32
C	400	100	10	14	12

Material types A and C are used regularly by the company in normal production. There is no current use for Material type B.

What is the total relevant cost of materials that should be included in the evaluation of the project?

A $33,800

B $34,400

C $35,200

D $37,400

(2 marks)

Q **57 The following data relates of 200 kg of material ZX in inventory and needed immediately for a contract.**

	$
Standard cost	3,220
Replacement cost	3,080
Realisable value	2,800

Within the firm the 200kg of material ZX can be converted into 200 kg of material RP at a cost of $140. Material RP has many uses in the firm and 200 kg costs $3,080.

What cost should be included for material ZX when assessing the viability of the contract?

A $3,220

B $3,080

C $2,940

D $2,800

(2 marks)

Q **58 100 hours of skilled labour and 200 hours of unskilled are required for a project. The company has plenty of spare capacity for unskilled workers who are paid at $5 per hour. The skilled workers are fully utilised. They are paid $8 per hour but the contract could be done in overtime which is paid at time and a half. The project will also require 10 hours of the existing supervisor's time. The supervisor receives a salary of $25,000 p.a which equates to an hourly rate of $14.**

What is the relevant cost of labour for the project?

A $400

B $1200

C $1340

D $2340

(2 marks)

Q **59** **A contract is under consideration that will require 250 machine hours. The variable overhead rate is $6 per machine hour and the company traditionally absorbs fixed overhead at 50% of the variable overhead rate. If the contract is accepted, $800 of other indirect costs specific to the project will be incurred.**

What is the relevant cost of overheads for the project?

A $800

B $1550

C $2300

D $3050

(2 marks)

Q **60** **The following data apply to a non-current asset.**

	$
Net realisable value	5,000
Historic cost	6,000
Net present value in use	7,500
Replacement cost	10,000

What is the relevant cost of the asset for decision making purposes?

A $10,000

B $7,500

C $6,000

D $5,000

(2 marks)

Q **61** A company is considering undertaking a project which will require 400 kg of a special material, Anignora. The company has 400 kg of Anignora in inventory but cannot obtain any further supplies. If this project is not undertaken, then the company could undertake project II which would also require 400 kg of Anignora. The revenues and costs associated with project II are as follows.

Project II revenues and costs

	$	$
Revenues		55,000
Less Costs – original purchase cost of 400 kg of Anignora	20,000	
Costs – other direct costs	25,000	(45,000)
Profit		10,000

The 400 kg of Anignora could also be sold as it is for $16,000.

What is the opportunity cost of using 400 kg of Anignora in the first project?

A $10,000

B $16,000

C $20,000

D $30,000

(2 marks)

Q **62** In the recently prepared annual accounts of an organisation, closing inventory of finished goods includes $5,800 for item Q, calculated as follows:

	$
Materials at cost	2,300
Direct labour	2,200
Production overhead	
Variable with labour cost	440
Fixed	860
Factory cost of producing item Q	5,800

Soon after the year end, item Q was stolen and the management wishes to know the relevant cost. A replacement could be made during normal working hours as Adam has spare capacity. Labour is paid on the basis of hours worked. The cost of replacement would be as in the schedule above except for materials, the replacement cost of which is now $2,600. The item sells for $9,000.

What is the relevant cost of item Q?

A $9,000

B $6,200

C $5,240

D $4,940

(2 marks)

Q **63 The budget for the year for a single product firm, was as follows:**

	$000
Materials (replacement cost)	3
Direct labour	5
Fixed overheads	4
	12
Sales	16
Profit	4

10% of the year's production was lost due to a strike by direct labour. Sales were made from inventory during the strike. The lost production is not to be made up due to excessive inventory holdings.

What was the incremental cost of the strike?

A $1,200 benefit

B $800 benefit

C $400 cost

D $800 cost

(2 marks)

Chapter 10: Dealing with limiting factors

Q **64 A company makes four products W, X, Y and Z. Labour is limited in the forthcoming year to 125,000 man-hours. Each W takes 1 hour to produce, each X takes 2 hours, each Y takes 2_ hours and each Z takes 6 hours. Equal numbers of W and Z must be produced and equal numbers of X and Y must be produced.**

	W	X	Y	Z
Contribution per unit ($)	10	18	20	50
Maximum demand	15,000	10,000	10,000	15,000

What is the optimum production plan?

	W	X	Y	Z
A	15,000	4,444	4,444	15,000
B	11,429	10,000	10,000	11,429
C	15,000	10,000	10,000	15,000
D	-	5,000	10,000	15,000

(2 marks)

Q **65 A company has the following production plan for the coming four weeks. The plan utilises capacity fully. Planned output is equal to the maximum demand per product. Product information is as follows:**

Per Unit ($)	**W**	**X**	**Y**	**Z**
Selling price	40	50	25	35
Direct labour	12	18	9	6
Raw material	7	14	5	13
Variable overhead	8	6	8	6
Allocated fixed costs	4	5	2	6
Output (units)	100	500	250	400

Direct labour is currently paid $3 per hour and the number of labour hours is expected to be severely curtailed during the coming month due to industrial action.

Which product should be placed first in the production scheduling for the next month?

A W

B X

C Y

D Z

(2 marks)

Q **66 A company has a maximum demand of 1,000 units for each of its four products W, X, Y and Z. Selling prices and costs are given below:**

Per Unit ($)	**W**	**X**	**Y**	**Z**
Selling price	80	60	65	90
Direct labour (@ $5 per hr)	10	15	5	15
Raw material (@ $6 per unit)	18	6	18	24
Variable overhead	12	7	7	6
Allocated fixed costs	9	7	7	6

Labour and materials are in short supply. Labour is limited to 10,000 hours and materials to 9,000 units.

Which garment should be chosen first in the production schedule?

A Garment W

B Garment X

C Garment Y

D Garment Z

(2 marks)

Q

67 A manufacturing business has correctly scheduled production of its two products, so as to maximise profits, using the 7,500 labour hours currently available.

	Product A $ per unit	**Product B $ per unit**
Material	25	15
Labour (@ $10 per hr)	15	20
Variable overhead	12	16
Selling price	82	75
Maximum demand (units)	5200	3800

What is the effect on profit if another 500 hours become available at the normal rate of $10 per hour?

A 6,000

B 8,400

C 9,200

D 10,000

(2 marks)

Q

68 A company is faced with a scarce labour resource. Profit will be maximised by allocating that resource to the products that make the most profit per labour hour.

Is this statement TRUE or FALSE?

A True

B False

(1 mark)

Q

69 A company, which aims to maximise profit, manufactures two products, X and Y.

Product information is as follows:

Per unit	**Product X $**	**Product Y $**
Selling price	55	45
Material	10	20
Labour	15	10

Spending is limited to $400,000 and $300,000 on material and labour respectively.

What is the optimal mix of production (in thousands of units) for the next period?

	Product X	Product Y
A	0	20
B	10	15
C	20	0
D	40	0

(2 marks)

The following information relates to questions 70 and 71

The following diagram is an accurate representation of a linear programming problem for a company facing a shortage of both labour (600 hours) and material (560 litres).

The company manufactures two liquid products, X and Y which have contributions of $25 and $10 respectively. There is a maximum demand for product X of 45 units.

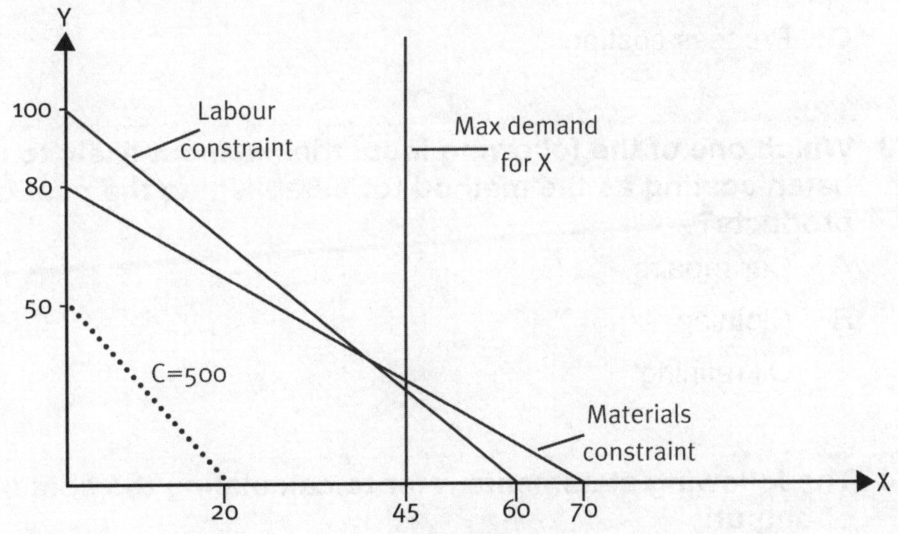

70 What is the amount of labour (in hours) used in each unit of product?

	Product X Hrs per unit	Product Y Hrs per unit
A	6	7
B	6	10
C	10	6
D	10	8

(2 marks)

71 What is the contribution for the period if the company selects the optimal production plan?

A $800

B $1318

C $1375

D $1500

(2 marks)

Chapter 11: Job batch and process costing

72 The cost of output goods is found by calculating the costs of the manufacturing process and dividing by the number of units produced.

What is this approach known as?

A Job costing

B Batch costing

C Process costing

(1 mark)

73 Which one of the following industries is most likely to use batch costing as the method for establishing the cost of products?

A Car repairs

B Clothing

C Oil refining

(1 mark)

74 The following statements refer to calculating the cost of a unit of output:

(1) In process and batch costing the cost per unit of output is found by dividing total costs by the number of units produced.

(2) In process and job costing the cost per unit of output is found directly by accumulating costs for each unit.

Which of the following is true?

A Only statement (1) is correct.

B Only statement (2) is correct.

C Both statement (1) and statement (2) are correct.

(1 mark)

75 The following data relates to a process for the month of May:

	$
Input materials (500 litres)	3000
Labour and overhead	2670

Normal output is expected to be 9 litres for every 10 litres input.

Actual output was 460 litres.

What is the cost per unit of finished output (to 2 decimal places)?

A $11.33

B $11.67

C $12.33

D $12.60

(2 marks)

76 4000kg of material are input to a chemical process. Normal losses are expected to be 10% of input and because of their toxic nature will incur a disposal cost of $2 per kg.

The process cost $11,800 and actual output was 3550kg

What is the total cost of the abnormal loss (to the nearest $)?

A $53

B $153

C $175

D $275

(2 marks)

The following information available for a process for the month of December relates to questions 77 and 78.

WIP @ 1 December	12,000 units (40% converted) Material element $33,600 Conversion costs $22,980
Materials added	48,000 units at a cost of $144,000
Conversion costs	$307,500
WIP @ 31 December	15,000 units (60% converted)

All material is input at the start of the process whereas conversion occurs evenly through the process.

Q

77 What is the value of closing WIP @ 31 December, using the Weighted average method of valuation?

A $84,680

B $99,480

C $101,250

D $136,200

(2 marks)

Q

78 What is the value of finished production in December, using the FIFO method of valuation?

A $305,250

B $406,830

C $408,600

D $416,250

(2 marks)

Q

79 Which of the following is not a possible method of apportioning the joint costs of a manufacturing process?

A Physical quantity

B Market value at point of separation

C Net book value

(1 mark)

Q

80 A process produces 3 chemicals X,Y and Z and a by product, B. Joint process costs in February were $22,500 and overhead is absorbed at 25% of process costs. Products X,Y and Z can only be sold after further processing and Data for the period is as follows:

	Output Tonnes	Futher processing costs $ per tonne	Final sales value $ per tonne
X	600	15	50
Y	500	10	40
Z	700	20	35
B	200	-	5

Joint costs are apportioned based on net realisable value and the sales proceeds of the by-product are used to reduce the cost of the main products.

What are the costs of the joint process attributable to chemical Y ?

A $6935

B $7282

C $8750

D $9073

(2 marks)

Chapter 12: Service and operation costing

Q 81 The principles used to calculate unit costs in manufacturing industries can equally be applied to service industries.

Is this statement TRUE or FALSE?

A True

B False

(1 mark)

Q 82 Which of the following would not be an appropriate situation for the use of service costing?

A Power supply industry

B Oil refinery

C Restaurant in a factory

D Haulage business

(2 marks)

Q 83 Which of the following statistics is unlikely to be used by the Rooms department of a hotel business?

A Room occupancy

B Cleaning cost per room

C Meals served per guest

D Average cost per occupied bed

(2 marks)

Q 84 Many service applications involve high fixed costs and the higher the number of cost units produced the higher the fixed costs per unit.

Is this statement TRUE or FALSE?

A True

B False

(1 mark)

Q

85 A transport business has 6 lorries in operation, 5 days a week for 50 weeks of the year. Each vehicle is expected to make 4 journeys a day, delivering an average load of 5 tonnes to each customer. The average customer is located 25 kilometres from the transport headquarters. Fuel and other variable running costs per kilometre travelled (laden or unladen) are budgeted to be $0.50. Other fixed running costs amount to $225,000 per annum.

What is the standard running cost per tonne kilometre?

A $ 0.45

B $0.50

C $0.77

D $1.25

(2 marks)

Chapter 13: Budgeting

Q

86 The following statements relate to budgeting:

i A forecast is an attempt to predict what will happen

ii A budget is a plan of what is intended to happen

iii All budgets are prepared in financial terms

iv The master budget consists of a budgeted profit and loss account and budgeted balance sheet

v A flexible budget adjusts both fixed and variable costs for the level of activity

Which of the following is true?

A All statements are correct

B Statements i and ii are correct

C Statements ii, iii and iv are correct

D Statements i, iii and v are correct

(2 marks)

Q

87 Which of the following statements is true?

A The principal budget factor is the person who is responsible for controlling and coordinating the budget process

B A business must always produce its sales budget first, before any other budgets can be decided on.

C The budget committee consists of managers with final responsibility for agreeing the budget.

(1 mark)

Q 88 An organisation is preparing its sales budget for the year ended 31 December 20Y1. It expects to sell 2000 units of product A per month. The current sale price is $500 per unit and this will increase by 10% in June. Demand for Product B is declining. First quarter sales are expected to be 4000 units in total and this will drop by 1000 units per quarter for each of the next three quarters. The selling price will be constant at $300 per unit. Product C will be introduced in September. Sales are expected to be 500 units per month at a selling price of $100 per unit.

What is the budgeted sales revenue for the year?

A $15,800,000

B $15,850,000

C $15,900,000

D $16,800,000

(2 marks)

Q 89 An organisation is preparing its quarterly budget. It has consistently maintained stock levels at 10% of the following month's sales. Budgeted sales for January are 2000 units and sales are expected to increase by 500 units per month for the following three months.

What is the budgeted production in units for February?

A 2050

B 2450

C 2500

D 2550

(2 marks)

Q 90 **The management accountant is preparing the master budget for her retail firm. The following information has been supplied.**

Sales	$300,000
Opening stock	$40,000
Closing stock	$60,000
Mark-up	25%

What amount should be budgeted for purchases?

A $220,000

B $225,000

C $240,000

D $260,000

(2 marks)

Q **91 An extract from next year's budget for a manufacturing company is shown below.**

	Month 3	Month 4
Sales	100,000units	120,000units
Closing stocks of finished goods	6,000units	8,000units
Closing stocks of raw materials	22,000kg	12,000kg

Each unit requires 2kg material.

What is the budgeted material usage for month 4?

A 230,000 kg

B 234,000 kg

C 240,000 kg

D 244,000 kg

(2 marks)

Q **92** The following information has been supplied in connection with an organisation's labour and overhead budget:

	Product alpha Cost per unit	**Product beta Cost per unit**
	$	**$**
Unskilled labour (@$5/hr)	15	10
Skilled labour (@ $8/hr)	16	24
Total labour cost	31	34
Budgeted production	8,000 units	12,000 units

What is the total amount of skilled labour hours required in the period?

A 40,000 hours

B 48,000 hours

C 52,000 hours

D 60,000 hours

(2 marks)

Chapter 14: Standard costing

93 A company's standard labour rate for its factory workers is set at $5 per hour.

The standard time allowed for producing one unit is 20 minutes.

During the period 4,800 units were produced and the factory workers were paid $5.25 per hour. The actual hours worked were 1,560.

What was the total labour cost variance?

A $390 adverse

B $190 adverse

C $190 favourable

D $390 favourable

(2 marks)

94 Which of the following would explain an adverse materials usage variance?

A The volume of activity was more than originally expected

B A higher quality of materials than anticipated was used

C There was a major spillage resulting in the loss of raw materials

(1 mark)

The following information relates to questions 95 and 96:

The materials budget for producing 5,000 units of product is 25,000 litres at $3.30 per litre. In the first month of production the company purchased 30,000 litres at a cost of $105,000, of which 28,000 litres were used to produce an actual output of 5,900 units.

95 What was the material usage variance?

A $9,900 adverse

B $650 adverse

C $4,950 favourable

D $5,250 favourable

(2 marks)

96 What was the material price variance?

A $6,000 adverse

B $12,600 adverse

C $6,000 favourable

D $12,600 favourable

(2 marks)

The following information relates to questions 97 and 98:

A company's product results for the month are as follows:

	Actual	Budget
Sales units	9,500	9,000
	$	$
Sales revenue	104,500	108,000
Manufacturing costs at standard	76,000	72,000
Contribution	28,500	36,000

97 What was the sales price variance?

A $3,500 adverse

B $9,000 adverse

C $9,500 adverse

D $9,500 favourable

(2 marks)

98 What was the sales volume contribution variance?

A $1,500 favourable

B $2,000 favourable

C $6,000 favourable

D $7,500 adverse

(2 marks)

99 A company's standard variable overhead rate for manufacturing is $7 per hour and the standard time allowed for production is 2.5 hours per unit.

During the period 3,200 units were produced in 8,320 hours. The variable overhead expenditure variance was $1,664 favourable.

What was the actual variable overhead rate per hour?

A $6.53

B $6.80

C $6.93

D $7.20

(2 marks)

Q **100 If a manufacturing organisation is absorbing fixed overheads on a labour hour basis, the fixed overhead volume variance can be split into expenditure and efficiency variances.**

Is this statement TRUE or FALSE?

A True

B False

(1 mark)

Q **101 A company's budgeted fixed overhead for the last quarter of the financial year was $280,000 for 7,000 units of output. It actually spent $284,400 manufacturing 7,200 units.**

What was the fixed overhead volume variance?

A $ 8,000 adverse

B $ 4,400 adverse

C $ 7,900 favourable

D $ 8,000 favourable

(2 marks)

Appendix: spreadsheets

Q **102 The benefit of using a spreadsheet to prepare a budget is that estimates can be varied without everything having to be recalculated manually.**

Is this statement TRUE or FALSE?

A True

B False

(1 mark)

Q **103 A spreadsheet is more useful that a database when the primary objective is to store large amounts of raw data that needs to be accessed by multiple users.**

Is this statement TRUE or FALSE?

A True

B False

(1 mark)

104 Which of the following is not a disadvantage of using spreadsheets?

A Spreadsheets are restricted to a finite number of records, and can require a large amount of hard-drive space for data storage.

B There can be sharing violations among users wishing to view or change data at the same time.

C Spreadsheets do not have the ability to generate graphs and charts for the analysis of data.

(1 mark)

105 Which of the following is the least suitable application of a spreadsheet package?

A Budgeting and forecasting

B Maintenance of customer records

C Inventory valuation

D Variance analysis

(2 marks)

Answers

MULTIPLE CHOICE ANSWERS

Chapter 1 The nature and purpose of management accounting

A 1 **The correct answer is B FALSE**

Data consists of numbers, letters and raw facts that have been recorded but not yet processed into a suitable form. Data that has been processed so as to make it meaningful is known as information.

A 2 **The correct answer is B**

A 3 **The correct answer is C**

A 4 **The correct answer is C**

A 5 **The correct answer is B**

A 6 **The correct answer is B**

Chapter 2 Types of Cost and Cost Behaviour

A 7 **The correct answer is B**

B is a non-production costs and as such should not be used to value stock.

A 8 **The correct answer is D**

A Indirect and fixed

B Indirect and fixed

C Direct and variable

D Indirect and variable

A 9 **The correct answer is B**

A 10 **The correct answer is D**

A 11 **The correct answer is B FALSE**

Telephone costs are likely to consist of a fixed element for line rental and a variable element for calls, hence are semi-variable.

A 12 **The correct answer is C**

A **13 The correct answer is C**

A **14 The correct answer is B**

Take the highest and lowest output and associated costs.

	Output (units)	Cost ($)
High	2000	8750
Low	800	3950
Change	+1200	+4800

Hence VC = $4800/1200 = $4 per unit.

FC = 3950 – (800 x 4) = 750 this year and therefore 850 next.

So cost of 1500 units = 850 + (1500 x 4) = 6850

A **15 The correct answer is B**

Take the highest and lowest output and associated costs.

	Output (units)	Cost ($)
High	12000	141000
Low	7000	86000
Change	5000	55000
Due to stepped FC		15000
Variable element	5000	40000

Hence VC = $40000/5000 = $8 per unit.

FC = 141,000- (12000x8) = 45,000 at output over 10,000 units.

So cost of 14,000 units = 45,000 + (14000x8) = 157,000

Chapter 3 Business mathematics

A **16 The correct answer is B FALSE.**

Expected values are an average measure based on a series of likely outcomes. They are most useful when used to predict a long term average and do not have a practical meaning when used to forecast a one-off outcome.

A **17 The correct answer is B**

sales = 0.6(200) + 0.3(300) + 0.1(400)
= 250,000

18 The correct answer is A.

The correlation coefficient measures the strength of the connection between two variables. A correlation coefficient of 0 suggests that the two variables are unrelated and as a result there is no linear relationship between them. The closer the value to +1 or -1 the greater the correlation and the more reliable the line of best fit.

19 The correct answer is B FALSE.

Using the line to predict values within the range observed is known as interpolation.

20 The correct answer is C

$$b = \frac{5(83920) - (520x755)}{5(61000) - (540)^2} = 0.89$$

21 The correct answer is C

y= (10x19) + 150 = 340

Chapter 4 Ordering and accounting for inventory

22 The correct answer is C

23 The correct answer is B

Material inventory account

	$000		$000
Opening balance (bal fig)	25	Issued to production	215
Creditors for purchases	240	Materials returned to suppliers	2
Materials returned to stores	6	Written off	12
		Closing balance	42
	271		271

24 The correct answer is FALSE.

The statement refers to periodic stocktaking.

In continuous stocktaking a business counts and values selected items of inventory on a rotating basis. Specialist teams count and check certain stock items on each day.

25 The correct answer is B FALSE.

Such waste may be written off but an alternative treatment is to increase the issue price to production to compensate for the expected waste.

Chapter 5 Order quantities and reorder levels

A 26 **B FALSE – the objective of holding buffer inventories is to reduce the risk of a stockout occurring e.g. where supplier lead times are uncertain (the time taken between placing and receiving an order).**

The availability of quantity discounts would affect the order quantity not the reorder level.

A 27 **The correct answer is C, which is a cost of ordering and obtaining the inventory.**

A 28 **The correct answer is C**

EOQ = √ (2fs/h)

f = 10, s=100,000, h= $0.005

EOQ = √ (2 x10 x 100000 / 0.005) = 20,000

A 29 **The correct answer is B**

f=10, s= 50x12 = 600, h=0.2 x $6

EOQ = √(2fs/h) = √(2x10x600/1.20)

EOQ = 100

Therefore place 6 orders p.a (600/100).

A 30 **The correct answer is B**

ROL = demand in the lead time

Demand per day = 1,000,000 / 250 = 4,000 units.

So expected demand in the lead time and hence ROL is 8,000

C is the EOQ and A the number of orders that would be placed p.a.

A 31 **Correct answer is C**

Cost of capital	9% x $30	=	$2.70
Rent lost	2 x 1.5 x$10	=	$30

(needs to be doubled as h relates to average inventory level but space needs to be kept for the maximum number ordered)

So h = $32.70

Fixed costs of rental and storeman are irrelevant. Annual purchase price and admin cost will depend on the level of demand and not the order quantity.

Chapter 6 Accounting for labour

A 32 **The correct answer is B**

A 33 **The correct answer is A TRUE**

A **34 The correct answer is C**

Idle time = 150 hours @ $5 = $750

Overtime (premium only) = 100 x 5 x 4 @ $2.50 = $5000

Total indirect labour element = $5,750

A **35 The correct answer is D**

Basic rate = 40/60 x $6 = $4
Bonus = 40/60 x $6/60 x 20 = $1.33
Total payment = $5.33

Note: Under Halsey scheme, bonus payment would be:

$$\frac{60-40}{2} \times \frac{\$6}{60} = \$1.00$$

A **36 The correct answer is A**

No. of leavers requiring replacement = 600
Employees at 1 April 20X0 = 5400 + 750 – 600 = 5550

Average no. of employees = $\frac{5550 + 5400}{2}$ = 5475

Labour turnover rate = 600/5475 x 100 = 10.96%

A **37 The correct answer is C**

Expected hours to produce actual output (standard hours):

600 units x 20/60 = 200 hours

Labour efficiency ratio = 200/220 x 100 = 90.91%

Labour capacity ratio = 220/ 210 x 100 = 104.76%

Production volume ratio = 200/210 x 100 = 95.24%

Chapter 7 Accounting for overheads

A **38 The correct answer is B**

		Primary hours		Finishing hours
E 9,000	x $^{36}/_{60}$	5,400	x $^{25}/_{60}$	3,750
F 6,000	x $^{30}/_{60}$	3,000	x $^{40}/_{60}$	4,000
		8,400		7,750

Rate per hour $\frac{\$84,000}{8,400}$ = $10 $\frac{\$93,000}{7,750}$ = $12

E $10 x $^{36}/_{60}$ + $12 x $^{25}/_{60}$ = $11

A

39 The correct answer is D

Machining hours = 4,000 x 0.5 hours + 4,000 x 1.0 hours = 6,000 hours

Assembly hours = 4,000 x 0.2 hours + 4,000 x 0.25 hours = 1,800 hours

Machine absorption rate = $\frac{\$120,000}{6,000 \text{ hours}}$ = \$20 per hour

Assembly absorption rate = $\frac{\$72,000}{1,800 \text{ hours}}$ = \$40 per hour

Fixed overhead per unit of Zonk = 0.5 hours x \$20 + 0.2 hours x \$40 = \$18

A

40 The correct answer is C

Monthly costs:	$
Rent & Rates	3,000
Supervisors salary	7,000
Machine depreciation	11,000
	21,000

Dept y share = (3000 x 5250/12000) + (7000 x 8/35) + (11000 x 275/1000) = $ 5937.5

A

41 The correct answer is B

	Production	Finishing
Allocated and apportioned fixed costs	$ 55,000	$ 63,000
Total Direct labour hours:		
Product alpha	1.5 x 8000	2 x 8000
Product beta	1 x 10000	0.5 x 10000
	22,000 hrs	21,000 hrs
Fixed overhead per labour hour	$2.50	$3.00

Product beta: (1 hr @ $2.5) + (0.5 hrs @ $3) = $4

A

42 The correct answer is A

A

43 The correct answer is C

44 The correct answer is C

Pre-determined overhead rate = $504,000/42000 = $12 per hour

	$
Overhead absorbed (45,000 hours @ $12) =	540,000
Overhead incurred	515,000
Fixed overhead overabsorbed	25,000

45 The correct answer is B

1) Q = 140000 + 0.3M
2) M = 113000 + 0.2Q
Substitute 1) in equation 2):
M = 113000 + 0.2 (140000 + 0.3M)
M = 113000 + 28000 + 0.06M
0.94M = 141,000
M=150000

Substituting this into equation (1)
Q = 140000 + 0.3(150000) = 185000

Total overheads for departments

	Machining	Finishing
Primary apportionment	220,000	160,000
Share of QC (45%/35%)	83,250	64,750
Share of maint (30%/40%)	45,000	60,000
TOTAL	348,250	284,750

Chapter 8 Marginal and absorption costing

46 The correct answer is C

Contribution per unit = Price – variable costs = $20 – $12 = $8.

$$\text{BEP} = \frac{120{,}000}{8} = 15{,}000 \text{ units}$$

47 The correct answer is A

Selling price per unit (36 ÷ 0.75)	=	$48
Contribution per unit (48 – 36)	=	$12
Fixed costs	=	$18,000

∴ Break even point ($18,000/$12) = 1,500 units

A 48 The correct answer is A

Break-even volume $\frac{79,104}{12}$ = 6,592

Margin of safety = $\frac{7500 - 6592}{7500}$ = 12.1%

A 49 The correct answer is D

Contribution (£000) = 5,000 – (1,400 + 400)
3,200

Contribution/unit = £3,200,000 ÷ 20,000
£160

Fixed costs (£000) = 1,600 + 1,200
2,800

therefore BEP = £2,800,000 / £160
17,500

A 50 The correct answer is C

Sales package = 1A + 2B

Contribution per package = 30 + 2x16 = $62

Fixed costs = (30,000 x 13) + (60,000 x 9) = 930,000

Break even point = 930,000/62 = 15,000 packages

= 15,000 Alpha and 30,000 Beta.

A 51 The correct answer is D

i) Incorrect. Smaller volume products often cause a disproportionate amount of cost.

ii) Correct

iii) Incorrect. Marginal costing gives a higher profit.

iv) Correct

A 52 The correct answer is A

A 53 The correct answer is B FALSE.

The absorption costing approach charges fixed overheads to units produced and as a result achieves a better matching of sales and costs during a period and a more realistic measure of profit.

A **54 The correct answer is C**

Closing stock = 5,000 units

Under full costing a proportion of the fixed manufacturing overhead will be carried forward in this stock.

$\frac{5,000}{75,000} \times \$90,000 = \$6,000$

This is the difference in annual net income

Chapter 9 Relevant costing

A **55 The correct answer is B as these will change depending on the decision**

A **56 The correct answer is B**

		$
A	200 x 22	4,400
B	500 x 36	18,000
	200 x 32	6,400
C	400 x 14	5,600
		34,400

A **57 The correct answer is C**

Material ZX could be sold for $2800 or used instead of material RP which would save $3080-140 = $2940.

Therefore the best alternative without contract is to use instead of RP to save $2940.

There is no point buying more of ZX as the replacement cost is higher than its value in use.

This can be shown diagrammatically as:

Opportunity cost is

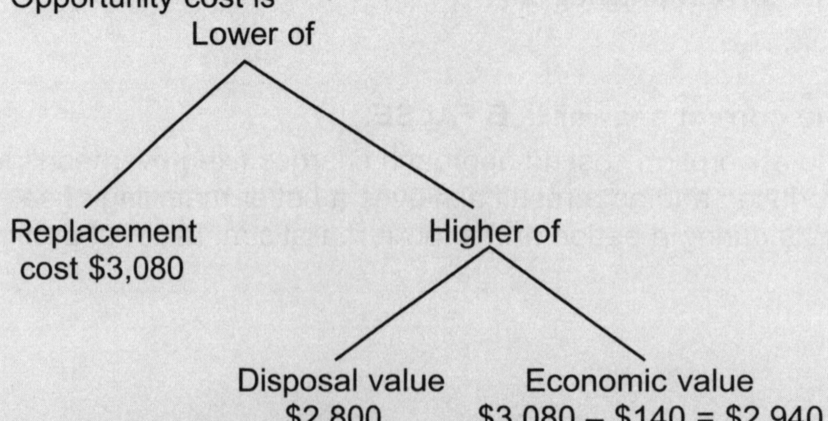

Therefore relevant cost of ZX is $2,940 (the net saving to the company on material RP).

A **58 The correct answer is B**

Unskilled labour	Nil	(spare capacity)
Supervisor	Nil	(fixed cost)
Skilled labour		
(100 hours @ $8 x 1.5)	$1200	

A **59 The correct answer is C**

Variable overhead (250 @ $6)	1500
Specific indirect costs	800
	2300

Arbitrary absorption of fixed overhead is not relevant

A **60 The correct answer is B**

The relevant cost of the asset is the:

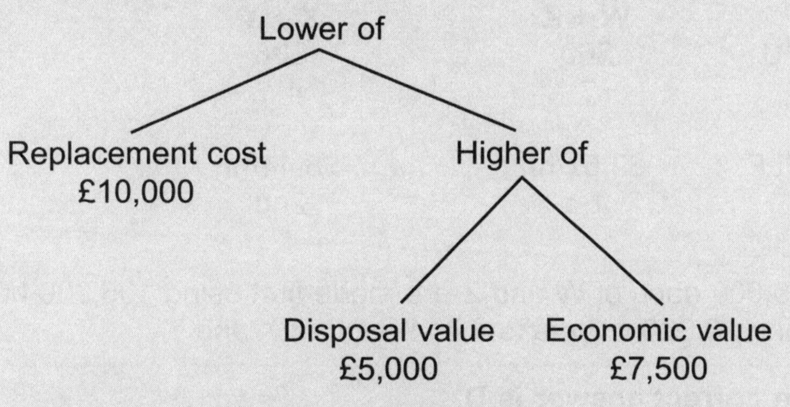

Therefore relevant cost is $7,500

A **61 The correct answer is D**

The original purchase cost of Anignora is irrelevant as it is sunk.

The choice is therefore to sell for $16,000, or to use in project II to yield contribution of $55,000 – $25,000 = $30,000.

Hence we would choose project II, the relevant cost being $30,000.

A **62 The correct answer is C**

Replacement cost of item Q = $(2,600 + 2,200 + 440) = $5,240

Fixed overheads are incurred anyway and therefore ignored.

Item Q could have been sold for $9,000.

Item Q is worth replacing as replacement cost is lower than the disposal value, hence relevant cost = $5240

A

63 The correct answer is B

There is no loss of sales revenue as sales are maintained by running down excess inventory. Therefore there is a benefit to the company equal to 10% of the variable costs which are now saved of 3 + 5 = $800

Chapter 10 Dealing with limiting factors

A

64 The correct answer is A

	W	X	Y	Z
Contribution per unit	10	18	20	50
Limiting factor (hours)	1	2	2½	6
Contribution per limit factor	$10/hr	$9/hr	$8/hr	$8.33/hr

	W + Z	X + Y
CPU	$60	$38
LF	7	4½
CPLF	$8.57/hr	$8.44/hr
	1st	2nd

Thus 15,000 each of W and Z are made first using 105,000 hours. The remaining 20,000 will make 4,444 each of X and Y.

A

65 The correct answer is D

Product	**W**	**X**	**Y**	**Z**
Contribution ($)	13	12	3	10
Labour hours	4	6	3	2
Cont/hour ($)	3.25	2	1	5
Rank	2	3	4	1

A

66 The correct answer is B

Labour is not a scarce resource as the requirement at maximum demand is 9,000 hours.

Ignore allocated fixed costs.

Product	**W**	**X**	**Y**	**Z**
Contribution ($)	40	32	35	45
Material units	3	1	3	4
Cont/unit material ($)	13.3	32	11.7	11.25
Rank	2	1	3	4

A **67 The correct answer is B**

	Product A $ per unit	Product B $ per unit
Contribution	30	24
Labour hours	1.5	2
Cont per labour hr	20	12
Ranking	1	2

Max demand A is 5200 units, requiring 7,800 hours of labour.

So current production plan with 7,500 hours is to make 5,000 units A

An additional 500 hours can be used to complete A (200 units taking 300 hours) and start B (100 units taking 200 hours)

Contribution = 200 @ $30 + 100@ $24 = $8400

A **68 The correct answer is B FALSE.**

As fixed costs will be incurred anyway, the company needs to consider the contribution per labour hour in order to maximise total contribution and hence profit.

A **69 The correct answer is C**

Contribution X = 55 – 10 – 15 = 30
Contribution Y = 45 – 20 – 10=15
Let x and y = number of product x and y to be made respectively ('000 units)

Maximise C= 30x + 15y gradient = -30/15 = -2
Subject to
10x + 20y = 400 (material constraint) gradient = -10/20 = -0.5
15x + 10y = 300 (labour constraint) gradient = -15/10 = -1.5

By considering gradients, optimum point is at intersection of x axis and labour constraint

So manufacture 20x and 0y

A **70 The correct answer is C**

60 units of X with all of the 600 hours labour = 10 hours per unit

100 units of Y with all of the 600 hours labour = 6 hours per unit.

71 The correct answer is C

Contribution line: maximise C = 25X + 10Y, gradient = -2.5

By moving the sample contribution line on the graph (gradient = -2.5) it can be seen that optimum plan is at the intersection of the two constraints:

10x + 6y = 600 (labour)
and x=45 (max demand)
If x = 45, then in labour constraint 450 + 6y = 600
So y = 150/6 = 25
Contribution = 45 @ $25 + 25 @ $10 = $1375

Chapter 11 Job batch and process costing

72 The correct answer is C

73 The correct answer is B

74 The correct answer is A

Statement (2) is true for job costing but not process costing.

75 The correct answer is D

Expected output = 90% x 500l = 450l

Cost per unit = (3000 + 2670)/450 = $12.60

76 The correct answer is D

	$	Units
Process costs	11800	4000
Normal loss @ disposal cost	800	(400)
Total	12600	3600

Cost per unit = $12600/3600 = $3.50
Abnormal loss = 3600 – 3550 = 50kg
Cost of abnormal loss = 50 @ ($3.50 + $2) = $275

A

77 The correct answer is B

Physical flow:

Opening WIP + Units added Finished units + start closing WIP
12,000 + 48,000 = 45000 + 15000

Equivalent units calculation:

	Completed units	Start closing WIP	Total EFU
Uts (MEMO)	45000	15000	
Material	45000	15000	60000
Conversion	45000	9000	54000

Cost per EFU:

	Material	Conversion
Costs in op WIP	$33600	$22980
Costs of period	$144000	$307500
Total costs	$177600	$330480
EFU	60000	54000
Cost per EFU	$2.96	$6.12

Value of finished output:

Completed units = 45,000 @ (2.96 + 6.12) = 408600
Closing WIP:
Material 15000 @ 2.96 = 44,400
Conversion costs 9000 @ 6.12 = 55080
Total closing WIP = 99480

A

78 The correct answer is B

Physical flow:

Opening WIP + Units added Finish Op WIP + units start to finish + start closing WIP
12,000 + 48,000 = 12000 + 33000 + 15000

Equivalent units calculation:

	Finish opening WIP	Start to finish	Start closing WIP	Total EFU
Uts (MEMO)	12000	33000	15000	
Material	0	33000	15000	48000
Conversion	7200	33000	9000	49200

	Material	Conversion
Costs of period	$144000	$307500
EFU	48000	49200
Cost per EFU	$3	$6.25

Value of finished output = value of units start to finish + completed opening WIP:

Units start to finish = 33,000 @ (3 + 6.25) = 305250

Completed Opening WIP:
Costs b/fwd 56580
Material added 0
Conversion costs (7200@6.25) 45000
Total value = $101,580

Hence total value of finished production = 305250 + 101580 = 406830

Note: Closing WIP
Material 15000@3 = 45000
Conversion 9000 @ 6.25 = 56250
Total value = $101,250

A **79 The correct answer is C**

A **80 The correct answer is C**

	$
Costs of process:	
Joint costs	22500
Overheads	5625
less by product sales 200 @ $5	(1000)
Total costs	27125

	NRV $ per tonne	Tonnes output	Total NRV $	Apportioned costs $
X	35	600	21000	12250
Y	30	500	15000	8750
Z	15	700	10500	6125
			46500	27125

Chapter 12 Service and operation costing

A **81 The correct answer is A TRUE**

A **82 The correct answer is B, which would use process costing to establish the cost of a physical product.**

A **83 The correct answer is C which would be of use to the Restaurant/ Kitchen**

A **84 The correct answer is B FALSE.**

Many service applications do involve high fixed costs but a higher number of cost units will result in a lower fixed cost per unit.

A **85 The correct answer is B**

Total km travelled per vehicle per day = 4 journeys x 25 km (one-way) x 2 = 200km

Total km travelled p.a. = 200km x 5 days x 50 weeks x 6 vehicles = 300,000 km

Total VC = 300,000 km @ $0.50 = $150,000

Total Running costs = $150,000 VC + $225,000 FC = $375,000 p.a.

Total tonne km per vehicle per day = 4 journeys x 25 km x 5 tonnes = 500 tonne km

Total tonne km p.a = 500 x 5 days x 50 weeks x 6 vehicles = 750,000 km

Standard cost per tonne km = $375,000 / 750,000 = $0.50

Chapter 13 Budgeting

A **86 The correct answer is B**

i Correct
ii Correct
iii Incorrect, eg budget for number of employees required
iv Incorrect. Master budget also includes budgeted cash flow
v Incorrect. Adjusts variable costs. Fixed are fixed.

A **87 The correct answer is C**

A **88 The correct answer is C**

Product A:
2000 units x 5months @ $500 = 5,000,000
2000 units x 7 months @ $550 = 7,700,000

Product B:
(4000+3000+2000+1000) @ $300 = 3,000,000

Product C:
500 units x 4 months @ $100 = 200,000

Total sales = 5000000 + 7700000 + 3000000 + 200000 = 15,900,000

A **89 The correct answer is D**

	Jan	Feb	Mar
Sales	2000	2500	3000
-Opening stock	(200)	(250)	(300)
+Closing stock	250	300	350
Production	2050	2550	3050

A **90 The correct answer is D**

Margin = $^{25}/_{100}$ = 20%

COGS = \$300,000 x 0.8

= \$240,000

Purchases = \$(240,000 + 60,000 – 40,000)

= \$260,000

A **91 The correct answer is D**

Month 4 production = 120,000 +8,000 – 6000 = 122,000 units

Month 4 usage = 122,000 units @ 2kg = 244,000 kg

A **92 The correct answer is C**

Total hours required = 16000 + 36000 = 52,000

	Alpha	Beta
Skilled Hours per unit	2	3
units	8000	12000
Total hours	16000	36000

Chapter 14 Standard costing

A **93 The correct answer is B**

$\frac{4,800 \times \$5}{3}$ – 1,560 x \$5.25 = £190A

A **94 The correct answer is C**

95 The correct answer is C

Actual materials used x standard rate		
28,000 x 3.30	92,400	
Standard cost of actual production		
5,900 x 5 x $3.30	97,350	
	4.950	favourable

96 The correct answer is A

$105,000 – 30,000 x $3.30 = 6,000 adverse

97 The correct answer is C

Budget selling price = $108,000/9000 = $12

$104,500 – 9500 x $12 = $9500 adverse

98 The correct answer is B

Standard contribution = $36000/9000 = $4 per unit

Volume variance = 500 x $4 = $2000 favourable.

99 The correct answer is B

	$
Actual hours x standard rate 8,320 x $7	58,240
Less favourable expenditure variance	(1,664)
Actual expenditure	56,576

Therefore actual rate per hour = $56,576/8,320 = $6.80

100 The correct answer is B FALSE

The fixed overhead volume variance can be subdivided into a capacity and an efficiency variance.

101 The correct answer is D

Standard fixed overhead rate per unit = $280,000 / 7,000 = $40 per unit

Fixed overhead volume variance = 200 units x $40 = 8,000 favourable (over-absorbed)

Appendix: spreadsheets

102 The correct answer is A TRUE

A **103 The correct answer is B FALSE**

A database would be more useful.

Spread sheets are designed to analyse data and sort list items, not for long-term storage of raw data.

A **104 The correct answer is C**

Spreadsheet packages do include a graphical function.

A **105 The correct answer is B**

Where a database would be more suitable.

Index